BRITISH
AMERICAN
PUBLISHING

SUBWAY GUNMAN

A JUROR'S ACCOUNT
OF THE
BERNHARD GOETZ TRIAL

by MARK LESLY

WITH CHARLES SHUTTLEWORTH

Published by British American Publishing
3 Cornell Road
Latham, NY 12110

Manufactured in the United States of America

93 92 91 90 89 5 4 3 2 1

Library of Congress Cataloging in Publication Data

Lesly, Mark, 1959–
    Subway gunman : a juror's account of the Bernhard Goetz trial
/ Mark Lesly with Charles Shuttleworth.
        p.   cm.
    ISBN 0-945167-08-3 : $18.95
    1. Goetz, Bernhard Hugo, 1947- ——Trials, litigation, etc. 2.
    Trials (Assault and battery)—New York (N.Y.) 3. Self-defense
    (Law)—New York (N.Y.) 4. Subways—New York (N.Y.)
    I. Shuttleworth, Charles, 1958- . II. Title.
    KF224.G63L47   1988
    345.73'04—dc19
    [347.3054]   88-17754
                                                       CIP

Acknowledgments

Our deepest thanks and eternal gratitude to those in the Office of the District Attorney of the County of New York, without whose assistance this book could not have been written.

Special thanks also to the court reporters who recorded the transcript of this case, especially Joel Machlis, Stephen Cohen, Nina Koss, and Hilda Wall. This book is a testament to their great work.

And thanks to Joel Milner, Larry Camburn, Tom Echevarria, Lenny Sanders, Jim Anthony, Richard Spitaleri, Jean Coonan, Ira Blutreich, Robert Hamkalo, Mike Axelrod, Edward Chase, Oscar Collier, and Susan and Margi Clifford for their contributions and encouragement.

The Indictment

The People of the State of New York v. Bernhard Goetz

THE GRAND JURY OF THE COUNTY OF NEW YORK, by this indictment, accuse the defendant of the crime of CRIMINAL POSSESSION OF A WEAPON IN THE THIRD DEGREE, an armed felony, in violation of Penal Law § 265.02(4), committed as follows: The defendant, in the County of New York, on or about December 22, 1984, possessed a loaded firearm, to wit, a pistol, said possession not being in the defendant's home or place of business.

AND THE GRAND JURY AFORESAID, by this indictment, further accuse the defendant of the crime of CRIMINAL POSSESSION OF A WEAPON IN THE FOURTH DEGREE, in violation of Penal Law § 265.01(1), committed as follows: The defendant, in the County of New York, on or about December 30, 1984, possessed a firearm, to wit: a .38 caliber revolver.

AND THE GRAND JURY AFORESAID, by this indictment, further accuse the defendant of the crime of CRIMINAL POSSESSION OF A WEAPON IN THE FOURTH DEGREE, in violation of Penal Law § 265.01(1), committed as follows: The defendant, in the County of New York, on or about December 30, 1984, possessed a firearm, to wit: a nine millimeter semiautomatic pistol.

AND THE GRAND JURY AFORESAID, by this indictment, further accuse the defendant of AN ATTEMPT TO COMMIT THE CRIME OF MURDER IN THE SECOND DEGREE, in violation of Penal Law §§ 100/125.25(1), committed as follows: The defendant, in the County of New York, on or about December 22, 1984, with intent to cause the death of Troy Canty, attempted to cause the death of Troy Canty by shooting him with a pistol.

AND THE GRAND JURY AFORESAID, by this indictment, further accuse the defendant of AN ATTEMPT TO COMMIT THE CRIME OF MURDER IN THE SECOND DEGREE, in violation of Penal Law §§ 100/125.25(1), committed as follows: The defendant, in the County of New York, on or about December 22, 1984, with intent to cause the death of Barry Allen, attempted to cause the death of Barry Allen by shooting him with a pistol.

AND THE GRAND JURY AFORESAID, by this indictment, further accuse the defendant of AN ATTEMPT TO COMMIT THE CRIME OF MURDER IN THE SECOND DEGREE, in violation of Penal Law §§ 100/125.25(1), committed as follows: The defendant, in the County of New York, on or about December 22, 1984, with intent to cause the death of James Ramseur, attempted to cause the death of James Ramseur by shooting him with a pistol.

AND THE GRAND JURY AFORESAID, by this indictment, further accuse the defendant of AN ATTEMPT TO COMMIT THE CRIME OF MURDER IN THE SECOND DEGREE, in violation of Penal Law §§ 100/125.25(1), committed as follows: The defendant, in the County of New York, on or about December 22, 1984, with intent to cause the death of Darrell Cabey, attempted to cause the death of Darrell Cabey by shooting him with a pistol.

AND THE GRAND JURY AFORESAID, by this indictment, further accuse the defendant of the crime of ASSAULT IN THE FIRST DEGREE, an armed felony, in violation of Penal Law § 120.10(1), committed as follows: The defendant, in the County of New York, on or about December 22, 1984, with intent to cause serious physical injury to Troy Canty, caused such injury to Troy Canty by means of a deadly weapon, to wit, by shooting him with a pistol.

AND THE GRAND JURY AFORESAID, by this indictment, further accuse the defendant of the crime of ASSAULT IN THE FIRST DEGREE, an armed felony, in violation of Penal Law § 120.10(1), committed as follows: The defendant, in the County of New York, on or about December 22, 1984, with intent to cause serious physical injury to Barry Allen, caused such injury to Barry Allen by means of a deadly weapon, to wit, by shooting him with a pistol.

AND THE GRAND JURY AFORESAID, by this indictment, further accuse the defendant of the crime of ASSAULT IN THE FIRST DEGREE, an armed felony, in violation of Penal Law § 120.10(1), committed as follows: The defendant, in the County of New York, on or about December 22, 1984, with intent to cause serious physical injury to James Ramseur, caused such injury to James Ramseur by means of a deadly weapon, to wit, by shooting him with a pistol.

AND THE GRAND JURY AFORESAID, by this indictment, further accuse the defendant of the crime of ASSAULT IN THE FIRST DEGREE, an armed felony, in violation of Penal Law § 120.10(1), committed as follows: The defendant, in the County of New York, on or about December 22, 1984, with intent to cause serious physical injury to Darrell Cabey, caused such injury to Darrell Cabey by means of a deadly weapon, to wit, by shooting him with a pistol.

AND THE GRAND JURY AFORESAID, by this indictment, further accuse the defendant of the crime of CRIMINAL POSSESSION OF A WEAPON IN THE SECOND DEGREE, an armed felony, in violation of Penal Law § 265.03, committed as follows: The defendant, in the County of New York, on or about December 22, 1984, possessed a loaded firearm, to wit, a pistol, with intent to use the same unlawfully against another.

AND THE GRAND JURY AFORESAID, by this indictment, further accuse the defendant of the crime of RECKLESS ENDANGERMENT IN THE FIRST DEGREE, in violation of Penal Law § 120.25, committed as follows: The defendant, in the County of New York, on or about December 22, 1984, under circumstances evincing a depraved indifference to human life, recklessly engaged in conduct which created a grave risk of death to another person by discharging a loaded firearm in an occupied subway car.

Language of the consolidated indictments numbers 476 and 1914 of 1985 of the State and County of New York.

The Charges

COUNT 1: Weapons possession,   CLASS D FELONY
          third degree.   maximum: 2 1/3 to 7 yrs.

COUNT 2: Weapons possession,   MISDEMEANOR
          fourth degree.   maximum: 6 mos. to 1 yr.

COUNT 3: Weapons possession,   MISDEMEANOR
          fourth degree.   maximum: 6 mos. to 1 yr.

COUNT 4: Attempted murder   CLASS B FELONY
          in the second degree.   maximum: 8 1/3 to 25 yrs.

COUNT 5: Attempted murder   CLASS B FELONY
          in the second degree.   maximum: 8 1/3 to 25 yrs.

COUNT 6: Attempted murder   CLASS B FELONY
          in the second degree.   maximum: 8 1/3 to 25 yrs.

COUNT 7: Attempted murder   CLASS B FELONY
          in the second degree.   maximum: 8 1/3 to 25 yrs.

COUNT 8: Assault with a   CLASS C FELONY
          deadly weapon.   maximum: 5 to 15 yrs.

COUNT 9: Assault with a   CLASS C FELONY
          deadly weapon.   maximum: 5 to 15 yrs.

COUNT 10: Assault with a   CLASS C FELONY
          deadly weapon.   maximum: 5 to 15 yrs.

COUNT 11: Assault with a   CLASS C FELONY
          deadly weapon.   maximum: 5 to 15 yrs.

COUNT 12: Criminal possession   CLASS C FELONY
          of a weapon in the   maximum: 5 to 15 yrs. and
          second degree.   a mandatory minimum of
                                       1 1/2 yrs.

COUNT 13: Reckless endangerment   CLASS D FELONY
          in the first degree.   maximum: 2 1/3 to 7 yrs.

The New York *Daily News,* June 16, 1987.

Preface

Judge For Yourself

Tuesday, June 16, 1987, about three o'clock in the afternoon.

There was a sense of subdued excitement when the last not-guilty vote was counted, as the deliberations wound down and we, the jury, unanimously found Bernhard Goetz innocent on the thirteenth and final count against him, reckless endangerment in the first degree.

We breathed a collective sigh of relief, knowing that our work was almost complete. I remember smiling but remaining silent. We weren't yet finished; there was still more to do.

In keeping with the same meticulousness we'd followed throughout our deliberations, James Hurley, our foreman, led us through a review of all thirteen charges again, making sure that no lingering doubts remained in anyone's mind about any of our votes. In each case another vote was taken, and this time Hurley recorded them on the official verdict sheet. The final results: guilty on count one, possession of a weapon in the third degree; not guilty on each of the twelve other counts.

When this was finished (finally!) we were free to celebrate. We applauded ourselves, shook hands, hugged; several jurors openly cried. After thirty hours of deliberation over a four-day period, locked up together in a cramped, cluttered, windowless room; and after having been sequestered for six nights and seven days, moving from hotel to hotel, isolated from the rest of the world—all of this to fairly decide the fate of one man whose case was our charge—we were releasing a lot of pent-up emotion and congratulating each other for a job well done.

From inside the jury room we knocked on the door, informing the court officers stationed outside that we had another message for the court. This time we sent out two notes: one saying we'd reached a verdict, the other expressing our gratitude and praise for the work of the court officers, several of whom I had come to consider my friends. The other jurors had become like family to me after the seven weeks of trial, during which we heard from forty-one witnesses, and our seven days of sequestration together. It was an intense, exhausting, exhilarating experience that none of us will ever forget: a once-in-a-lifetime chance to be a major player in a case of far-reaching importance and to see firsthand how our justice system works.

Then we went out to deliver our verdict, entering the courtroom in single file, myself first, and taking our seats. Even knowing the results didn't detract from the tenseness of that scene. There was a particular feeling that ran through that courtroom whenever the case reached a dramatic high. At these times the room was emotionally charged, and you knew that the thoughts of every person were focused on the drama unfolding before them. Ears strained to listen; eyes ached to see.

The regular ritual then took place that was done every time we reentered the courtroom once deliberations had begun. The court clerk, Robert Hamkalo, asked Hurley and the defendant, thirty-nine-year-old Bernhard Goetz, to rise. This time, though, Goetz seemed to know what was coming and stood up with some difficulty, as if it was taking all his concentration. His face looked strained at that moment; but once he was standing, though his knees appeared weak, his face became wooden. I'm sure we were all as expressionless as he.

"Now, ladies and gentlemen of the jury, through your foreman, just answer yes or no please," Hamkalo said. "Have you agreed upon a verdict?"

"Yes," Hurley said.

Hamkalo read count one from the indictment and then asked, "[H]ow do you find the defendant . . . guilty or not guilty?"

Hurley answered for us in a flat monotone: "Guilty."

Goetz dropped his head and said something to himself, then looked back up, appearing nervous, taut. If there was a

reaction from the crowd, I didn't hear it, nor did I hear one
after count two, the first of the twelve successive times when
Hurley, his voice growing stronger as he went along, replied,
"Not guilty." There were loud gasps, though, after Hurley's
responses to the seventh and eleventh counts. Those were the
ones that involved the shooting of Darrell Cabey, who had
been paralyzed and brain damaged from the incident, when
Goetz shot four youths in a New York City subway car on
December 22, 1984, at about 1:40 on a Saturday afternoon.

Goetz himself remained rigid but then finally slumped
forward against the defense table as an expression of relief
when acquitted of the eleventh count, the first-degree assault
charge concerning Cabey, and a weak smile played on his lips.
Then he looked down and shook hands with his lead attorney,
Barry Slotnick, and with Frank King, a former New York City
Police Department detective who headed the defense's investigation team. I saw that Slotnick's partner, Mark Baker, and
several court officers were teary-eyed by then, and Gillian
Coulter, the defense's law clerk, had tears spilling down her
cheeks.

Hamkalo then asked each of us if we agreed without reservation with the verdict. We all responded, in turn, "I do."

"If Your Honor please, the verdict has been taken and
entered," Hamkalo stated. "The jury has been polled individ-
ually and unanimously agreed upon the verdict, Your Honor."

Before Justice Crane discharged us, he first read the note
we'd sent, signed by James Hurley, the jury foreman, with the
one that announced a verdict had been reached:

> We, the jury, would like to enter into the record our thanks to
> the many court officers who have helped smooth the way for us
> over the difficult past six months of this case. . . . These officers
> have shown patience and enthusiasm far exceeding the levels required
> by the job as they guarded us, escorted us, lifted our flagging spirits,
> maintained order and even modeled for us in the courtroom.
>
> In addition, we have been treated with complete respect by
> Your Honor, the court clerk, and all counsel concerned from our
> first encounters as potential jurors.
>
> Again, to all parties, please accept our gratitude.

"Thank you very much for that note," Justice Crane said.
"I remark that this has been one of the most difficult cases of

our time and its emotions will last long beyond this verdict, and there will be factions and criticism and there will also be support. . . .

"Whatever is thought about your verdict, you have the confidence of this Court that you have done your duty in the finest tradition of jury service, and you have been one of the finest juries I have ever had the privilege of serving before me. . . .

"I tell the parties and I say this has been a hard fought case. It was done with professionalism, was done with thoroughness, and . . . no attorney in this courtroom need ever have misgivings about anything that was performed before me.

"I thank you all very much and congratulate you all, whether the result is to your liking or not."

The judge's dismissal was not really much of an ending for us, though, in terms of our lives returning to normal. Just trying to get out of the building, past the media and both pro- and anti-Goetz demonstrators, was an event in itself. It reminded me of scenes from the movie "A Hard Day's Night" as we hurried down several flights of stairs and through a maze of hallways and doors, then boarded a minibus that took us away while a pack of reporters chased us on foot. A carload of reporters and photographers also gave chase, and when we dropped Hurley off in front of his building in Battery Park City, several of them jumped out of the car and raced after him. I saw Hurley's lead dwindle as he entered the lobby, but I'm pretty sure that he got away safely.

Later, of course, the media did catch up with all of us at one time or another, as did people who either supported or despised our decision. We all had to contend with a certain amount of congratulations and criticism that people tried to heap upon us for reaching the decision that we did.

I found reporters waiting on the stoop of my apartment building when I got home from the courtroom. For the next several hours I gave dozens of interviews, in addition to accepting an offer to appear on "Good Morning America" the next day. I went to bed after 2:00 a.m., and a limousine picked me up and took me uptown to the ABC studio about four hours later, at 6:15. That afternoon I did a local television interview on my stoop, another with the Cable News Network in their studio, and then went back to ABC for their five o'clock news program. A car was waiting there for me to take me down to the *New York Post*'s offices, where (with some help) I wrote the first of a three-day series of articles on the trial based on observations and impressions I'd recorded on tape at the end of each day.

I found it really exhilarating to be able to communicate through the media to millions of people and believe that they were interested in what I had to say. And I didn't mind facing the tough, probing questions that challenged the decision we had reached. The journalists to me were very polite, and I wasn't confronted by other people until the following week, when I appeared with three fellow jurors on "Donahue."

A few of the other jurors, though, found themselves under fire in their neighborhoods. One was Michael Axelrod, who was living then in Hell's Kitchen, an area that is more racially mixed than mine.

One incident I read about that Mike later confirmed occurred while he was being interviewed on the day of the verdict by a hoard of television camera crews and newspaper reporters who surrounded him in front of his apartment building on West Fifty-fifth Street. He was answering their questions, and several people who were passing by interjected comments that were supportive. One middle-aged man from a neighborhood dry cleaner offered to clean a suit of Mike's for free. Another young man wanted to shake Mike's hand. "I'm proud of you," he said.

Most notable, though, was a seventeen-year-old black man who was angered by the perceived racial implications of our verdict. Newspaper columnists, black leaders, and others have insisted since the trial ended that our verdict has paved the way for an open season on black youths, giving anyone who feels paranoid or in any way threatened by blacks in the subway the sanction to shoot them. They have also asserted that our verdict was a racist one, and that if Goetz had been black and the youths who accosted him had been white, we would have quickly found him guilty on every single count.

Mike tried to explain to the youth—as he also tried to do later that day on ABC's "Nightline," when he was grilled by New York *Daily News* columnist Earl Caldwell, and as I contended later on "Donahue"—that our verdict should not be interpreted as having *any* racial implications, because race or racism was in no way a factor in our deliberations or in our decision.

"I wish you could have been there," Mike said to the youth. "I wish the whole city could have been there every day listening to the testimony."

So do I, and that's what I hope to accomplish by writing this book.

My story is composed of personal recollection aided in part by the tape-recorded diary I kept throughout the trial and my written notes from during the deliberations, combined with the actual transcripts of the trial that I have relied on to ensure accuracy and because direct quotation has proved more eloquent and telling than my interpretation of what was said could be. Also, my use of transcripts allows a more complete chronicle of the events of the trial than what I as a juror was allowed to know. Included as they occurred, then, are the on-record conferences between the judge and the attorneys that took place at the sidebar (the side of the judge's bench away from the witness stand and the jury box) and were heard only by those who were within earshot, and the open-court occurrences which took place with the jury absent. I have tried to set down here simply the truth; it is no more sensational than the events themselves.

What this will allow, I hope, is that in telling the story of what I saw and heard and thought and felt during my six months of involvement with this case, you who listen will be able to imagine yourself in my place, so that you can judge for yourself whether our verdict could have been anything other than what it was. Keep in mind that *our* charge was to determine Goetz's guilt or innocence according to the law as given to us by the judge and based only on the evidence we saw and heard. Beyond that, *you* can decide what you think really happened in that subway car on December 22, 1984, and whether you feel that justice has been served.

Mike Axelrod felt a bit disheartened, I think, after his encounter with the youth. He said then, "It's not my job to go around convincing eight million New Yorkers. It's not my job to make peace in New York."

I first heard that story when I read it in *New York Newsday* the next day. And I've thought ever since then that maybe, just maybe, through this book, I can.

Contents

Chapter 1

⚖

Voir Dire: I Am Selected

Who likes jury duty? From everything I'd ever heard, it sounded awful. A crowd of people, bored out of their skulls, sit around all day on wooden benches in one large room, waiting to get called for jury selection. Then when you do get called the chances are less than half that you'll be chosen for that case, so you're sent back to the jury room to start the process all over again. If you ever do get on a case, well, maybe it would be interesting. But I always had the impression that the majority of cases are extremely dull, especially civil suits. At least when I got my notice for jury service it specified that I was to report to criminal court.

The notice came in early November 1986, telling me to come for two weeks' service beginning on December 12. Although I was twenty-seven and had lived in New York City continuously since 1977, this was the first time I'd ever been summoned to serve. I had never stayed in one apartment long enough for them to catch up with me.

Had I ever served before, I might have realized that the address on my summons was an unusual one. Rather than directing me to go to the main jury room of the criminal court building at 100 Chambers Street, I was sent instead to the court building at 111 Chambers Street, courtroom number 572. And so the whole prospect of my jury service changed almost from the moment I arrived.

By the time I got there, the courtroom was packed. Not only were there not enough seats for everyone, but some people hung out in the hallway and others were two deep along the

1

walls. From the conversations I heard going on around me, I was made aware that this was highly unusual. In most criminal cases, no more than about fifty jurors are sent to a courtroom at one time.

Then we found out what was going on. From a door to the left of the judge's bench, several people entered the well of the court, including Gregory Waples, the assistant district attorney assigned to prosecute the case; the defense attorneys, Barry Slotnick and Mark Baker; and the defendant, Bernhard Goetz.

I was in the back of the courtroom and didn't recognize him immediately, but Goetz's entrance caused quite a stir. I would say thirty or so of the three hundred prospective jurors in the courtroom responded by applauding the man, which, I take it, is something else that doesn't happen during your average criminal case.

After the trial, Waples said he did not recall hearing any applause for Goetz, but James Moseley, another juror who was also there that first day, remembered the incident as I did; perhaps it was more audible in the back of the room. It was a spontaneous display of support for the defendant, and, I believed, a vivid demonstration of how difficult the task would be to select a jury for this case that could truly be impartial. Waples had the unenviable job of prosecuting Goetz on behalf of the People while a large percentage of New Yorkers, black or white, right or wrong, supported what Goetz had done.

I was not one of those who applauded Goetz, but I was excited by the prospect of being selected. I remember thinking to myself, "All right! This isn't just some boring case"; and that if I had to do jury duty at all, this was the case I wanted to be picked for.

Acting Justice Stephen Crane then entered the courtroom. The court clerk, Robert Hamkalo, swore us in en masse as prospective jurors, and Justice Crane briefly detailed the charges against Goetz and introduced us to Goetz and the attorneys. The jury selection process was to begin, Justice Crane explained, with an individual screening of prospective jurors that would take place in another room. The five men then promptly retreated through the door they'd entered, along with a court reporter who was stenotyping the transcript of all the proceedings.

Hamkalo drew names out of a rotating canister and called people to enter the screening room, one at a time, for interviews that lasted five to ten minutes. This also, I learned, was not the usual procedure, but rather was an extra step that had been added for this case. Normally people are chosen and seated in the jury box, where they are then interrogated twelve or more at a time. This was Friday, December 12; I was not questioned while seated in the jury box until three months later, in the middle of March.

I was not called into the screening room on either of the first two days. After lunch on the third day—Tuesday, December 16—I still had not been called when a long list of names was read that included mine. We were excused and told to return on Friday, January 23.

In January the room was no less crowded, the stock of prospective jurors having been replenished with first-time people for every person who'd been dismissed the month before. I joined a group of three other people who were talking with each other and seated next to me. One was a black, middle-aged man, a city bus driver with the relaxed air of someone who spends a lot of his time making small talk with strangers. The other two were attractive women: a tall, black woman in her early twenties and a white woman, around thirty, with long brown hair.

I mention these people because I think it amazing that, of the many hundreds of people who went through the voir dire proceedings, the four of us who were talking together in January, shooting the breeze to help the time pass by, would later constitute one-third of the entire jury-in-chief. We were all taken: the man was Robert Leach, and the women were Erniece Dix and Diana Serpe.

When my name finally came up, I grabbed my coat, walked through the well of the courtroom, and went in the same door that I would come out of almost five months later with the other jurors, verdict in hand. A hallway led to the small screening room; I entered and stepped toward the empty seat at the head of a rectangular table. To my left and closest to me was Justice Crane. Seated to his left were Waples and a court reporter. On my right were Slotnick, Baker, and, farthest from me, Goetz. The judge and the attorneys stood up and said hello; then we sat down, and the questioning began.

I tried to act as relaxed as possible and to look at anyone who asked me a question squarely in the eyes as I answered. I resisted the temptation to look directly at Goetz, in part because I didn't want him to feel uncomfortable or that he was being scrutinized, and because I didn't want to seem overly interested. From the corner of my eye, though, I did glance at him occasionally. For the most part he sat looking down at the yellow legal pad in front of him, listening intently and jotting down notes. Once or twice I noticed him staring my way, his face expressionless and pale as a ghost.

The interrogation began with Justice Crane who asked me very basic questions: my name, age, and occupation (I'm a writer and actor, and I work as a word processor to pay the rent); what neighborhood I live in (SoHo); whether I use the subways and what particular lines I ride (almost all, usually the E train to my job in the Wall Street area); and whether I or any relatives or close friends had ever been arrested (no). I was then asked what I'd learned through the media about the case, and I explained that I knew very little. I believe I was as ignorant of the case at that point as anyone in Manhattan could have been, given the intense amount of publicity that surrounded it from the start.

"I remember seeing headlines about it," I said, "but I rarely read anything but the sports section in the papers." The newspapers I read are tabloids, and I explained that I read them from back to front, the back page being the front page of the sports section, "and when I get to the comics I stop reading."

Justice Crane and then Waples asked several more questions, probing my memory about what I'd read. I remembered only that there had been "an altercation on the subway and people got shot," and that several days passed before the press knew who did the shooting. I said I thought there were "two or three" people involved besides Goetz.

"I had the impression that there was . . . a certain amount of intimidation going on," I added. "I don't know what to say more than that."

"Did you form any views or opinions as to . . . the rightness or wrongness of what happened?" Justice Crane asked.

"No," I said.

"Do you have any opinions as you sit here today?"

"No."

"Do you think you can be a fair and impartial juror in this case?"

"Yes."

"To both sides?"

"Yes, sir."

"No problem not talking to anybody about the fact that you're being considered for jury service in the Goetz case?"

"I have no problem with that," I replied.

Then came the defense's turn to question me. "You read the sports section. Essentially you go from the back forward," Slotnick said. "Are the Giants going to win on Sunday?" He was referring to the Super Bowl, which was two days away.

"By seventeen, I think," I answered.

With that he stood up and started walking slowly toward the door before he turned and said, off the record, "'Scuse me, Judge. I have to call my bookie!"

Everyone laughed, myself included, even though his joke had startled me. Until that moment, the interview had been conducted in an entirely solemn, serious manner. Slotnick's easy humor had caught me by surprise.

The interview basically ended there, and I left with the feeling that it had gone well. Before I left I was asked if my employer would continue to pay me if I was away on jury duty for an extended period of time. The trial, I was told then, would likely last two months, and I was told that I wouldn't be forced to serve if I would be cut off from my primary source of income. I said I wasn't sure and was instructed by Justice Crane to find out. I looked into it the following week and learned that it was my company's policy to pay employees who were on jury duty.

Six weeks later I got the callback telling me to report on Friday, March 20. I had made it to the next step.

Once again the courtroom was full, although no longer to the point of overflowing. I recognized Bob Leach and Diana

Serpe from the proceedings in January, and Erniece Dix was also there.

Late that afternoon my name was called. This time the interviews took place within the courtroom, at the sidebar of the judge's bench: the same place where during the trial the attorneys and judge would huddle to argue over points of law. From there people were either dismissed or asked to take a seat in the jury box.

The cast was the same. At the sidebar were Justice Crane; attorneys Waples, Slotnick, and Baker; and a court reporter. Goetz was seated at the defense table, so he was behind me as I spoke.

Not a lot of questions were asked. Justice Crane asked if I felt I could still be a fair and impartial juror. I said I could. In fact, I had consciously avoided reading or hearing anything about the case since I'd first been called in December. He also asked again if my company would pay me were I to be picked and I told him they would.

Waples asked if I had ever learned through news reports "whether anyone involved in this case had any prior criminal record."

"No," I said.

"I didn't asked you this last time," Waples went on. "Based upon what you know to date from the media, which you understand is not fact, do you have any inclination one way or the other, are you leaning one way or the other, as to whether Mr. Goetz was right or wrong in what he did on the subway?"

"No, I'm really not."

"So, you're really right in the middle?"

"I really am."

"And you haven't prejudged the question of self-defense . . . ?"

"No," I replied.

Slotnick asked if I had "any position on gun control." I said no.

"And do you accept the concept that someone can use force to protect himself who, objectively, believes he's in danger?"

"Yes, I do."

"And you understand that there's a difference between possessing a gun that may be illegal—which may be a crime, may not be a crime, that's something you have to determine—and using it . . . ? You understand that somebody can use a gun in self-defense and [that may] not be a crime?"

"Sure. I'll take your word for it," I answered.

"Well, you're going to take the judge's word for that," Slotnick said. "Do you have any compunction whatsoever about finding Mr. Goetz guilty if you found that he fired a gun that was illegal at people?"

"Whatever the law tells me is right, that's where I'll go," I said.

Then Mark Baker asked, off the record, "So, are you still reading the sports pages?"

"Yes," I said. "And if you remember, I told you the Giants would win the Super Bowl by seventeen points. They won by nineteen. If it hadn't been for George Martin's safety, I would have hit that point spread right on the nose."

"Who do you like in college basketball?" Slotnick followed. The NCAA tournament was down to its final four.

"Indiana," I answered.

The attorneys compared notes and I passed another hurdle. I was the seventeenth person asked to take a seat in the jury box; the box contained eighteen seats. Apparently the defense team liked Indiana too.

When the eighteenth seat was filled, we were told to return on Monday, March 24, and to wait by the fifth-floor elevator bank until we were called for. A court officer came out and ushered us through a side door near the elevators that led directly into the back of the courtroom, and we took our seats in the jury box. Already we were being separated from the other prospective jurors.

The whole of Monday was spent answering Justice Crane's questions. The judge read a list of the prospective witnesses in the case to see if we knew any of them personally. He asked us to discuss any prior experiences in jury service, and whether we'd ever been robbed or been a victim of a violent crime. I didn't respond to that question, although I would have if I had been asked whether I'd ever been *involved* in that kind of situation. Three times in my life I have used my martial arts skills to thwart purse snatchings: twice before this interrogation and once since then. But in those cases I came to the aid of crime victims; I was not a victim myself.

We were asked if any of our family members or close friends worked in law enforcement or as lawyers. I explained that I knew a few lawyers but that none of them was really a close friend, and that I'd worked at law firms occasionally as a freelance word processor or typist. Justice Crane then asked me if, as a result, I had any "attitudes about lawyers," and I got a big laugh from the courtroom full of prospective jurors when I answered, "I watch 'L.A. Law.'"

We were also given a mimeographed sheet with ten questions written on it, and one by one we were asked to answer them. They were all very routine and many I'd answered before:

"My name is Mark Lesly. I'm a word processor; have been for six years. I've lived at my present address for two years. I was born and raised in Westchester County. I've lived in New York for ten years. I've never been married; have no children. I'm a high school graduate. I got a Bachelor's degree in drama at New York University. I've never had any military service. I've never had any legal training. And I study tae kwon do in my spare time."

That last answer was in response to the question, "What hobbies do you have?" I was never asked about the extent of my study, which has been practically continuous since I was fourteen. I am now a second-degree black belt in tae kwon do and have been teaching it for the past four years. I also have experience in kendo (a sport form of martial art in which people wear body armor and fight with bamboo swords) and the use of nunchakus and Okinawan sai swords.

Apparently my interest in the martial arts did not disturb the prosecution, because there were no follow-up questions from Waples on the subject. I know that it was an extremely favorable point with the defense. Slotnick told me the day after the trial, when we were both at ABC to appear on "Good Morning America," that he knew immediately that he wanted me as a juror and that he could tell I was a martial artist from the way I walked into the screening room. Also, the only reference made to my martial arts skills came from Slotnick the next day.

On Tuesday the prosecution and defense were each given a chance to question us, and in so doing discussed certain facets of the case, providing glimpses of what was to come.

Waples discussed the fact that some of the youths Goetz shot would likely be called to testify against him, and that the youths had criminal records. Two of the youths actually had been convicted of "serious felonies" since the date of the subway incident, Waples explained, one for "attempted robbery for his participation in a chain snatch," and the other for "a very serious rape and robbery, involving a gun." Waples asked whether as a result any of us would "automatically disbelieve" their testimony, and whether we could "follow the judge's instructions" in assessing witnesses' credibility. He also asked whether anybody thought "that if you convicted the defendant you'd be sending the wrong signal to society" in lieu of the fact that "in some quarters" Goetz "has been perceived as standing up to crime."

Waples inferred that Goetz had overreacted to the threat he faced when he shot the youths, and that his response was inappropriate and/or excessive. He made the distinction between fear and anger, asking if we could accept that anger alone may not legally justify Goetz's actions. He also asked if we could accept that a person's "honest fear" may not provide the legal justification for shooting someone if that fear proved to be unreasonable.

The example Waples used to explain this last concept was an interesting one. "Let's assume, because of the very particular way my mind operates, that I believe that everyone who smiles at me is secretly plotting to kill me and some day, when I go back to my hometown in the Midwest, I'm walking down the street and the first man I encounter smiles at me and I kill him because I'm in mortal fear of my personal safety. My belief is genuine, it's sincere, it's honest to the marrow of my bones," Waples said, "but you can accept the proposition that that fact alone . . . may not necessarily in the eyes of the law allow me to throttle that farmer who is simply saying good day."

Waples's "smiling farmer" hypothesis was to me particularly interesting in light of what I later learned: that in his tape-recorded statements Goetz said he made the decision to shoot the youths because of the way Troy Canty was smiling at him. It was also extremely effective in that throughout the trial I often recalled the image of that smiling farmer even though Waples never referred to him again.

Waples concluded by asking whether any of us thought we would sympathize or identify with Goetz. "It's possible, . . . after you listen to all the evidence in the case, you may conclude that if you were in Mr. Goetz's shoes you would have done exactly the same thing that he did on the subway," Waples stated. "But it's also possible that you may conclude that even though you would have done the same thing, applying the law that Justice Crane gives you, you would have to conclude that what you [would have done] and what Mr. Goetz did would not be legally justifiable under those circumstances. Could you return . . . a verdict of guilty," Waples asked us, "even if that, in effect, meant condemning what you yourself would have done in exactly the same situation?"

"I don't expect miracles," Waples added a few minutes later. "But I do expect justice from a jury that's impaneled in this case and hope that each of you could assure me that whatever feelings of sympathy [you may develop] for any party in this case would be set aside and you could base your verdict solely on the evidence. Is there anyone who could not make that promise to me at this time?"

After a five-minute break it was the defense's turn, and Slotnick questioned whether any of us were predisposed against Goetz for having carried a weapon and used it against people to defend himself from them. He told us that the defense would argue Goetz's use of the gun "was proper and appropriate," but he wanted our assurances that we would not castigate Goetz if we decided that, were we in Goetz's stead, we wouldn't have chosen to shoot the youths. Slotnick also asked us whether we would vote Goetz not guilty if we found his actions morally wrong but legally allowed.

"Mr. Lesly, you mentioned that you're involved in martial arts?" Slotnick asked me specifically.

"Yes, sir."

"You understand that not all of us have your ability and your talent?"

"Yes, sir."

"All right. I presume that you could face four people and probably give them a big surprise."

"Perhaps," I said.

"But the possibility of your doing it as against a lot of other people is stronger and better?"

"I would think I probably have a better chance than the average person."

"In view of that fact—and you may find that Mr. Goetz had never had any martial arts experience and had been mugged and beaten before and just didn't want it to happen again—the fact that you have the ability to subdue people, the fact that he felt and perceived the necessity to use a gun, would you hold that against him?"

"Not at all," I replied.

"You have any strong feelings about guns?" Slotnick continued.

"No," I said.

After Slotnick's interrogation was completed, the attorneys and the judge left the courtroom, and in an adjacent room decided our fates. When they were through, Hamkalo called the names of thirteen of the eighteen people in the jury box, and those thirteen were told they were excused. My name was not one of them.

That was a very exciting moment: when I first realized I had been accepted, that I had made it all the way. I also believed they had made a good choice. I had convinced myself that for several reasons the court couldn't have a better juror. First, the whole case was centered around self-defense, an issue. I had thought a lot about in my fourteen-year involvement with martial arts. I had to do a lot of soul-searching as I became capable of inflicting mortal damage on a person through the skills I had learned. And besides having a knowledge of self-defense techniques, I also felt I would understand better than most people the nuances of the Goetz scenario and be able to judge more precisely the nature and extent of the threat he faced.

Most important, I knew in my heart I'd be completely open-minded and fair in this case; that I harbored no presuppositions about Goetz's guilt or innocence If I had been he, I would've wanted me.

The five of us who remained were then repositioned so that we sat in seats one through five and were told that these would be our permanent seat positions. The man who sat in seat number one, James Hurley, was named foreman of the jury. I was given seat number five. We—Hurley, Erniece Dix, Catherine Brody, D. Wirth Jackson, and myself—were the first five jurors chosen, and, after returning the next day and the following Monday, were excused until the trial date, April 27, because the selection process was to last at least another week.

Before we were excused, we were asked to stand and swear our oath as jurors. The oath proved extremely significant in our deliberations three months hence. "Do each of you solemnly swear to try the action of the People of the State of New York against Bernhard H. Goetz, the defendant at the bar, in a just and impartial manner to the best of your judgment and render a verdict according to the law and the evidence so help you God?"

Justice Crane also repeated his instructions that we were not to discuss the case with anyone from then until the trial was over, and not even among ourselves until we began deliberating. That was going to be a difficult task, especially because, when the final jury was selected, both the *New York Post* and the *Daily News* printed a list of the names of the jurors who'd been chosen, along with a brief biographical profile of each. Several friends of mine saw my name and phoned to tell me about it, and I had to ask them to please not mention the case again to me until after it was over.

I was surprised that the newspapers would have published such a list, but it gave me a clue as to how extreme the extent of the media coverage of this trial was going to be. Just avoiding the reports in the newspapers and on television was going to take a major effort, and the back page of the *Post* would have to remain my front page for the next two months at least.

I decided then that if I couldn't talk to anyone else about it, I would at least talk to myself at the end of each day if for no other reason than to keep my pent-up thoughts from bursting my brain. I borrowed a pocket-size tape recorder from a friend, along with a couple of microcassettes, and with it kept a tape-recorded diary that I am, in part, utilizing here. I was already dying to talk about my impressions of the major players in the trial just based on my observations of them during the voir dire proceedings: Justice Crane; attorneys Waples, Slotnick and Baker; and of course the defendant, Bernhard Goetz.

The first time I was really near any of these men was at the January screening, when we were all sitting together at the one long, rectangular table in the small room to the rear of the courtroom.

Never in my life had I so immediately trusted a person as I did Justice Crane. The man absolutely oozed integrity, as well as intelligence, fairness, and concern. He was a short, stocky man in his late forties, bespectacled and balding, although he combed his hair over the top of his head to cover the bald spot. The warmth he exuded came from the way he looked at people. His eyes soft but focused, face etched with compassion yet pensive, composed; he seemed to try not only to see you but to see into your soul.

Gregory Waples seemed, in comparison, a harder, more calculating man. I remember thinking when he first started speaking to me, "This guy is *serious.*" When he was working he was all business, totally concentrating on the matter at hand. He also proved to be equal to the challenge that his opponent presented, where a lesser attorney might have fallen completely apart. A studious man whose integrity I thought was also unchallengeable, Waples handled himself well when confronted with the wily brilliance of Slotnick's tactics and throughout the trial remained relatively composed.

Younger than Justice Crane, in his late thirties, Waples's appearance fit his billing: a star prosecutor of the Manhattan district attorney's office who'd been at the top of his class at Columbia Law School. He clearly believed in what he was doing and was not a cop-out corporate type, although he could easily look the part. Tall and handsome, with wavy brown hair, eyeglasses, and the sinewy physique of a man who runs marathons, Waples reminded me a little of Clark Kent. The only hint of his unusual nature that didn't quite fit the corporate mold was the bright orange backpack he occasionally carried so that at the end of the day he could change from his business suit into running clothes and, pack on his back, head for home.

Barry Slotnick was Waples's antithesis. Also tall and lean but older and distinguished looking in $2,500 suits and with streaks of gray in his trim, full beard, Slotnick was the quintessential smoothie. He had a flair for the dramatic, an ego as large as his string of legal victories, and a personality as formidable as those of his famous clients, who include the alleged former Mafia boss Joseph Colombo, Sr., and Rabbi Meir Kahane, the leader of the militant Jewish Defense League. The Goetz case was delayed until the trial of John Gotti, the reputed head of the Colombo family, was concluded because Slotnick was representing a codefendant. And the moment the Goetz trial ended he went to work on his next big case, defending Rep. Mario Biaggi (D.-Brooklyn) from charges of bribery, fraud, and conspiracy.

Slotnick clearly relished the spotlight that his high-profile cases consistently provide. And where Waples seemed to shun publicity and was extremely reluctant to talk about himself, Slotnick reportedly had once proclaimed that he was the best criminal defense lawyer in America. And who knows? He may be right.

What impressed me throughout the voir dire proceedings was Slotnick's easy, relaxed manner compared with Waples's ever-serious air. I was surprised at how effortlessly and how often he would change his tack and slip into humor, using it to ease tension or as a probing device.

Although Slotnick was the leader and public voice of the defense team, I was always aware of Mark Baker's presence. And once the trial began, while Slotnick was the interrogator, summator, and showman, it was always Baker who approached the sidebar to contest specific points of law for the defense.

As unassuming as Slotnick was imposing, in his late thirties and average in height and looks, what was unusual about Baker was his extraordinary powers of observation. He was forever alert and saw absolutely everything, so sharp was his focus and his concentration so strong. Justice Crane once introduced him to us as "the brains of the outfit," and his contribution should not be underrated. His razor-sharp legal mind and attention to detail were two attributes that Slotnick must have found invaluable. He was the coach and Slotnick the quarterback, and they were a very formidable team indeed.

Then of course there was Goetz himself, whose silent presence dominated my attention during the voir dire proceedings, yet he would have been a lot less noticeable than Baker were he not the defendant, the subject of all the hoopla and the reason we were there. Although he was tall, he was a wan and meek-looking man, and his shoulders were stooped as though he had literally been trod upon all his life.

As I said before, I had made a point of not looking at Goetz during the first screening, but before the selection process was over I had many opportunities to observe the man. He was, I thought, almost entirely unreadable. His face was expressionless, betraying no emotion, and he displayed little if any reaction to anything that went on around him. Sometimes he would hunch over the defense desk, writing on a notepad, or else he would sit upright and silently observe. Clearly, though, he appeared intelligent, and I got the feeling that his opinions about the prospective jurors were being put to use by his counsel. He wasn't just their pawn, along for the ride.

The final juror was chosen on Tuesday, April 7, two weeks after I'd been picked. The selection proceedings took place over a period of three and a half months, during which 320 prospective jurors were questioned. The jury consisted of eight men and four women, six of whom were crime victims. Three of those six had specifically been the victims of subway crimes. The trial date was set for Monday, April 27. Here are the short biographies of the twelve jurors selected, as published in the *New York Post*:

> James Hurley, 29, a financial analyst who will serve as jury foreman. He's a subway mugging victim.
>
> Erniece Dix, 23, an administrative aide for the Police Department.
>
> Catherine Brody, 59, a college English professor. The target of an attempted subway mugging, she told the judge, "I resisted, and that surprised me."
>
> D. Wirth Jackson, 74, a retired engineer. Victim of several burglaries, including one in which an armed intruder threatened his

wife and dog. "We managed to talk him out the back door. . . . We were lucky," he said.

Mark Lesly, 27, a word processor and martial arts expert who proclaimed, "I'm not afraid of anything."

James Mosely, 23, a technical sales representative. Noting that his girlfriend was a mugging victim, he said, "It's my belief that in a situation like that, if you don't have a weapon, it's best to cooperate."

Carolyn Perlmuth, 31, a financial journalist. Her mother was mugged while walking with her in the street.

Diana Serpe, 33, an airline sales agent. She believes she escaped being mugged because "I walk in the center of the street where it's well lighted."

Robert Leach, late 40s, a city bus driver. When asked if he's ever afraid, Leach said, "Every time you get on a bus . . . [t]he driver has no chance. If some kids surround you, you're trapped."

Francisco Figueroa, 32, a computer operator. The victim of a burglary, he said the police never showed up to investigate.

Michael Axelrod, 34, a telephone technician and speech therapist. During questioning, he said, "I have no problem with the concept of self-defense."

Ralph Schriempf, 63, a World War II veteran, word processor and part-time tap dancer. A subway pickpocketing victim, he said, "I think the day of turning the other cheek is behind us."

James Moseley was actually twenty-seven. I don't know where the *Post* got its quote about me.

The day after the final jury was selected, television reporters tried to contact many of the jurors by telephone, and Justice Crane had a fit about that. Cathy Brody received two messages from reporters, one wanting to schedule a postverdict interview two and a half months ahead of time, and the other simply asking her to return the call. She promptly notified Justice Crane's office of this, as did several other jurors who had also received phone messages from reporters that they did not return.

This was extremely serious, and the judge called an emergency hearing to decide if the tampering was significant enough to warrant a mistrial. He met with the laywers on both sides and they ultimately agreed that it was not.

Justice Crane was so angry, though, that he threatened to sequester the jury for the whole length of the trial. The result was that the television stations the reporters represented— WNYW-TV (Channel 5), WABC-TV (Channel 7), and the Cable News Network—apologized profusely, and an understanding was reached between the judge and the media that lasted the duration of the trial. He reportedly warned newsmen, "Stay away from my jurors," and they kept their promise to leave us alone.

Chapter 2

The Trial Begins

April 27

On the first day of the trial I arrived promptly at 9:30 a.m. on the sixth floor of the court building at 111 Center Street and waited by the elevator bank until everybody was there. Then Dan Doelger, the court officer who was assigned to us almost exclusively throughout the trial, led us down to the fifth floor and into the jury room, which was where we would wait whenever we were dismissed from the courtroom during the proceedings, and where we deliberated at the trial's end.

We were summoned from the jury room at about 10:00 a.m. and entered the courtroom through the side door we'd been using since the latter part of voir dire, to the right of the judge's bench and to the left of the jury box. We always entered and exited in single file, but we did not have to be in any particular order, so 95 percent of the time I went in first, just because I liked the drama of it, the added thrill. We jurors were always the focus of attention whenever we entered the room, and it felt just like we were walking out on stage: I could sense that all eyes were trained on me. Toward the end of the trial I even remember other jurors saying, "C'mon, Mark" as we were assembling in the hallway outside the jury room, before we would reenter the courtroom; my going first became a part of our routine.

On this first day of the trial, the difference in the courtroom from voir dire was perceptible. During voir dire, for instance, the press had sat in the first few rows of one side of the courtroom. This day they filled both sides and were four rows deep. In the first row on the side of the jury box were five or six artists assigned to draw sketches, and one or two more were on the opposite side. Later in the trial attendence thinned a bit, but today there was not a spare seat to be had.

The room was abuzz even though no one was speaking above a whisper, and Justice Crane apologized to us for the lack of a better amplification system. "The room is an echo chamber," he said, "despite the numerous people absorbing the sound." Justice Crane had a microphone and there was one attached to the witness stand, but there were none for the attorneys and there was only one speaker in the room. He advised us that if we had any difficulty hearing statements or testimony, we should indicate this by raising our hands.

Justice Crane then delivered his opening remarks, discussing the procedures the trial would follow and the rules of evidence by which we had to abide.

The next step in the trial would be each side's opening statement. The prosecution's would be delivered first, during which Waples was required by law to indicate what he intended to prove, by way of evidence, to support the charges against Goetz. The defense then could follow but was not required to make an opening statement. The judge explained that the opening statements were not to be taken as evidence but merely as a preview of what each side intended to prove.

The prosecution would then present its case, using witnesses whom Waples would question and Slotnick would have the right to cross-examine, and physical evidence entered as exhibits during such examinations. Again, the defense could choose to present evidence, but it was not obligated to; the prosecution has the burden of proof.

After both sides rested their cases, the defense would make a closing argument, followed by the prosecution's. The judge would then charge us with the law, explaining what it stipulates and providing us with the guidelines we had to follow in reaching our verdict.

Evidence, the judge explained, consists primarily of the testimony of witnesses: their answers coupled with the questions to which they respond. We were not to infer facts from the mere posing of a question; questions by themselves are not evidence. During the trial the attorneys would object to a question or an answer because it was somehow legally improper or inadmissable. If the judge sustained the objection, we would be instructed to disregard what had been said. Often, though, Slotnick used the tactic of asking questions that clearly were improper and were bound to be objected to, undoubtedly because he believed that jurors cannot completely discount what they've heard. He would try to press his points with us in this way while Waples, appearing exasperated, would strenuously object; and it was our job to sort out what questions were answered and what statements were stricken and not to confuse inferences with facts.

Justice Crane then concluded by repeating a speech he'd made when he had charged us as jurors: "You are the sole judges of the facts, and I am the sole judge of the law. You must accept the law, as I give it to you, without hesitation or reservation, even if you privately disagree with me.

"You've got to keep an open mind. You must not converse amongst yourselves or with anyone else on any subject connected with the trial. You must neither offer nor express an opinion as to the guilt or lack of guilt of Bernhard Goetz until I finally give the case to you.

"You must not read or listen to any accounts or discussion of the case in the event it's reported by newspapers or other media. . . . And you must promptly report to the court any incident within your knowledge involving an attempt by any person improperly to influence any member of the jury.

"Now we're going to proceed to the next step, which is an opening statement by the People. Mr. Waples."

Chapter 3

The Opening Statements

There was a rail along the front of the jury box, and attached to the rail was a collapsible wooden counter on which the attorneys could place their notes when addressing the jury directly. Waples walked up to us with a large stack of papers which he referred to during his statement. He stood directly before us, shifting slightly on occasion from side to side. His look and his tone were both extremely serious, and he was so intense that at times during his speech his hands would shake. He sounded throughout just like the outraged prosecutor who's got the goods on the villain, and there was certainly some calculation in his statement's emotional ebb and flow.

Waples began by describing the shootings from the prosecution's point of view.

"At first, December 22, 1984, seemed a day much like any other day to the twenty or so passengers who were seated in the seventh car, car number 7657, of a ten-car IRT number 2 downtown express train.

"The train had begun this particular journey at White Plains Road in the Bronx at 12:36 p.m., and, about 1:40 p.m., this grimy, graffiti-smeared car was lurching and swaying in the noisy and peculiar rhythm that's almost unique to the New York City subway system as the train holed underground from the Fourteenth Street station towards its next stop at Chambers Street.

"Most of the passengers in that car were preoccupied with their own affairs: minding an infant child, reading, dozing,

23

staring blankly out into outer space, or lazily contemplating the holiday season.

"Suddenly, however, that day that had begun so ordinarily, turned into a nightmare. Suddenly, every passenger on that train, every passenger in that car, was jolted by the electrifying and terrifying spectacle of Bernhard Goetz—this gentleman on trial here—standing on his feet, firing shots in every direction from a gun he was holding in his hand.

"In a brief convulsion of violence, the defendant deliberately shot and seriously wounded four young men who had been riding on that train long before he boarded that car. He also fired a fifth shot, which missed its intended human target, struck the metal wall of the subway car, and then ricocheted about the car's interior. Providence alone prevented any of the innocent men, women, and children from being killed or seriously injured by the defendant's wild shooting.

"By the defendant's own admission—tape-recorded admissions that will be played for you at this trial—at least two of the four young men whom he shot were trying to run away or [were] in the process of running away from him when he gunned them down. In fact, you will hear medical evidence in this case that two of the four young men whom the defendant shot were shot in their backs, one squarely in the center of the back as he tried to flee, another shot under the shoulder blade by a shot that then traveled laterally across his body.

"One of the two individuals who was shot in the back, and by far the most severely injured of all of the four wounded youths, was a nineteen-year-old young man by the name of Darrell Cabey. The evidence will show that the defendant fired two separate shots at Darrell Cabey. That same evidence will show, beyond the slightest shadow of a doubt, that when the defendant fired the second of these shots at Cabey, Darrell Cabey was sitting down in the subway seat, much like you are sitting in your jury seats now, absolutely helpless and doing absolutely nothing to threaten or menace Bernhard Goetz.

"Shockingly, you will hear the defendant admit [that] before his last shot was fired at the seated and helpless Darrell Cabey, the defendant advanced on him, as he was sitting in the seat, and said, 'You look all right; here's another.' You will learn that the bullet which actually did strike Darrell Cabey caused massive injuries to his body. It severed his spinal cord. As a consequence, since December 22, 1984, Darrell Cabey has been paralyzed from above his waist down, and can look forward to the rest of his life, if that is the best way to characterize it, living in a wheelchair.

"Now, during the voir dire you heard Mr. Slotnick constantly refer to the people who were shot by Mr. Goetz as thugs and hoodlums; and perhaps, during the trial, you will hear similar . . . colorful expressions used to describe these individuals. But the resort to pejorative characterizations—shock words really—cannot paper over the fact, which will be proved largely through the defendant's own tape-recorded admissions, which you will hear, that the shooting of Darrell Cabey was little more than a cold-blooded execution or an attempted execution and is as far from being a legitimate act of self-defense as heaven is from hell. . . .

"[W]hile the defendant has claimed that this subway shooting was a legitimate act of self-defense, the truth is much more vulgar and infinitely more complex," Waples argued. Then he challenged us to "confront the reality that these shootings were totally unnecessary, vicious, and even sadistic acts of violence undertaken not in the spirit of self-defense but in a cold, almost incomprehensible wave of aggression. You must confront the sad but inescapable truth in this case, because the evidence will support it, that these terribly destructive shots that were fired on December 22, 1984, were fired not by a typical New Yorker, not by a reasonable person, such as yourselves, who responded to provocation in an appropriate and limited manner, but by an emotionally troubled individual . . . who became obsessed, if only for a brief period of time, on December 22, 1984, with the consuming desire to inflict as much pain and suffering on these four young men as he possibly could.

"The evidence will show that there is much more to this case than some people would have you believe. To *really* understand what happened in this case, ladies and gentlemen, you have to look beyond the objective facts. To *really* understand what happened in this case, you have to take a long, hard look at the defendant in this case. You have to take a long, hard look at Bernhard Goetz."

Waples made a very subtle half-turn of his body at this moment, an extremely slight gesture meant to guide our eyes in Goetz's direction. Goetz, who was as always seated at the far end of the defendant's table, facing the judge, did not visibly react to this. His head was bent slightly downward, eyes aimed at the table as he listened stoically, just as he had throughout the voir dire. Goetz did react several times, though, as Waples proceeded on this tack, portraying him and depicting the events surrounding the shootings with passionate words in a harsh and condemnatory light.

Speaking about the two confessions Goetz made when he gave himself up nine days after the shootings, on New Year's Eve, by walking into the police station in Concord, New Hampshire—one on audiotape, and the second on videotape—Waples said they would be "graphic and horrifying depictions explaining in excruciating detail exactly how the defendant shot these four men in succession," and that they would "prove absolutely devastating to any claim of self-defense. . . .

"They will reveal a very troubled man, a man with a passionate but very twisted and self-righteous sense of right and wrong. But above all, these tapes will show in exquisite detail just how unnecessary . . . and hence unjustifiable it was for the defendant to shoot any of these young men in the manner he did. . . .

"[Y]ou will come to realize from the evidence that these four young men were really shot because in the defendant's mind they were the kind of people he hated with a ferocious and all-consuming passion. Quite simply the evidence will show that on December 22, 1984, for no legally sufficient reason, the defendant decided . . . that Troy Canty, Barry Allen, James Ramseur, and Darrell Cabey deserved to die. And so on that busy Saturday afternoon, in front of half a carload of subway passengers, the defendant tried to kill those four young men, not because it was necessary as an act of self-preservation or self-defense, [but] because, according to the defendant's twisted set of values, this was right and this was just."

Waples described Goetz as "something of an enigma, a contradiction, a man who on the inside is quite different from what he appears to be on the outside. For beneath this quiet and simple and scientific, aloof exterior that you have seen in court for the past several weeks lies the real and very complex Bernard Goetz. It is an incendiary mixture of raw, nervous tension, of incredibly rigid opinion, and of explosive, self-righteous anger.

"Long before he descended the steps into the subway system on December 22, Bernhard Goetz was a tormented man, an emotional powder keg one spark away from a violent explosion. And greatly adding to the danger that this walking powder keg would reach his flash point and explode was the fact that . . . before leaving his apartment . . . the defendant armed himself with a loaded, illegal, unlicensed handgun . . . , one of three handguns—illegal, unlicensed—that he kept in a small arsenal in his apartment."

Goetz's "attachment to this gun developed into some kind of strange obsession that ultimately came to dominate [his] life," Waples said; and he called Goetz's unwillingness to travel anywhere in New York City outside of his apartment without his gun "pathetic." He spoke of Goetz's "fanatical contempt for the criminal justice system in New York City" that he said was spawned "as a consequence of his mugging incident in 1981," and that developed into a "gnawing and consuming frustration" that was "abnormal, if not really bizarre."

"And even more disturbing was the defendant's reaction to this corrosive frustration that was eating away inside of him, a reaction that made this explosion of violence . . . virtually inevitable, I submit to you, ladies and gentlemen," Waples said.

"Convinced that the criminal justice system had totally collapsed, this defendant, with moralistic and self-righteous zeal, resolved to take the law into his own hands, like a self-appointed vigilante, answerable only to a higher call." Goetz had evolved, according to Waples, "from crime victim to avenging angel"; and the most impassioned part of Waples's speech followed as he spoke about Goetz's "smug defiance of the laws of New York," his "warped vision of right and wrong," and his "jaundiced mind," a term that Slotnick objected to as "inappropriate."

Justice Crane sustained the objection. "I caution you," he said to Waples, "stay with the evidence."

"Thank you, Judge," Slotnick said.

Waples continued on the same course, however. Referring to the victims and the moments preceding the shootings, he said, "So, when one of them inadvertently provided the provocation, provided the spark, this human powder keg went off."

"Objection, Your Honor, one more time," Slotnick interjected. "Those invectives are to be ignored by the jury as irrelevant to this case."

"The jury is not to be influenced on the basis of invectives or emotion," Justice Crane addressed us. "Let's stick with the evidence without wavering, okay, Mr. Waples?"

As I mentioned, Goetz did visibly react during Waples's onslaught against his character. He broke out several times into what I can only describe as a hideous grin. This was the first time in the perhaps half-dozen occasions I'd been in court with him that I had ever observed any emotion on his otherwise stone-faced countenance, but even these grins were enigmatic to me. I couldn't tell exactly whether he was reacting with disbelief at the way he was being depicted, or if he was smiling in recollection of the actions that had occurred as the scenes were being described.

Slotnick maintained a bored expression throughout Waples's opening statement, which lasted over an hour. It concluded with what the prosecution considered some of the most damning facts against Goetz: his use of a quick-draw holster and hollow-point bullets, which are designed to cause more severe damage to a person upon impact; and Goetz's own admission that the four youths were not carrying weapons, only one of the four had spoken to him, and not one "ever laid so much as a finger on [him], or even tried to" before he shot. Waples told us that despite Goetz's taped statements, in which he said all four of the youths surrounded him on the train, the prosecution would prove that at least two of the four "never even approached the defendant, much less encircled him in a threatening manner." One of these two, Waples contested, was Darrell Cabey, who, he said, was a "sitting duck" when he was shot, according to Goetz's own admission, while sitting motionless in the car. Waples said Goetz had also admitted in his taped statements that he walked over to Cabey, saw that his first shot had missed and that Cabey was uninjured, and said, "You look all right; here's another" before firing at him at almost point-blank range.

As he discussed the four youths, Waples didn't portray them as innocent saints, but he did describe them from a standard liberal point of view: they had "not been dealt a very good hand" in life; and they were poor, unemployed, had criminal records, and used drugs "almost as a matter of life's routine." He admitted that "they had not labored particularly diligently to overcome the disadvantages" they had been born with and said that "in all probability you folks will . . . find very little in common with any of these four young men. . . . Their lifestyle is, perhaps, totally alien . . ." But, Waples said, "this clash of values will present you, the jury, with a real personal challenge, because just as it is your constitutional duty to accord Mr. Goetz a fair trial, so, too, is it your duty as jurors in this case to accord any witness a fair hearing when they come to the witness stand."

Darrell Cabey, Waples said, would not testify because of the brain damage he suffered during a two-month coma he went into several days after he'd been shot. And he focused our attention on the shooting of Cabey throughout his statement as he argued that Goetz's use of force had been unreasonable and excessive. Just showing the gun would have been enough to ward off the attack, he stated. But even if Goetz had felt justified in shooting Troy Canty, the youth who had first approached him and asked him for five dollars, Waples insisted there had been no need to shoot Allen and Ramseur, who, he said, were attempting to flee, and absolutely no justification in shooting Cabey.

"What you are here to decide is whether New York law will condone one individual walking up to another person when he is sitting in a seat and totally helpless and saying, 'You look all right; here's another,' before firing a shot point-blank that leaves that individual paralyzed for life," Waples concluded. "You are here to decide whether the idea of equal justice under the law for all people is a reality or is an empty dream."

After a five-minute recess it was the defense's turn, and almost immediately I was conscious of the sharp stylistic con-

trasts between Waples and Slotnick. Where Waples had directed
his opening exclusively to us and had stood in front of us and
moved and gesticulated very little, Slotnick was all over the
place, talking to everyone. He addressed not only us in his
speech but also the judge, the courtroom at large—especially
the reporters—and even Waples, all at the same time. His was
a much broader performance with a lot more motion and
dramatic technique, which I as a trained actor could especially
appreciate. I was almost surprised at the end that there wasn't
a burst of applause.

As convincing as Waples was at playing the part of the
outraged prosecutor, Slotnick was equally good as the offended
defense attorney, stung by the prosecutor's strong and unfair
accusations. But where Waples's speech had been emotionally
dramatized, with the pitch of his indignation rising and falling
on certain cues, Slotnick's was fully choreographed, as if he'd
rehearsed his blocking as well as his lines. It was like seeing
a Pinter play and then a Cole Porter musical: Waples played
it straight while Slotnick did the whole song and dance.

Slotnick also seemed a much more polished performer. He
was far more relaxed, and he oiled his speech with an easy
humor that made me smile several times in spite of myself. I
noticed that Waples began to emulate Slotnick's use of humor
a bit, as if he were afraid of appearing too intense and serious
when compared with his opponent and even Justice Crane,
who also used humor to lighten the tension and weight of the
proceedings.

These contrasts in the two mens' styles were also evident
in their overall appearance. Waples dressed properly but not
flashily, in a suit and tie that, although not shabby, gave the
impression of his being a hardworking, up-and-coming assistant
district attorney, definitely down here with us mortals. Slotnick,
however, in his beautifully tailored suits and his $15,000 solid-
gold Piaget wrist watch, luxuriated in his success. Another small
point that I thought revealing was that while Waples addressed
us, he drank water from a paper cup which was also what the
jury was provided with. Slotnick, though, had a nice, tall glass
to drink from. Occasionally Slotnick's style made him appear
aloof, but I think the demeanor of each man was calculated
somewhat to score different points with the jury. Waples tried

to win favor by being "one of us," while Slotnick sought to dazzle us with his showmanship. He was, clearly, an established star.

"Justice Crane, members of the bar, Bernhard Goetz, ladies and gentlemen of the jury: As you know by now, my name is Barry Slotnick, and I represent Bernhard Goetz.

"I have just sat and listened to over an hour of the district attorney's summation that might indicate to you that Bernhard Goetz was the citizen Rambo. I also wish to indicate to you that during the course of the summation I scratched my head and wished I had a tape recorder so that, when this case [is] over, I might come back and play that opening statement to you so that you will be totally insulted, as I was, because I know what this case is about.

"It is not about a vicious, angry human being who pervaded this city, running around shooting people. It is not a testimonial to the likes of Allen, Canty, Cabey, and Ramseur—and remember those four names. There were times when I sat back there and I believed that I was sitting at a testimonial dinner for those four thugs and hoodlums. . . .

"Bernhard Goetz is neither Rambo nor a vicious predator. He was approached by four individuals who surrounded him with the intent to rob him and he took what . . . you will see [was] proper and appropriate action. Justice Crane will tell you at the end of this case that someone who is the victim of a robbery has no duty to run away or retreat. You will see under the facts of this case that Bernhard Goetz had a right to pull his weapon and fire at those four individuals who were robbing him because the law will mandate—and you will see the facts as put to the law—that that's the alternative that he had and that was the choice he had and that's what the law allows."

In addition to conjuring up images of Rambo, Slotnick said that the trial itself recalled " 'The Twilight Zone.' In this courtroom you will find that everything is wrong and displaced. You will find that the victim of a crime, the victim of a December 22, 1984 robbery, sits here as a criminal defendant. You will find that the vicious predators who attempted to rob this man, who surrounded him, who said, 'Give me five dollars'—the prelude to a mugging—some of them will take the witness stand with the good immunity bath given to them by the district attorney of this county and testify to lies and testify to things that didn't occur because they know they have a right to do it without [fear of] prosecution."

Slotnick discussed at length the granting of immunity to two of the victims, Troy Canty and James Ramseur, saying that it was done after the first grand jury had refused to indict Goetz and by an "embarrassed" district attorney, Robert Morganthau, who was "pressured by fringe elements" into seeking new information that could lead a second grand jury to indict. He did not mention, it was pointed out to me after the trial, that these "fringe elements" included editorials by *The New York Times* and the *Daily News*. What he did say, though, which was quite convincing, was that their immunity gave Canty and Ramseur a "license to lie" because "they know they will never be prosecuted" for perjury; and that they would have a motive for lying because of the multimillion dollar civil suits they had pending against Goetz.

The destruction of the youths' credibility was clearly one of Slotnick's major tasks, and he made a great show of how he proposed to go about it. If the prosecution did not call them as witnesses, he declared at one point, he would call them for the defense, and once he had them there, he would go over their backgrounds.

"Mr. Ramseur will take this witness stand . . . [a]nd he will be asked the following: 'James Ramseur, where do you live?' And he'll tell you, 'state's prison.' 'How long have you lived in state's prison, Mr. Ramseur, or how long do you expect to live in state's prison?' And he'll tell you, 'I recently got sentenced to eight and a third to twenty-five years.' It's a long time to go to jail for this decent witness that Mr. Waples will give you."

Slotnick would change the inflection in his voice to separate the questions and answers, and after each answer he would look aghast, then cup his hand behind his ear and lean toward the witness stand as if astounded by what he'd heard. He'd then ask the next question in an incredulous tone: " 'Mr. Ramseur, what were you convicted of? Was it rape, robbery, and sodomy of a pregnant woman . . . ?' And the answer will be 'Yes.' And was it this same [woman], when you got done with her, who needed eighteen stitches in her anus, was taken off a rooftop and spent time in a hospital?' And the answer will be 'Yes.' And that's your decent, law-abiding young lad who has been dealt a bad hand by society."

I remember particularly that when Slotnick told us about the eighteen stiches, he was looking right at us with an expression that said, "Can you believe this?," wanting us to share his disgust and horror. Making eye contact with the jurors was a consistent ploy of his. During his cross-examination of a witness, or even when Waples was asking the questions, Slotnick was always looking over at the jury box with an ironic look on his face that said, "Yeah, right," whenever he wanted us to disbelieve testimony. It was all part of his effort to try to gain the jurors' confidence and to try to make us fellow conspirators who saw things his way.

Slotnick referred to Ramseur's rape conviction a number of times to make several other points. The fact that it happened five months after the shootings showed that Ramseur was "convicted of continuing a life of crime," he said. And Slotnick argued that since the woman had been first accosted by Ramseur and another in an elevator, her situation was analogous to Goetz's. "We know what happened to her," Slotnick said. "We don't know what would have happened to Bernhard Goetz. We can only speculate because he aborted the robbery at its beginning. But we know that . . . when James Ramseur and his partner closed in on [that woman] in the elevator, she was no different than Bernhard Goetz. . . . But she knew, she understood. She saw the body language and realized she was in deep trouble."

He referred to Troy Canty over and over as "the leader of the gang of four," an image he kept repeating, I took it, to hammer home the idea that the youths were acting as a gang and were not to be considered separately. This was important because of the Darrell Cabey issue. He also called Canty "a major drug addict" before he put Canty hypothetically on the stand.

"Now, you can say, well, Mr. Goetz makes his living by being an electrical engineer. 'Mr. Canty, how did earn your living? Tell us about all the good jobs you had. Tell us how you purchased your narcotics. Tell us where you got your spending money from.' I trust there will be a major silence on this witness stand because you will find that Troy Canty got the money for his drugs, got the money to survive, because he was a street urchin."

Slotnick spewed invectives against the four youths relentlessly. In his hour-long statement, which was split in half when we recessed for lunch, he called them "thugs"; "hoodlums"; "predators of society"; "vultures"; "mean, vicious-looking men, without pity in their eyes"; "low-lifes"; "hooligans"; "savages"; "punks." Referring again to his twilight zone image, he said, "We might as well switch tables, because I'm going to prosecute those four. And you're going to see that those four were committing a robbery. They're not on trial here. [For] some strange reason, which is not explainable, Bernhard Goetz is. But I'm going to try them for robbery. I promise you that. And you're going to convict them and acquit him. . . .

"They went about their life stealing and cheating and robbing from other people. And they assumed the risk that when you go out to rob somebody, . . . he may take a position and fight back. And they assumed the risk that a citizen like Bernhard Goetz would lawfully, justifiably fire a weapon in the protection of his property. And that's what this case is all about. . . .

"[N]o one, no one has a right to ask you to give them money. No one has a right to instill fear in you. No one has a right to tell you you have no obligation to resist my threats and my robbery. No one has that right. . . . [T]hose four individuals assumed the risk that among their victims one might fight back. And one did. And his name is Bernhard Goetz. And he acted within reason, within the law."

Beyond his inflammatory rhetoric, Slotnick did discuss the defense's interpretation of the facts in the case and the differences between what the prosecution and the defense would have us believe were thereby delineated for us in these two opening statements. Ultimately what we would have to decide was whether Goetz acted reasonably and within the parameters of the law in response to the threat he perceived when he shot the four youths on the subway that day.

Waples would have us believe that Goetz was not really threatened, that only Troy Canty faced him, that Ramseur and Allen were shot as they attempted to flee, and that Darrell

Cabey was then shot execution style as he cowered in his subway seat, pretending to be an innocent bystander. He portrayed Goetz as someone who had shot in anger as opposed to fear, that his was not an act of self-defense but rather an act of revenge against the four youths whom he perhaps perceived as symbols of the three men who had attacked him in 1981. In that attack he apparently had been beaten severely and suffered a permanent injury. Slotnick told us his meniscus, which is part of the knee, had been crushed. This was a detail I could especially relate to because I too have suffered a severe knee injury. Goetz's injury, as described by Slotnick, sounded like it must have been exquisitely painful.

The prosecution's case seemed to rely predominantly on Goetz's taped confessions. Waples quoted from them extensively and, realizing that he was going to have a credibility problem when the youths testified, told us, "You can totally ignore, if you wish, the testimony of one or more, any or all the young men who were shot by Mr. Goetz . . . because in the final analysis it's the defendant's own tape-recorded statements that prove far more than any single piece of evidence just how guilty he is." In these confessions, Goetz, we were told, said he wanted to kill the youths. " 'My intention was to murder them, to hurt them, to make them suffer as much as possible,' " Waples quoted him as saying.

Waples particularly focused attention on Goetz's description of how he shot Darrell Cabey to support his contention that the shootings weren't justified. Goetz said on tape about Cabey, "If I was thinking a little bit more clearly, if I was a little more under self-control—I was so out of control—I would have put the barrel against . . . his forehead and fired." Goetz also said, "If I had more bullets, I would have shot 'em all again and again." And Waples told us Goetz said that after the shooting stopped, he reached into his pockets and contemplated for a moment, before his anger finally subsided, gouging out Troy Canty's eyes with his keys.

The defense, of course, contended that Goetz was threatened, that he was about to be robbed and very likely beaten, and that he was sensitized to the situation by his previous mugging. Slotnick quoted Troy Canty as telling a police officer after the shootings, " 'We surrounded the white guy. We were

going to rob the white guy, but he shot us first' ": a statement
that Canty presumably would deny. When Canty and Ramseur
went before the grand jury, Slotnick told us, "[T]hey said—
completely ignoring their prior statements to police—'I don't
know, I was just sitting there and this crazy man shot me.'
Does that sound reasonable?" Slotnick asked us. "Do you really
believe that?"

According to the defense, Goetz walked onto the train and
as he walked past Canty, Canty said to him, "How's your day?"
These words, Slotnick said, were "very significant . . . code
words [that signaled] the beginning of a mugging." Goetz sat
down and ignored him, but then the four of them came and
surrounded him, and Canty "stuck his face in his face" and
said, " 'Give me five dollars.' "

"They didn't work for Bernhard Goetz," Slotnick said.
"They didn't ask him for a check. They asked him for money.
And what did they say? And you will learn that, in the mugger's
manual, there are certain things that you do. You walk up to
somebody and you ask him for change of a quarter, so he
reaches in his pocket. You walk up to somebody and you ask
him—and it's a common scheme—'Do you have change of five
dollars?' And if you want to be bolder, to let the man know,
to instill fear in him, you stick your face in his face and you
say, 'Give me five dollars,' surrounded by your other friends.
So there he was. And when you reach in for your billfold,
whether it be in your back pocket or . . . out of your pocketbook, what's the next thing that happens? It all goes. It all
disappears."

As for the brutal admissions Goetz made in his taped
statements, Slotnick contended that they were taken out of
context. "Yes, Mr. Goetz did say he became like an animal.
Yes, Mr. Goetz did say terms like that. However, when you
listen to the entire thing, . . . you will understand it." Goetz
"bared his soul" in his confessions, Slotnick said. But he contended that Goetz's mind at the time of the shootings, "full of
stress and fear, may have recounted a lot of things that didn't
actually happen."

About the shooting of Darrell Cabey, Slotnick said, "I tell
you now there are witnesses who will come forward who will
indicate to us quite clearly what happened on that train. And

the so-called cold execution, as he calls it, I tell you you will not see.

"There may be one witness who testified to it," Slotnick then admitted. "And you're going to have to determine his credibility." But, Slotnick insisted, Goetz's memory was flawed on this point.

"Maybe it was something he wished he did. Maybe, when it was all over, the anger that built up in him, the idea that he was now being put in this position, that he was not the victim, according to the district attorney, but that he was the criminal, that he was the hunted; maybe that's what put his mind into a frenzy. Maybe his anger overcame him at that point.

"So when you see the statement, when you see his video-tape, please, I ask each and every one of you, analyze it carefully together with the facts because it's totally and wholly in points inaccurate. . . . I trust you will see from the evidence . . . [t]here was no, quote, 'You don't look bad; here's another.' Bang. Maybe it's something he wanted to have done. There was no key that was stuck in somebody's eye. That was the anger, . . . the stress, the frustration, the height of what this man was going through at this time in his life. Would he have a hatred now for Messrs. Canty, Cabey, Allen, and Ramseur? Wouldn't you? You bet."

Slotnick contradicted himself, though, when he surmised that Goetz's frenzy began after the shootings, because he also contended that Goetz's frenzy caused him to continue shooting once he'd started. His frenzy began, Slotnick had argued earlier in his opening, once Goetz realized he was surrounded and trapped, that he had "no place to go" to escape the youths.

Where Waples was arguing that the shootings were cold-blooded and perhaps even premeditated, and that they were performed in a deliberate, calculated manner, Slotnick contended that everything had happened by reflex, in a flash. And, according to Slotnick, the people Goetz was shooting even ceased to be people but rather became "nothing but blobs in this moment of great stress and tension."

"You take the gun out and before you know it, it's empty. And before you know it, all the bullets are gone . . . and it's over. And that's what happened," Slotnick said. "And you will hear that police officers in the same position—seasoned and trained law-enforcement men—suffer the same, the absolute same type of reaction. You will hear that when a police officer fires his gun and he's asked thereafter how many times, he won't know. In the eminent moment of stress, the human mind betrays itself."

As the trial unfolded, it became more and more clear to me that this case would all boil down to the shooting of Darrell Cabey. All the rest was window dressing. The prosecution was placing a heavy emphasis on Goetz's own admissions, and if we were to accept those admissions as credible we would be accepting his version that he had been in fact surrounded and was being threatened. The one truly criminal act he described on the tapes was the way he shot Cabey, execution style. Slotnick would argue that it didn't really happen in that way. There would be witnesses who would support both sides of the argument, and we would ultimately have to decide which rendition of the events on that subway was the one to be believed.

Chapter 4

Early Evidence and Nonevidence

We also heard two witnesses testify during the last hour of the first day, as the prosecution began its case. The first was Marie Venticinque, who worked for the district attorney's office, and her testimony concerned a three-dimensional scale drawing of a subway car that was the same type as the one in which the shootings had occurred. She was not the person who actually made the drawing—her boss, Harry Best, had made it and he was on vacation in Europe—but she was qualified to describe its particulars so that we could understand the direction in which the car was traveling, the dimensions of the car, and the symbols used that specified the poles, the seats, and the doors. The drawing was then entered into evidence as People's exhibit one and was used throughout the presentation of the prosecution's case. Every witness who testified to being at the scene of the shootings was asked to refer to the drawing to detail what he or she had seen, and, with a red grease pencil, to indicate where he or she and others had been positioned at various times within the car.

The other witness, John Filangeri, was one of the paramedics who was called to the Chambers Street subway station after the shootings, and he went over for us what he did and what he saw. He and his partner were the first paramedic team to arrive at the scene, and they made the initial examination of the four wounded youths. "Troy Canty and Darrell Cabey appeared to be in severe shock, and James Ramseur was also in shock, but I don't believe his was quite as severe as the other two," Filangeri told us. He explained that "shock" in this case referred to a physical rather than emotional condition, where "[t]he individual becomes cold, clammy; [his] pulse [rate] begins to [increase]. As the shock becomes more profound, . . . the person becomes weak, dizzy. If he tries to sit up, he may pass out. His mental status becomes clouded. He may become confused, combative, and finally lethargic and unconscious, if allowed to proceed."

Filangeri detailed the locations of each of the four youths' bullet wounds, which was important because the ballistic evidence of the trajectories of the gunshots was going to be crucial concerning whether or not Goetz had shot one or more of the youths in the back as they were trying to flee. Troy Canty was initially deemed to have suffered the most life-threatening wound: a single shot to the left-center of his chest, very near his heart. A single bullet had gone through the left arm of James Ramseur, just above his elbow, and then entered the left side of his chest, causing internal injuries. Barry Allen was shot an inch or two to the left of his spine and four inches below his shoulder, clearly in the back. And the bullet that hit Darrell Cabey entered from his left side, behind the arm, and passed laterally across his back, severing his spine.

When Filangeri first arrived he saw Barry Allen "on his hands and knees, crawling along the floor of the car." Darrell Cabey was "slumped" in the short seat next to the conductor's cab; and to Filangeri's right as he entered the northwest door of the car were Troy Canty and James Ramseur, both lying motionless, face down on the floor.

The two most seriously hurt, Canty and Cabey, were taken to St. Vincent's Hospital in separate ambulances, while Ramseur and Allen were taken to Bellevue Hospital for treatment. Filangeri alone drove Cabey to St. Vincent's; and after court recessed for the day, a sidebar conference was held concerning what Cabey had said to Filangeri in the ambulance, which he, according to standard procedure, had noted in his report. Cabey's statement was that "[t]he guys I was with were hassling this guy for some money. He threatened us and then he shot us." Waples contended that the statement was inadmissable under hearsay rules, while Slotnick argued that it was allowable as an exception to those rules because it was an "admission

. . . made during the course of a treatment to a doctor who is treating him. He has no reason whatsoever to fool or lie."

The issue of whether the statement was allowable was made murkier because Cabey was unlikely to be able to testify on his own behalf. Waples contended that Cabey could not testify because of the brain damage he'd suffered, though at this point the defense was still insisting that if Waples wouldn't call Cabey to the stand, they would, in order to interrogate him on his criminal past. In this case, they could ask Cabey directly whether he had made the statement to Filangeri.

At the same time, however, Mark Baker argued that the statement should be allowed because Waples said Cabey was unavailable. "Mr Waples is building his case around Darrell Cabey," Baker said. "Since Darrell Cabey is a crucial individual in this trial, to the extent that there is a piece of evidence here that bears upon his state of mind at the time and what he thought he was involved in and the group he was involved in, the jury should hear it and determine it in terms of weight."

Waples then asked, "Does this mean I can put in Darrell Cabey's statement to the detectives a couple of days after the shooting in which he says Allen and Canty approached Goetz and Ramseur and Cabey remained sitting on the bench until the shooting started?" Baker consented, saying, "Let's put all of Cabey's statements in." Still, Waples said, "I feel I'm getting flim-flammed here because Mr. Slotnick is arguing [Cabey's] availability to get certain statements and Mr. Baker is now using his unavailability to get other statements." Justice Crane said that he'd think about it and give them an answer the next morning.

⚖

April 28

There was a two-and-a-half-hour delay before we were called out of the jury room on this second day to hear the defense's cross-examination of John Filangeri. For the first hour and a half, before proceedings could begin, some technicians worked to improve the sound system and acoustics in the courtroom both for our benefit and for the audience, particularly the press. Several of the jurors had had trouble hearing the witnesses on the first day and kept having to ask for testimony to be read back. So in addition to the one microphone attached to the witness stand and the one speaker it was connected to, a second speaker was added on the opposite side of the judge's bench, the judge got a microphone, and another microphone was set up on a stand between the prosecution's table and the jury box for the attorneys to use during their examinations. The result was an improvement, although voices echoed for much of the day and witnesses constantly had to be reminded to speak up and talk closer to their microphone throughout the trial. At least after this the sound system caused no more major delays.

Then there was a sidebar discussion concerning one eyewitness, Garth Reid. On the first day of the trial, apparently, the defense had presented a motion to dismiss the charges against Goetz to Justice Crane, a major part of which, according to Mark Baker in the sidebar, was that Garth Reid did not testify before either the first or the second grand jury when they indicted Goetz. Baker quoted a police report made a few days after the shootings in which Reid said he overheard another passenger say, " 'Look at those four punks, they're bothering that guy.' " Reid then looked over and, according to Baker, "said he saw the kids hassling the white guy who was doing nothing, with his hands in his pockets or at his side." Baker argued that this constituted "crucial" and "highly exculpatory" evidence, that Reid had been "always available," and that his testimony had been purposely concealed from the first grand jury by the assistant district attorney who was then in charge of the case, Susan Braver.

"It is our position that Miss Braver obviously saw the value of the information to the defense, purposely did not put it into the first grand jury, surprisingly got the verdict that she did—which we always contend the district attorney is very upset about—and that Mr. Reid was not put into the second grand jury for the same purposes," Baker said.

Waples, in rebuttal, argued that from the time of the shootings Reid had been "evasive" and "cagey" with the district attorney's office and had tried to understate what he knew. The police originally had gotten Reid's statements only because he called to try to get back a baby carriage that he'd left in the subway car. He later spoke to Braver in her office before the first grand jury, but she found his testimony unessential as he admitted to knowing even less than what was on the police report. Waples couldn't find Reid at the time of the second grand jury, in March 1985; but when he did finally speak to Reid that August, Waples explained, "He was very cagey when I said, 'Look, I don't think you're telling me the entire truth, because you don't want to be involved.' He said, 'Yeah, that's basically true.' "

Justice Crane ruled that because Reid had been subsequently persuaded by Waples to cooperate and testify in spite of his original evasiveness, the prosecution could not be accused of having "breached responsibility" in presenting its case before the two grand juries. "In any event, I don't think Garth Reid's testimony, if it would appear here in court, is exculpatory," Justice Crane said.

Baker argued that "more diligence should have been required" to find Reid in time for the second grand jury and said of Reid's interview with Braver, "My understanding of the witness is that he was not evasive at that time."

"Then we have an issue of fact," Justice Crane replied, and deemed that when Reid was called to testify there would be a hearing concerning "his cooperation or noncooperation with Miss Braver before the first grand jury."

Next, John Filangeri was questioned about the Cabey statement in open court. The jury was not present so that Justice Crane could explore whether it was evidence we should hear. Slotnick asked if Cabey had been lucid at the time he made it, and Filangeri answered, "I believe so." He explained that Cabey had made his statement when responding to Filangeri's questions ("Do you know what happened to you? Do you remember . . . ?"), which were asked in order to test his lucidity. Filangeri conceded during Waples's examination that Cabey's mental acuity could have been affected by his state of shock. But when asked by Justice Crane for his professional opinion, Filangeri said, "I believe at that point his mental state was clear."

Slotnick tried to get Filangeri to confirm his contention that Cabey was including himself as part of the group in the first part of his statement when he had said, "The guys I was

with were hassling" Goetz. Filangeri did not, however, and
Waples argued that "in every statement . . . without exception" Cabey had "disassociated himself from any activity by
any of his friends on the subway car that day."

Despite these efforts by both sides to depict Cabey's statement in a favorable light, Justice Crane ruled the statement
inadmissible on two grounds. First, the rules of evidence on a
statement against the declarant's "penal interest" requires that
"the declarant be unavailable." Justice Crane said that this
"once again shows you how topsy-turvy everything is in this
case" because the defense—the side requesting that the statement be admissible—was still contending that Cabey was available. He asked Slotnick if he were willing to stipulate that
Cabey was, in fact, unavailable, and Slotnick was not. Second,
the evidence rules also state that the declarant must be aware
that the statement he makes is against his penal interest, and
Justice Crane said, "I don't think we have shown that Mr.
Cabey was aware" of this.

The judge allowed that the admissibility status of the statement could later change if Cabey proved unavailable, and ruled
that for the present time Slotnick could question Filangeri
during his cross-examination in our presence only about Cabey's
lucidity at the time a "certain statement" was made. Slotnick
acceded to the ruling but told the judge of his "desperation
to bring this statement before the jury."

"I need this statement for my case, Your Honor," Slotnick
pleaded.

"I know, Mr. Slotnick," answered Justice Crane. "I'm taking great care. It's very uncharacteristic in terms of a trial to
stop and examine to a clinical degree each and every aspect
of the rules of evidence. I'm doing that because I know it's
important, and I'm doing that because I don't shoot from the
hip ordinarily."

"I know that," Slotnick replied. "Your Honor is quite
scholarly in his approach. I think both of us join in what Your
Honor is doing."

All of this is what we jurors missed while we sat together
through the morning in the jury room. The long delay was

helpful, though, because we got into the habit of figuring out good ways to kill large blocks of time early on.

The first day had been a little disorganized in the jury room, with no arrangements having been made for coffee or to accommodate the smokers among us, no decks of cards, and nobody really knowing each other. But that situation was quickly remedied, thanks especially to Augustine Ayala. Augie was one of the four alternate jurors, and he proved to be a real team leader, a take-charge kind of guy, whom we soon were referring to as Mr. Coffee. He brought in a coffeepot from home, took up the collection for coffee supplies, and also brought in poker chips and cards. The court officers allowed us to keep the pot and supplies in the room overnight, which made life much easier. They also refrigerated the milk and any food we brought in for the day.

Soon we had a pretty good system worked out and enjoyed the delays despite the cramped quarters. There were sixteen of us in the one narrow room with two adjoining bathrooms, a rectangular table, sixteen wooden chairs, and one metal coatrack. We decorated one long wall with a couple of posters: an advertisement for Jamaica that Augie brought in featuring a bikinied woman on a beach; and a Mets poster, courtesy of Mike Axelrod. On the other long wall we put a six- or seven-foot-long computer printout made by D. Wirth Jackson of the jurors' admonition not to talk about the case. It was the same admonition that the judge repeated to us every time he excused us from the courtroom; words that I heard over and over again.

Smoking was limited to one side of the room, and a large ventilator on the ceiling over the center of the table provided good enough air circulation so that those of us who didn't smoke weren't bothered by the fumes. The air stream was so powerful, though, that card players, especially the poker players, who always sat at the center of the table, had to be careful that it didn't flip over their cards. A second card group sat at the far end of the table—the smoker's side—and played fan-tan.

I mostly tried to sleep during the breaks for the first few days. I was suffering through a bout of insomnia caused, I suppose, by the excitement surrounding the beginning of the trial. But later I joined the poker game, whose regular members were Mike Axelrod, James Mosely, Carolyn Perlmuth, Bob Leach, Frank Figueroa, and myself. We divided up the chips at the beginning of each day and maintained a fair degree of seriousness about the way we'd bet, even though money was not at stake, so the game was competitive and fun to play.

Ralph Schriempf and John Patten, another alternate, did a lot of crossword puzzles. D. Wirth Jackson brought in trivia games that Ralph would play with him; the two of them also liked to discuss old songs. Sometimes Ralph joined the fan-tan game with John Patten; our foreman, James Hurley; Erniece Dix; and alternate number three, Lou Vereen.

Diana Serpe for the most part sat in a corner by herself and read a lot, mostly paperback novels and *New York* magazine. For the first week or so I noticed Moseley, who sat at the table next to me, looking in Diana's direction a lot. After a while he stopped and I thought he'd lost interest. I did not know until after the trial that the two had become romantically involved and were making an effort to play it cool.

Cathy Brody, the English professor, was another big reader. Brody also took copious notes on the proceedings. I'd always see her writing on a yellow legal pad in the jury room, in the hallways, in the mornings, during the lunch break—wherever and whenever she could.

I also did a decent amount of reading over the weeks: "The Holcroft Covenant" by Robert Ludlum and James Clavell's "Shogun" for the third or fourth time. There was time to do a lot of things, we had so much of it to kill; yet we'd never know if a break was going to last five minutes or a few hours, so often we'd just sit around and talk, telling stories about ourselves to help pass the time. Or we'd talk about sports or other neutral subjects since we were prohibited from speaking about the trial, that which was foremost on all of our minds.

Then, lo and behold, we'd be called back out; and we'd assemble in the hallway, with me first, of course, to return to the stage for another dramatic scene. This, in essence, was our routine.

In his cross-examination of Filangeri, Slotnick followed Justice Justice Crane's ruling and elicited only that Cabey had spoken about the incident and that Filangeri believed him to be lucid at the time he spoke. He questioned Filangeri about where he had found the four youths when he arrived on the scene in an effort to infer where they had been when they were shot and thereby to prove that Goetz had been surrounded. Slotnick made important points in this regard, I thought, concerning Darrell Cabey and James Ramseur.

"[L]et's assume that the first individual on [Goetz's] left was Troy Canty and he took out a gun and he fired at Troy Canty. Would it be consistent with the wound that you found on Troy Canty and where Troy Canty was lying?"

"I believe it would be," Filangeri said.

* * *

"And where Mr. Ramseur was lying would not be inconsistent with the fact that he may have been standing next to or within close proximity of Troy Canty and Bernhard Goetz, is that correct?"

"That's correct."

* * *

"Would that shot have been inconsistent with Mr. Cabey standing around Mr. Goetz and turning when he saw a gun . . . ?"

"It's possible it could have been incurred that way."

"Would that shot that you saw on Darrell Cabey have been consistent with someone walking over to an individual seated in front of him, taking out a gun and saying, . . . 'You don't look bad; here's another,' and firing directly at his front?"

"I don't believe so."

Filangeri could not speculate as to where Barry Allen was when he'd been shot because he'd found Allen crawling in the subway car when he arrived. Slotnick asked in reference to Allen, "He was hopping around?"

"He was crawling around," Filangeri responded.

I thought it was funny how Slotnick tried to characterize Allen as "hopping" to suggest, I suppose, that he was not as seriously injured as he was. Slotnick had already made this same characterization twice in questions to Filangeri in the examination he'd made while we were out of the room, and each time Filangeri replied that Allen had been crawling, not hopping. Slotnick was relentless when he wanted to make a point.

Filangeri was not a ballistics expert, however; and although these speculations seemed logical, their value was limited in that Filangeri was not an eyewitness and so could not know where Goetz had been positioned when he fired at the youths. In redirect examination, Waples reiterated that Filangeri had been making "assumptions" based on where the victims were found.

"So, in the case of Barry Allen . . . , [y]ou only know that he was shot in the back?"

"That's correct."

Concerning Darrell Cabey, Filangeri said that Cabey was paralyzed when he found him slumped in the small seat by the conductor's cab, and "judging from the paralysis" it was "highly impossible" he could have crawled or lifted himself up into that position.

Waples then borrowed an empty chair that was next to the court reporter, positioned it between the witness stand and the jury box, and sat down to demonstrate his theory of how Cabey was shot. "In fact," Waples said, "if he were sitting in that small seat, much like I am sitting in this seat now, and a person advanced from his left with a gun in his hand, who had already shot three individuals, the wound in his back would be entirely consistent, would it not, with a flinching motion to his right, away from the gun, causing a wound to be inflicted in the side of the back that traveled laterally across his back and severed the spinal column?

"That is correct," Filangeri said.

Slotnick then tried to counter on this point in his recross-examination by asking whether, assuming Cabey was shot while moving away from Goetz, his momentum might have propelled him into the seat. Filangeri answered, "I suppose that's possible. There are numerous possibilities." But Waples objected to the question as speculation, and Justice Crane sustained him; so we were told to discount both the question and the answer, and at this point the guesswork came to an end.

The next witness was Detective Charles Haase, a middle-aged man who bore an uncanny resemblance to the actor Dennis Franz, who played Lieutenant Bunz on "Hill Street Blues." Haase was a fifteen-year member of the crime scene unit, which routinely takes photographs of crime scenes and searches for trace evidence such as fingerprints, ballistics material, blood, etc., and then marks and packages the evidence and sends it to the proper labs.

Five eight-by-ten-inch black-and-white photographs that were taken after the youths had been removed by the paramedics were entered into evidence and shown to us. We passed them among ourselves in the jury box. Three were taken of different angles of the subway car, showing articles of clothing strewn about and patches of blood on the floor of the train. The fourth showed a large dent in the steel wall of the conductor's cab, which was perpendicular to the short bench on which Cabey was found; and the last was a picture of the seat itself on which lay the partial remains of a bullet: parts of the copper jacket and the lead core.

These two pieces of the bullet and another piece of the lead core that Haase found on the floor of the train were placed into evidence, as were the coats the youths were wearing and three screwdrivers that they presumably had in their pockets.

Haase was asked to point out to us the locations of the bullet holes in all of the coats. Cabey's coat, a blue parka, had two bullet holes in the left side of the exterior: one in the upper back area and the second lower and farther to the front, about five inches below the armpit. The holes on the inside of the thick, padded coat were not in precisely corresponding locations; they were closer together, just below the armpit. Ramseur's, a navy blue-and-maroon reversible jacket, had a hole in the exterior of the left sleeve and an exit hole on the interior side where the bullet entered his arm. It must have been unzipped at the time because there was no entrance hole in the body of the jacket to show where the bullet entered his side.

A reversible vest that Waples also sought to enter as evidence was objected to by Slotnick. He said in a sidebar that he didn't know for a fact that the vest had belonged to Allen, but it had a bullet hole in the center of the back, five or six inches below the collar, that clearly corresponded to Allen's wound. Slotnick's objection, though, apparently was a theatrical ploy, because he reversed his objection and entered the vest into evidence himself during his cross-examination. Instead of allowing all of the coats to be entered as evidence that was meant to incriminate Goetz, therefore, Slotnick wanted to turn the tables on the prosecution, just as he said he would do in his opening, and appear to be prosecuting the defendant's victims. He was suggesting that Ramseur's reversible jacket and Allen's reversible vest incriminated the youths because they had worn them with the intention of changing their colors after committing a crime to avoid being apprehended. Slotnick asked Haase during cross-examination, "By the way, . . . are you aware of the fact . . . that that's the uniform of a mugger, to wear a reversible jacket? Are you familiar with that fact?" Needless to say, the question was objected to and the objection was sustained.

Slotnick also tried to disparage the youths as drug addicts while cross-examining Haase. He pointed out the fact that Haase had also found twelve small zip-lock bags and a Vick's inhaler on the floor of the subway car in addition to the articles submitted as evidence. Of the zip-lock bags, Slotnick asked, "[I]s that indicative to you of someone dealing with drugs?"

"Not necessarily," Haase answered. "I carry them in my kit."

"You carry zip-lock bags?" Slotnick said, perhaps caught off guard for a moment. "Is there a possibility you had dropped them and they were yours?"

"No."

"Do you know that the perpetrators were drug addicts?" Slotnick then asked.

Waples objected to the question, but Justice Crane over-ruled. Haase then answered, "No."

Haase, when asked, did not remember the Vick's inhaler, although he'd listed it on his report as an item recovered from the car. Nevertheless, Slotnick asked him if he knew if the inhaler had been tested for narcotics.

"No," Detective Haase answered once again.

The other issue Slotnick wanted to stress was that the police had done a lousy job of safeguarding the evidence before

Haase arrived on the scene. This had been broached during Waples's direct questioning, and had been noted by Haase in his report. Only the detective in charge should have been in the subway car after the paramedics had gotten the victims out, yet several uniformed officers were there as well as members of the press. Evidence can be destroyed when too many people are allowed into a crime scene, Haase stated, and, in fact, no fingerprints were recovered from the three screwdrivers or from anywhere on the subway car, and the bullet fragment found on the floor was originally seen by another officer on the small seat with the other fragments.

Slotnick antagonized Haase a little on this point. "[I]n general," he asked, "up to the time you appeared, the investigation was sloppy because . . . what you found in the car was the media, the press, all sorts of individuals walking around, perhaps smearing fingerprints, kicking bullets, things of that sort. Is that correct? Yes or no?"

"I can't answer that yes or no," Haase replied.

"Would you say that there were people in that car that should not have been there prior to your arrival?"

"Yes."

"Would you say that the evidence was not safeguarded properly and adequately prior to your arrival?"

"Yes."

"Would you say the operation prior to your arrival was somewhat sloppy?"

"By the people—"

"Yes or no?"

"By whom?"

"By whoever was in charge of the investigation until you showed up."

"To a degree, yes," Haase said.

Slotnick wanted to rub this in, apparently, because it fell into the same category as the points he'd raised in his opening about other failings of the New York City Police Department, such as in the incident when Goetz had been mugged and beaten so badly. Goetz had been questioned by police for over six hours after the mugging and his assailant had been released after two and a half hours with a charge of mischievous conduct. The defense's contention that Goetz was an intended victim in

this case who had thwarted a mugging and that the victims
were the real criminals also followed this same line. Slotnick
was tying together the district attorney's office, the police
department, and the whole New York City judicial system and
making a case that the system was both inept and absurd.

I'll mention here two other witnesses who didn't appear
until the next week, on May 5, because their testimony was
mostly limited to the same physical evidence that Haase discussed.

The first was a transit officer, Richard Reip. Reip and his
partner were called to the Franklin Street subway station, one
stop north of Chambers Street, and took part in the hunt for
Goetz after the shootings, when he'd fled on foot by way of
the subway tracks. They searched the tunnel and then arrived
at the crime scene, where Haase handed over the evidence
he'd collected for them to voucher and deliver to the precinct.
Slotnick did not cross-examine Reip.

The second was a transit detective, Alejandro Torres, who'd
arrived at the crime scene shortly after the shootings, well
before Haase. The paramedics were already there.

Torres said he attempted to interview each of the youths
while the paramedics attended to them. "I asked them their
names and what happened, and none of them responded,"
Torres said, except Darrell Cabey, who "held onto my arm
and asked me to help him and not to let him die." The youths
all "appeared to be in pain," according to Torres. "They were
moaning. Their eyes would close and open."

As Cabey and Ramseur were moved onto stretchers, Torres
assisted in taking their coats off. He said he found a screwdriver
in each of Cabey's two front pockets; and, significantly, he
testified that the pockets were zippered shut. He found a third
screwdriver in one of the pockets of Ramseur's jacket. In cross-
examination Torres revealed that in that case, "I just pulled it
out. I didn't have to open the zipper."

Chapter 5

The Audiotapes

During the afternoon session of the trial's second day, Justice Crane, always considerate, discussed with us the physical problems we were having with the courtroom. The sound system was still bouncing voices around ("I'm hearing myself in stereo," Justice Crane complained), and he encouraged us to raise our hands if we were having trouble hearing. The court officers kept tinkering with the sound system, though, by repositioning the speakers and angling them in different directions, so that by the end of the day the problem was more or less resolved.

A lot of us in the front row of the jury box were also having trouble seeing much of what was going on because the front of the jury box was too high and the jury rail blocked our view. I had to crane my neck just to see the witnesses' faces while they testified on the witness stand, and I had to rise out of my seat to see certain exhibits as they were placed into evidence, or to see the witnesses when they stood beside the scale drawing of the subway car, which was on an easel between the witness stand and the jury box. This defect had existed for twenty-seven years, since the building was constructed in 1960, but due to the importance and publicity surrounding this case it was finally fixed in a single night, between the second and third days of the trial, by cutting off about ten inches of wood along the front of the jury box.

Until the jury box alteration was made, Justice Crane again advised us to "not be shy and speak up by raising your hand if you can't see anything, because we'll stop right then and there.

"You are important people in this trial," Justice Crane continued, sounding very paternal, "and we want you to be able to have a full view of everything you are supposed to see and be able to hear everything you're supposed to hear. So please keep that in mind. Even if it does slow us down, it's very important."

The next two witnesses were an officer and a detective from the Concord, New Hampshire police department, where Goetz had turned himself in at about noon on New Year's Eve, 1984, after nine days on the lam. First to testify was Officer Warren Foote, who was on duty at the station when Goetz walked in and had been assigned to speak to Goetz and hear what he had to say.

When Foote first realized that Goetz wanted to make some kind of confession, he advised him of his right to remain silent, to have an attorney present, and so forth; and he had him sign a Miranda warning sheet after Goetz stated that he wanted to waive those rights. The two then talked for an hour and twenty minutes, from 12:40 p.m. until 2:00 p.m., in a small interview room on the second floor of the police station. Asked by Waples to describe Goetz's emotional and psychological state, Foote said, "He was nervous, very nervous, at that time."

Then Foote was joined by Detective Christopher Domian, who asked Goetz if he would be willing to make an audiotaped statement. Goetz agreed, and then that interview lasted, with both Foote and Domian present, for two hours, from 2:00 p.m. to 4:00 p.m. A transcript of the audiocassette tapes from the interview was then typed by a secretary for Goetz to read over and sign. Later a third interview was held once New York City officials arrived, which also lasted two hours and was recorded on videotape. Goetz was formally charged with being a fugitive from justice by Detective Domian at about 1:00 a.m., New Year's Day.

April 29

The second day of the trial concluded with Officer Foote's testimony, and Detective Domian took the stand to begin the third day. The burden of the questioning was merely to establish the scenario in which Goetz's statements were obtained and then to enter the statements into evidence. At the end of Waples's direct examination of Domian, the audiotapes were played.

An amplifier allowed the audience to hear the tapes, while I and my fellow jurors were each given a lightweight pair of wireless headphones to wear that had a dial so we could control the volume ourselves, along with a copy of the forty-seven-page, single-spaced transcript of the tape so that we could read along. Justice Crane warned us, though, that the transcript was merely a guide and was not actual evidence. "It is the sounds on the tape that are evidence in this case," he said, and "if there's any discrepancy between the tape and the transcript, the tape controls."

It was strange to finally hear Goetz's voice for the first time, after seeing him always mute for so long. His voice was a little higher pitched than I had imagined; it was strained, with a slight whine, and betrayed his nervousness: he stammered a lot. The strain he had undergone over the nine days since the shooting was apparent; he sounded tense and emotional, though he was trying his best to choke his emotions, to not let himself get carried away. He struggled to remain analytical and to intellectualize what he had done and what he was feeling, but then he'd become upset about what he was describing and would start losing his grip, losing control.

I sensed that Goetz was riddled with guilt about what he'd done even though he felt justified or hoped he was justified. He spoke convincingly about wanting to find out the truth of the matter and feeling that he deserved to be punished if what he had done was wrong. Often in his anger he became defiant and self-righteous, but at other times he sounded angry and disgusted with himself.

Goetz proved to be such a complex individual in my mind that for almost every positive aspect of his psychological makeup a negative aspect would present itself as well. He was clearly upset and drained by his experience. Domian had to ask him initially to speak up to make sure he'd be understood clearly, and Goetz answered, "I—I—I'm just tired, you know? You get so tired."

At times he sounded resigned to what he was likely to face in giving himself up, yet he was horrified by its prospects and clung to the pitiable, impossible hope that somehow he could keep his anonymity. Domian asked him the name of his one-man electronics business, and Goetz resisted, answering: "You see, if you make all this pub—I just don't want this to be pub—You know, like, you see, I'll tell the truth, and they can do anything they want with me. But I just don't want to— I just don't want to be paraded around. I don't want a circus, you know, or something like that. . . . The flashcubes popping off in my face and stuff like that, that's—You see, I—I'm not ashamed of what I've done. I'm sure—I'm sure I've done it. I wish this were a dream. I wish this were a dream, but it's not. But, you know, it's nothing to be proud of. It's just—just, you know—It just is."

Domian reiterated to Goetz his right to have a lawyer present, and Goetz said, "Look, I know I can, but the issue, you see, the issue in my mind is right or wrong. Like, I don't want these, you know, like people have offered to defend me for free and stuff like that. And—And what they—what a lawyer would do . . . is tell me what not to say. He would say, 'Well, don't say this, and don't say that,' and—and you get off on the technicalities. And that just makes me sick. Because if you did it, and it's true, you should be judged, you know, on the truth, and what is right and what is wrong. If what I did is wrong, then—then . . . okay, and I have to live with that."

Later in the interview Goetz said again, "You know, I don't care what they do to me," and in the next breath uttered, "The truth is all I have."

The cynical view you could take of this, of course, was that here was Goetz on trial now armed with the likes of Barry Slotnick, who would never flinch at winning his case on technicalities. Also, though Goetz was without a lawyer, his confession was calculated to a degree. He had had nine days to think on this matter and had chosen to give himself up in New Hampshire because he trusted people from New England and wanted to tell his story to a more sympathetic audience. He said of the reason he'd driven to Vermont immediately after the shootings, "[I]nstinctively, somehow I kinda feel like heading north is the way to go if there's a problem. . . . I don't know . . . how to explain it; it's just a feeling." And, indeed, in obtaining his confession, perhaps especially because he had surrendered voluntarily, Domian was very tolerant as Goetz digressed to tell of his previous mugging and of the horrors of living in New York City. Goetz described his thinking when confronted by the youths in the subway as "cold-blooded" but then justified himself by saying, "[Y]ou have to think in a cold-blooded way in New York." Then he told Domian, "How can you understand that here in New Hampshire?" Goetz said he turned himself in because it was "the right thing to do" but also because "sooner or later I was . . . going to be caught anyway." He knew he was better off surrendering than being apprehended and felt in his mind that he was telling his story to someone who could not judge him for what he'd done.

Goetz also showed that he was aware of the law and of the issues on which he would be judged. He vigorously rebutted the news reports that had speculated that the shootings were premeditated on his part. "If this were premeditated," he argued, "why wouldn't I have simply put on a fake moustache and worn different glasses, or worn contacts? Why would I . . . just go around dressed like I'm always dressed? How can anyone be so stupid?" He became defensive when explaining how before he started shooting he "laid down [his] pattern of fire" in his mind, because he realized that sounded incriminating. "[T]his wasn't premeditated," he insisted. "I never knew those guys were on the train, you know? And like I said, I'm— I'm no good guy or anything like that, but if they had acted a little differently, if they hadn't cornered me—" Here he digressed and never finished the thought, but later he added, "I would have stayed in my apartment, or, you know, something, you know, if I'd had any hint that this would have happened."

Even more in Goetz's favor was that despite his awareness of the law concerning allowable self-defense, rather than using this knowledge to help try to exonerate himself, he often consciously did the opposite. Domian asked him if he was afraid when Canty was standing over him, asking him for money, and the other youths moved to surround him; and Goetz answered, "No, listen. You see, I know what the law is, and the law says . . . are you afraid [for] your life? But that isn't the issue." Goetz refused to mask the truth and to escape justice on "technicalities" by claiming he was afraid when he felt he hadn't been. He tried to act as if he hadn't been afraid until there was a real reason to be afraid.

"I just want to say something," he interjected at one point, and then explained that one of the youths who had a screwdriver in his pocket had shown Goetz the bulge in his coat to instill fear in him, pretending to have a gun. But Goetz said, "[A]nd I know this is going to incriminate me, that it isn't a threat. You know it's bullshit."

This is what Goetz contended happened on the subway that day: what he did and what caused him to do it. He entered the train at Fourteenth Street, traveling from his home to the Chambers Street station to meet some friends for a pre-Christmas drink. Domian asked if he ever met the friends. "No, of course not," Goetz said, "because the trip was—"

"It didn't go as planned?" Domian offered.

"Yeah, you could say that," Goetz replied.

As usual, Goetz was armed. He told Domian the story of his previous mugging, the resulting permanent knee injury, his dissatisfation with the police department's handling of the case, and of his subsequent effort to obtain a permit to carry a pistol in New York City. He had spent $2,000 and still had been turned down by an officer who said, " 'We can't go around giving a pistol permit to anybody who wants one. That would be irresponsible.' " Goetz called these incidents "an education" that taught him "that the city doesn't care what happens to you." He said he subsequently bought several handguns legally out of state, and confessed to owning more guns than the one he used and to having sold guns to other people at cost. In New York City, he said, "a lot of people feel you have to have a gun, but they don't let you." So, he said, "they have you trapped" because "you're in a situation where you must carry a gun."

"You see, I can't walk in New York without carrying a gun," Goetz said, and added, "In the winter time, in New York, like since I was attacked, I—I can't wear gloves anymore, because if you wear gloves, you can't get to the gun, you know?"

Goetz entered the southbound subway car by the northwest door because he had seen a vacant seat in this car, while the car behind it had been too crowded. He said he had figured out after the fact that the reason seats were available was because of the four youths, who had scared other people away. He sat down on the long bench across from the door he entered, and immediately one of the youths, Troy Canty, who was lying on the long bench across from where he sat, turned to face him and asked, "How are you?" Goetz said Canty's question was "a meaningless thing, but in certain circumstances . . . that can be a real threat. You see, there's an implication there."

In addition to Canty, one youth was on the short seat to the left of the door he entered, and the other two were seated across from the door, on the short seat by the conductor's cab. All three therefore were to Goetz's right when he sat down— two on his side of the aisle and another diagonally across.

When the train was out of the station and had reached full speed, Goetz said, Canty and the other youth seated across the aisle (presumably Barry Allen) "got up . . . and they came to my left-hand side." Goetz said their "body language" told him he was in danger. Canty held onto the hand strap above Goetz, leaned over him, and said, "Give me five dollars."

"These guys say they were joking and laughing, but it wasn't a joke, okay?" Goetz said, referring, I took it, to statements by the youths he'd heard through news reports. "I looked—You see, I looked at his eyes and, you know, I looked at his face and, you know, his eyes were shiny . . . , he was enjoying himself. You see? And then he had a big smile on his face, and, as I told Officer Foote, you know at that point you're in a bad situation, okay?

"Now I know, in my mind, I know what—well, who— who knows for sure, but I know in my mind what they wanted to do was play with me. . . . [T]he issue isn't the five dollars or something like that. That's unimportant, you know? . . . People who know me know that five dollars doesn't mean a thing to me. . . . It was they wanted to play with me. You know? It's kind of like a cat plays with a mouse before—You know? It's horrible, but, uh—"

"At that point, in my mind, I knew what they were," Goetz said a moment later. "The confrontation, that was the threat right there. It was seeing his smile and his eyes lit up and the presence of the other [three] and I knew . . . my situation."

"When I saw him smiling, I laid down my pattern of fire," Goetz said, deciding to shoot from left to right. "But before— before I was gonna start shooting, I needed absolute verification. So—So—I—I asked one more time. I—I was being deceitful. As I told Officer Foote . . . , you learn to hide your intentions. In the business world in New York, you have to hide—you know, to hide the person you are, and, I mean, I haven't for several years. I—I thought I'd become an honest person over these years. I hope I have been."

What Goetz did to get verification was to ask Canty what he'd just said, and Canty repeated his demand. "When I had —and I know this sounds horrible and cold-blooded and they're gonna wipe the floor with me for this—but when I had veri- fication, you know, what you do is, you don't think anymore. . . . [T]he upper level of your mind you just turn off. . . . You react. That's the important thing. You react. You go in a different state of mind and a lot of things change. . . . Your sense of perception changes. Your abilities change. Speed is everything. Speed is everything."

Goetz stood up and drew his gun; and, he said, "the whole situation speeded up. All hell broke loose, as soon as the gun came out." He then shot at each of the four, clockwise, from left to right. He aimed for the center of the body in each case. "I hardly heard the gun firing," he said. "You see, . . . your ears aren't important. . . . This is a combat thing. . . . You just follow your vision."

He fired at the first two, then spun toward the others. Of the third youth, Goetz said, "I think [he] tried to run through the—the wall of the train. But he had—you know, he had nowhere to go. He had nowhere to go."

The fourth youth, Darrell Cabey, "tried pretending he wasn't with them," Goetz said. "He just—He just kinda stopped where he was. He wouldn't even look—He wouldn't look at me. He kinda stood up and he—I think he held his hand or something. I don't remember clearly. . . . He reached up and held his hand on the railing, or on the, uh, excuse me, the hand strap. . . . I guess it was his reaction to fear."

Domian asked if he shot each person just once, and Goetz said, "That's one of the things that puzzles me." He tried to rationalize why he couldn't remember clearly, saying, "[I]f you can accept this: I was out of control. . . . It's true, maybe you should always be in control, but if you—if you put people in a situation where they're threatened with mayhem, several times, and then if—then if something happens, and if a person acts—turns into a vicious animal, I mean . . . what do you expect, you know?"

"Let's stick with the first two people. Lock yourself in on that," Domian said. The first two people. You shot each of them once, is that correct? Just once?"

"You—You see, that's what must have happened. That's what did happen," Goetz answered, showing his confusion. "Because that's the way to do it. It's—It's the only—It's the only logical way."

After he had shot at all four, Goetz said, he checked on the first two who had both fallen to the floor and saw that they were "cold, that they'd been taken care of." They were incapacitated and no longer a threat. "The guy who was standing up, or something like that, he was then sitting down," Goetz said, returning to Cabey. "I wasn't sure if I had shot him before, because he just seemed okay. Now, I said—I know this sounds—this is gonna sound vicious. And it is; I mean, how else can you describe it? I said, 'You seem to be all right; here's another.'"

"So this person is sitting down when you shot him, which you think may be again?" Domian asked.

"Excuse me?" Goetz replied. "But you see, the police say that four shots were fired. I fired five shots. And I admit something. If I—If I was thinking a little bit more clearly, if I was a little more under self-control—I was so out of control —I would have put . . . the barrel against his forehead and fired."

Listening to the tapes, I was surprised that Goetz had made such damning statements; and I was surprised also that, given these statements, the first grand jury had decided not to indict. I had not taken these statements to heart when I'd heard them from Waples in his opening because I'd been told opening statements were not evidence; but now I'd heard them from Goetz, and I found them to be incriminating indeed.

Goetz sounded sincere, though, and I became convinced by what he said and also by the evidence and the testimony of others that his version of the sequence of events in the subway car was essentially accurate. His recollection about what happened after he stopped shooting was amazing, I thought, given what his emotional state must've been. He remembered speaking to two women who he was worried had been hurt either by a bullet or otherwise in the chaos during the shootings, and he was able to describe them both in general terms. He also remembered speaking to the conductor who came in afterward from one car in front, and his account of these conversations was later corroborated to a large extent.

The conductor asked Goetz what had happened, and he answered, "They tried to rob me and I shot them." Goetz told Domian he'd said this because "I trusted him instinctively" and "[h]e was in a uniform. That's all that matters, you know? You respect the uniform." The conductor subsequently asked Goetz for his gun, though, and Goetz declined to give it up.

Goetz also said that after he stopped shooting he looked down at Troy Canty and said something to him like, "You better learn a lesson from all this." Then, he said, "I sat down and stood up a few times"—an action that I at first thought sounded unlikely, but that Victor Flores, one of the eyewitnesses, specifically remembered him doing as well.

At some point then the train slowed and stopped, and Goetz decided to flee the scene. "I had a choice of staying there," Goetz told Domian. But, he said, "if I stayed on that spot, they would have come and they would have gotten me and they would have wiped the floor with me, which is what is prob—almost certainly going to happen anyway." Goetz said he decided instead to try to "survive" by "think[ing] like a criminal": acting quickly, before police could respond, and running away. He went to the front of the subway car and, between cars, jumped off the train, then ran south in the tunnel to the Chambers Street station, stopped running once he reached the street, took a cab to Fifteenth Street and from there walked home. He showered and changed ("I was all dirty," he said, though he didn't know what from), then rented a car and drove north, stopping in a motel in Bennington, Vermont. The next night, some forty miles north of Bennington, he said, he parked on some side road, walked into the woods, and, as he put it, "ditched the gun."

Having heard the tapes, my opinion leaned slightly toward the prosecution, though I realized it was my duty to maintain an open mind. I had found Goetz credible and to a degree sympathetic. He seemed an honest, polite, and rather meek man in essence who was willing to cooperate yet was determined to try to tell his story his way. He apologized to Domian when he digressed too much, though, and repeatedly said, "Excuse me," "I'm sorry," and, complying to questions, prefaced his answers by saying, "Okay." When he was trying to remember the day of the shootings, he asked Detective Domian, "May I look at my watch?" And he even voiced concern that the meter had run out on his rental car, so that it was probably illegally parked.

Most baffling about Goetz, then, was his ambivalent attitude about violence, which is really at the core of the psychology of the man. In discussing the details of what he'd done—for instance, how he wore his quick-draw holster—he'd become squeamish: "Do you have to know these violent things?" he pleaded to Domian. "It's—It's—It's—It's so disgusting. . . . If you want to—Do you want to know? You know, it's so— it's so—To do what's necessary is so yukky."

"You don't know what it's like to be on the other side of violence," Goetz said to Domian, referring apparently to when he was mugged. "It's—It's like a picture. When it happens to you, you see, you see it. You know, people see, people have the craziest image. They see like Captain Kirk or someone like that getting attacked by several guys and boom boom boom, he beats 'em up and—and two minutes later he's walking arm in arm . . . with a beautiful woman or something like that. And that's not what it is. That's not what it is."

Later he said to Domian, "You see, you don't know what it's like to be a victim inside"; and he explained that "the worst part of being attacked . . . is that you do not know, from moment to moment, . . . what is going to happen the next moment. And you know anything can happen, and I mean anything, okay?" Again referring to the mugging, he said, "After that incident, I'm not—If someone just comes—If someone would come up to me and put a bullet in my head, I don't care. I'm not afraid of dying instantly. I don't have a family or anything like that. What I'm afraid of is being maimed and of—of these things happening slowly and not knowing what's going to happen from moment to moment." That was the fear that he held when the youths approached him on the subway, he explained; and that was the fear that made him carry a gun.

If his fear was understandable, though, I felt his compulsion to defend himself bordered on the obsessive. He apparently owned several handguns in addition to the guns he'd sold to others. That he felt he could not go out of his apartment without being armed and could not wear gloves in winter I thought was extreme, as was his use of a quick-draw holster ("You need speed"), hollow-point bullets (for "maximum stopping power") and low- and higher-velocity charges (for "reliability" and "the most options"). "You see, this is really combat," Goetz had said to Domian; and I felt there was a difference between being prepared to defend oneself and preparing oneself for war.

I also thought it strange how he talked about needing to feel fear, that it was "important to be afraid." He said that fear is "part of the animal response, because what being afraid does for you is it makes you think and analyze, and it speeds up your mind. . . . It builds up your adrenalin a little, okay? . . .

"The important thing is, once the time comes to act, you don't have—you don't think, you react. . . . The lower levels of your brain are going to take care of everything for you. It's—You have speed, you have your—your visual capabilities. . . . [I]t's all visual. Your perception changes, your field of view changes. You see everything. Your sense of hearing becomes unimportant. . . . What you see is important. You react not—not from second to second. You react from—from maybe a tenth of a second or a twentieth of a second. From— From— From moment to moment you react. You know, I've been trying to forget this. I've been trying to forget this. I've been trying—I've been trying to forget it. I'd like to."

Although Goetz felt extreme guilt over the incident ("You can never get away [from] what you do," he said), he was clearly fascinated with it, particularly with how his adrenalin affected or distorted his perceptions, his normal, conscious reality. "It's funny, you know? What's so funny about this is that you remember it afterwards, but from instant to instant you are seeing and forgetting the previous moment. It's so—It's so strange. You can't describe it. It's—It's—It's—"

Of course, how distorted and confused Goetz's recollection was would be a key issue in the trial, particularly concerning how he said he shot Darrell Cabey while Cabey was seated and perhaps from point-blank range. "There are issues," Goetz himself conceded. "People think it's more horrible about point-blank and maybe I did it point-blank, I don't know." About how he shot him, he said, "I was gonna shoot him anyway. I'm sure I had made up, I mean, in my mind, that I was gonna pull the trigger anyway, but he jerked his right arm, and on reflex he was shot instantly."

When Goetz talked about how he'd shot Cabey, more emotion poured out of him than at any other time. Had he been attached to a machine that recorded his emotional state, I'd say the graph lines would have jumped when he discussed shooting Cabey from slightly wavering (that is, fairly calm) to wildly erratic (extremely agitated). But it was hard to tell the reason for this. Either this was where his memory failed him so that he wasn't sure what had happened, and his uncertainty anguished him so; or else this was where his actions had overstepped what could be considered reasonable and justified, and he was feeling a sense of guilt. From the audiotapes alone there was no way to know.

I did agree with the defense's contention that a lot of Goetz's comments about his violent intentions concerning the youths ("My intention was to murder them, to hurt them, to make them suffer as much as possible," etc.) were taken by Waples somewhat out of context in his opening presentation. Goetz, as I said, was feeling extremely guilty, and a lot of his anger was self-directed, but some of it was also aimed at the city and at these youths for putting him in the position where he felt he had to shoot. So I disregarded this type of statement as the inflammatory rhetoric of an angry man and felt that my job as a juror was to see past these emotional tirades when they concerned what he was feeling, what he wanted to do, and study what it was that he really did, what actually happened. He could not be judged on his words, only his deeds.

If I couldn't approve of what he had done to the youths, I could at least feel sorry for what Goetz had done to himself. "It was so crazy," he commented. "These guys had—had trapped me and . . . isn't that something? They . . . trapped themselves." The truth was, though, that Goetz had been trapped in another sense as well. He found himself caught in a situation which he shot his way out of, and by shooting he put himself into a separate situation from which there was no escape. He was trapped forever by his conscience and would perhaps forever be trapped by the intense publicity surrounding the case. I could pity the man as he pleaded with Domian that all he wanted was to try to forget the incident and to be allowed to return to his normal way of life.

Goetz had been shocked at the extent of the news coverage surrounding the shootings. "[T]here was a completely wrong response," he said. "The city and the police and everybody . . . , they make it such a big thing, and to me—I know this sounds horrible—to me it's just one more crime."

"They called this the most violent crime of the year, or something like that," Goetz also said. "And that's—let them call it that. But when have they ever been concerned about violence before?"

He was upset with a news report that had called him a "madman"; furious with a psychological profile made of him by Dr. Joyce Brothers of him in the *New York Post*: he called her a "quack" and a "sham." But most of all he was concerned about how this publicity was going to affect his life. "You don't know what freedom means until you're actually facing losing it," he said. And his statement ended with his saying, "What I want more than anything—and I know the possibility is slim— I want to be— I want to be left alone and I'd—I'd like to live a normal life. I'd like to change my identity and move somewhere else. They're not gonna let me do it. I'm—I'm almost sure of that. But they might. There's a possibility. . . . You see, I've—I've got things to do. I've got to answer a lot of mail and stuff like that."

After lunch, Slotnick used his cross-examination of Domian ostensibly to question the detective's memory of what was said in the interview, but actually as a ploy to underscore the statements Goetz made that he wanted us to remember and take most to heart.

"Now, when you met Mr. Goetz, he appeared to be a quiet, meek individual, did he not?"

"Yes, sir," Domian replied.

Slotnick asked a whole series of questions to reiterate that Goetz had spoken without coercion, freely and voluntarily, that he'd waived his Miranda rights, that he was nervous, and so on. Then came another series of questions about Goetz's version of the incident: how Canty had spoken to him, how the four of them had surrounded him, how they all had been standing and bunched together, and how he had felt "threatened with mayhem" and had feared being maimed.

"There came a time when on—well, on several occasions, he began to speculate. He said things like, 'That must have happened; it's the only logical way I can explain it.' Do you remember that?"

"Yes, sir."

* * *

"And then you asked him, 'You shot two, and then you turned to your right, and you shot twice again.' "

"Correct."

"Remember that?"

"Yes."

"And he responded that he did, but he didn't remember whether he had done it point-blank or whether there was movement around him at that point. Do you remember that?"

"Correct."

"Remember asking him, 'At any point in time, did either one of these—any of these people that you shot attempt to get the gun away from you, or lunge at you in any way?' and his response was, 'I don't know'?"

"Yes, sir."

"Remember Mr. Goetz telling you that everything happens very quickly, and in order to be in this position, you have to be afraid?"

"Yes, sir, I do."

"And remember him telling you, when it was all over,

'Everything started to slow down; it was like putting on brakes; it started to slow down,' and he came back to reality?"

"Yes, sir, I do."

*   *   *

"And remember him telling you right afterwards, 'The gun—and I don't care if you believe it, or if anyone believes it, but the gun was for self-defense'?"

"Yes, sir."

"Those are exactly his words, are they not?"

"Yes, sir."

*   *   *

"And he also told you that under the circumstances that he found himself, that he was capable of things that he would not normally be capable of?"

"Correct."

"He explained to you that the mind sometimes takes over the body?"

"Correct."

"Do you remember him telling you, 'All I have is the truth, and all I'm going to tell you is the truth'?"

"Yes, sir."

*   *   *

"I have no further questions, no further questions," Slotnick said, ending his cross-examination with a dramatic flourish.

Waples began his redirect examination with the question, "Mr. Domian, did the defendant say certain things to you that Mr. Slotnick did not question you about on your cross-examination?"

"That's correct," Domian said, equally dispassionately.

Waples followed the same tack that Slotnick had, reiterating Goetz's more incriminating statements about shooting as the youths tried to run away, about how he shot Cabey, and about his use of hollow-point ammunition. He quoted the text more precisely than Slotnick, who had referred to Goetz's statements often more generally, allowing himself to interpret and characterize them a bit. He was also much briefer than Slotnick, taking only five minutes or so; and then Slotnick recrossed to let us hear Goetz's statement to the conductor—"They tried to rob me and I shot them"—one more time.

Chapter 6

A Short Chapter on Sally Smithern

Waples next called a woman named Sally Smithern to the stand. She was the first of nine people who testified to having witnessed the shootings on the subway that day, but she had been seated in the middle of the car behind the one Goetz and the youths were in and had seen what she saw through the windows of the doors between the cars.

Smithern's testimony was interesting mostly because she was the first person to relate to us what it was like to have been on that train when pistol shots were fired, and how difficult it would be for us to obtain an accurate report of what had happened from people who had been so frightened and traumatized, especially two-and-a-half years after the fact. I also for the first time got to see Slotnick cross-examine with the aim of discrediting a witness, how he would persist in pressing every possible point of contention far beyond what was needed to raise the necessary degree of doubt. He wouldn't set out to damage the credibility of a witness; he would try to completely destroy it. And not every time with every juror, but often enough, he would succeed.

Besides these insights, I doubted after I'd heard Smithern's testimony that she would prove a very pertinent witness. Her vantage point was very obscure, and I felt it was doubtful that she could have seen what went on from where she was seated with any great accuracy. Indeed, her memory of details was poor, and much of what she did remember contradicted previous testimony. That was clear through Waples's direct examination, even before Slotnick began his credibility attack.

Probably the most valuable point the prosecution wished to make through Smithern was her recollection that the car she was in had not been crowded. She, like Goetz, boarded the train at Fourteenth Street, and she said, "On my end it wasn't crowded at all. In fact," she elaborated, "I don't even remember anyone sitting on my bench, and I know across from me there were three people and that's about all." Goetz had said on the audiotapes that he'd entered the car he did because there were no seats available in the car behind his; and Goetz had theorized that the reason his car was relatively empty was that other passengers had cleared out in fear of the youths.

After the train left Fourteenth Street, Smithern said, "I was reading. I heard a loud bang that I perceived as a shot. I looked up, my eyes went directly to a very—a person standing, a very light image, puffy light coat, some kind of hat, light hat. His arm—this person's arm was pointed outwards, and I heard the shots. Then I saw the hand go like this, in a sweeping motion and, like, stop. And each time it stopped, three times, I heard another shot. And that's what I saw."

We had already heard from Officer Foote that Goetz said he was wearing a light blue jacket, a green-plaid shirt, and blue jeans on the subway that day, but there had been no mention of Goetz wearing a hat, so it appeared that Smithern was wrong in that detail. The major problem with her testimony, though, was that although Smithern said, "My eyes were peeled on this . . . person's arm," she said that the motion of the arm was from right to left, which was the opposite of what Goetz had testified to and which seemed to be corroborated by physical evidence. No one was contesting, for instance, that Troy Canty was the youth who had spoken to Goetz and who was the first one shot; and when Filangeri arrived on the scene, he found Canty lying farthest to the south end of the car and away from Smithern, on the side that would have been to Goetz's left. So Smithern remembered the whole thing backwards, which I felt by itself seriously undermined the value of her testimony. I didn't think Slotnick had to go to the extremes that he did to further discredit her account.

The defense's contention was that Smithern was never on that train; that she had made the story up after hearing all the news reports in the hope of making some money out of it.

Slotnick asked her, in order to imply this to us, "[D]id Mr. Waples tell you that a lot of people have come forward in this case that weren't on the train, that were just here to give testimony or to take the witness stand in a highly publicized case?"

"No," she answered.

"He didn't tell you that?"

"No."

"Did he ever question you whether you were ever on the train?"

"I'm not really sure what you're getting at," she said defensively.

"It's not important," Slotnick said. "Please answer my question."

"I don't remember," Smithern replied.

He also asked her a lot of questions about her background to make her appear a little flaky. She had moved around so much that she couldn't recall all the places she had lived (she rememered Los Angeles, Cincinnati, Akron, Ann Arbor, and Kalamazoo) nor all the apartments she'd sublet in New York City. Much of her moving had to do with her attending seminars in different undergraduate schools, also too numerous for her to recall, but including the University of Michigan, the Los Angeles College of Chiropractics, and Ohashi Institute here in New York, where she studied acupuncture and "holisticology," which she defined as "oriental diagnosis, Japanese school." Smithern said she had a list of all the addresses she had held that she would have to consult to remember precisely.

"And this list of your prior places of residence, you didn't happen to bring it to court with you today?"

"No," Smithern answered.

"Is it more than one page?"

"Probably not. I write pretty small."

"Now, when you were in Los Angeles," Slotnick asked a bit later, "did you learn anything about the making of movies?"

"No," Smithern said. "I was studying eight to five, Monday through Friday."

"What were you studying?"

"Chiropractics."

"And do you have any thought that if they ever make a movie of this trial, that you might be one of the people that would be depicted in the movie?"

"No. I doubt it," Smithern replied.

Slotnick went on to attack the discrepancies between her testimony and some known facts: the direction of the motion of Goetz's arm, and also the location of her car in relation to the train as a whole. The shootings took place in the back end of the seventh car, and Smithern had placed herself in the middle of the eighth car, which was the third car from the rear of the train. Yet she'd said during direct examination that after the shootings she ran through about a half-dozen cars to get to the rear, and then walked through the same half-dozen cars without passing through the car in which the shootings occurred when she finally got off the train. So again the accuracy of her version was impeached.

Smithern was so nervous and uncomfortable on the stand that I never believed she was lying to seek some measure of fame and fortune. I felt she was trying to cooperate and was doing her best to recall what she had seen. She really just seemed to have a lousy memory. She could not remember, for instance, from what station she had entered the subway that day; she said she had been probably somewhere on the Upper West Side. She also said she believed she had been heading for the West Fourth Street station, and she had gotten off an express train at Fourteenth Street to switch to a local. When the next express train arrived and the local hadn't come, she got on, thinking that the express might also stop at West Fourth. She was mistaken about even this, though; neither train goes to that station, which is a part of a separate subway line, and although the local would've gotten her within a few blocks, the express took her far out of her way.

She also became extremely flustered during cross-examination, as Slotnick contended that from a seated position she could not possibly have been able to see what she remembered seeing. The window of the storm door that she would have looked through was one of the old-style round ones, like a porthole, that is situated quite high up, at eye level on the door. Slotnick pulled out the prosecution's photograph of a subway car door with the same kind of window and first showed the photograph to us.

He handed it directly to James Hurley, which Waples objected to because the court officers are meant to do that, and Waples said, "Judge, I think the appropriate procedure is not for the attorney to approach the jurors."

"I'm sorry, Judge. I apologize. Nothing was meant by it," Slotnick said.

In my opinion, though, Slotnick never did anything that wasn't intentional. During his cross-examination of Smithern as well as all the later witnesses whose testimony he sought to discredit, Slotnick was always moving over to us and giving us those looks of his, priceless facial expressions that said, "Can you believe what you're hearing? Doesn't that answer insult your intelligence?" He approached us with the picture just then to be sure he had our attention and to reestablish eye contact as he began his final credibility assault.

"Now, Miss Smithern," he began, "you were seated and your eyes were glued on that hand and you watched the degree of angles as the shots fired from east to north, is that correct?"

"Yes," she said, fidgeting with her hands and looking as if she would rather be anywhere than in this courtroom being confronted by this man.

"Now, do you remember anything unusual about the hand?"

"No."

"How about the fact that for you to have seen what you say you saw, you would have had to be seven feet in the air. Did you notice that?" Slotnick said, smirking at us.

"Objection," Waples stood and said.

"Sustained," said Justice Crane.

Slotnick then presented her with the photograph and asked her to draw a line through the window representing the angle of her line of vision. Smithern was so flustered at this point that she tried with the purple marker she was given to enlarge and lower the window, saying she did not believe it had been that high on the door.

"Please don't draw an extra window. I know you would like to lower the window," Slotnick said, then took the photo from her and moved once again to hand it to us, to show us what she'd done. Justice Crane stopped him this time and made him give it to a court officer rather than to us directly. Again, Slotnick apologized.

"I'm almost finished," Slotnick then said to Justice Crane, and in his most condescending tone added, "I think it's about time Miss Smithern went home, Judge."

He continued, "Miss Smithern, have you ever been under psychiatric care?"

Waples used his redirect to ask Smithern if she was positive she'd seen what she saw and to allow her to deny she was seeking fame and fortune. Then he read the police report of her original call on a hotline number when she had anonymously told essentially the same version of what she'd seen that she testified to. Slotnick recrossed by asking, "Miss Smithern, that report doesn't change the size of the window does it?" Then, when there were no more questions from either attorney, Justice Crane said, "I have one. Did you ever make it to West Fourth Street that day?"

"I don't think I did. No, I didn't," she replied.

"You're excused. Thank you," Judge Crane said, and then he adjourned the case for the day.

Chapter 7

Canty, Allen, and Ramseur (Round 1)

May 1-5

For the next two-and-a-half days of testimony Troy Canty was on the stand. Waples's direct examination lasted over an hour, and then Slotnick's cross-examination took two full days. What we had seen in Slotnick's attack on the credibility of Sally Smithern's testimony, then, had been merely a warm-up for his assault on Canty: a wearying war of attrition that became tiresome to listen to and extremely tried the patience of both Waples and Justice Crane. Waples became so incensed by the tactics Slotnick resorted to that I felt the whole mood of the trial was irrevocably altered. The outward geniality and extensions of professional courtesies all but broke down between the two men because of what Waples considered Slotnick's flagrant violations of appropriate conduct. But I also wondered if Waples's show of outrage and moral indignation wasn't an equally calculated stance.

Canty was dressed in a business suit, and although he didn't look like a yuppie on his way to Wall Street, he did appear to be making an effort to get his life together and to better himself, trying to find a niche in this world. Waples asked him where he lived, and Canty said, "Phoenix Academy," a drug rehabilitation center in Westchester County. Canty had been there for over two years.

Before that Canty had lived in a twenty-story building in a housing project in the Bronx with his mother and older brother. He had dropped out of school after the ninth grade and admitted that he had supported himself by thievery from that time until the time he was shot. Mostly he robbed the cashboxes in video-game machines; he said he could make $150 to $200 "on a good day" doing this. He also said, "I used to buy items wholesale and sell them for retail, and occasionally I shoplifted in large department stores."

He had been arrested and convicted of misdemeanor charges several times before the shootings, when he was nineteen. He was sixteen when he was first arrested for possessing property that he stole with another youth from a midtown office of WOR-TV in January 1982. Three months later he was caught stealing eight shirts from Bloomingdale's in Manhattan, and two weeks after that $130 worth of merchandise from Macy's. A year later he was arrested for stealing money from the cashbox of a poker machine in a tavern in the Bronx, and then again, six months later, from video-game machines in a Penn Station arcade. Until that last arrest he had apparently been sentenced to nothing more than probation, but then he began receiving jail terms of never more than sixty days. In 1984 he was arrested twice again for robbing video-game machines, first in September from an Eighth Avenue bowling alley, and then on December 4 from a bar on Third Avenue and Twenty-third Street, eighteen days before the subway incident occurred.

The money he stole went for clothing and drugs, according to Canty. He said he started smoking marijuana when he was thirteen or fourteen; began sniffing cocaine about two years later; and then started smoking crack two years after that, when he was seventeen or eighteen. Waples asked him how the crack would make him feel, and Canty answered, "I can't really explain it. It was sort of like a rush." He said he went from smoking it two or three times a week to "pretty much every day" by December 1984, when his habit was costing him $50 a day.

"Before December 22, 1984, did you ever think about trying to get off drugs?" Waples asked him.

"Yes," Canty said. He answered Waples's questions extremely succinctly, usually in a word, a sentence at best.

"When did you first start thinking about that?"

"I don't remember."

"Did you do anything about it before December 22, 1984?"

"Yes. I tried to stop."

"How did you try to stop?"

"By not doing it."

"Just by doing it yourself, trying to stop?"

"Yes."

"Did that work?"

"No."

Waples then asked him about his prior relationship with the three other youths. He had had a long-time friendship with Barry Allen, had known Darrell Cabey for about a year, and was only somewhat friendly with James Ramseur. He said he had committed crimes with all of them before. On the day of the shootings Canty said he had been with Barry Allen, that the two of them had decided they were going to go to Manhattan to rob video-game machines, and that on their way they met up with Cabey and Ramseur, who then came along. The four of them boarded first the bus to the subway and then the subway to Manhattan without paying their fares, and Canty said that on the subway he and Barry Allen "horseplayed around" by "shadowboxing" and "hanging on the handle bars." He said he believed Ramseur and Cabey remained seated throughout. The four were heading for the video-game machines at Pace University in lower Manhattan, Canty said; and he explained that these robberies were done by groups of youths so that two or three could use their bodies to block the view of the person in charge while another used a screwdriver to pry open the box.

Canty said he remembered Goetz entering the subway car at the Fourteenth Street station. The four youths were all seated in the rear of the car, he said, he on the long bench just to the right of the door, Barry Allen on the short seat to the left of the door, and Ramseur and Cabey on the short seat across the aisle, by the conductor's cab. Goetz entered and sat on the long bench across from Canty. He did not remember exchanging words with Goetz, just that "he looked at me and I was looking at him." He then stood up and went over to Goetz shortly afterwards, Canty said, because he was aware that none of the youths had any money, and it was helpful to have money so that they could play video games while they stole from them to ward off suspicion.

Canty testified that he was between three or four feet from Goetz, hands empty and at his sides, when he asked Goetz, "Mister, can I have five dollars?" Goetz then got up from his seat and, according to Canty, said, "You can all have it." At this moment, Canty said that to the best of his knowledge all the other youths were sitting. If any had stood up and moved over toward where he was, they were behind him and he hadn't seen them.

"He got up and turned his back towards me," Canty said. "He walked and he was zipping down his jacket. Then he turned around and pulled out his pistol . . ."

"What were you doing when you saw the gun?" Waples asked.

"Standing."

"What happened?"

"He fired; I grabbed my chest. Then I went to the floor."

After he was hit, he said, Barry Allen came up to him and asked, "Troy, are you hurt?" Then he heard another shot and then two more. When all the shots had been fired, he heard James Ramseur, who was also now lying on the floor, "tell me to get my feet out of his face," a line that struck me as hysterically funny; I had to fight to control myself from laughing out loud. Canty said he also "heard Darrell Cabey crying, 'Why did he shoot me? Why did he shoot me?' " and Barry Allen "moving around, jumping, saying, 'It burns.' " He said that Goetz sat down across from where he was lying, and that Goetz was "shaking his head and saying he got to get out of here."

"What was your condition at this time?" Waples asked.

"I was on the floor holding my chest."

"And how did you feel at that time?"

"My legs and arms started getting numb."

"What else?"

"I was breathing slow. I couldn't hardly breathe."

Canty was taken to St. Vincent's Hospital and released eleven days later, on January 2. He said his chest still bothered him "sometimes when it rains and sometimes when I shower it irritates me." He said his intention when he walked up to Goetz was "to get some money to put it in the video machines."

When asked if he was intending to rob him, Canty said no. The reason he had approached Goetz specifically, he said, was because "he was closest to me."

After the shootings, Canty still had a sentence pending concerning his arrest on December 4. He was given a conditional discharge and was allowed to enter the drug rehabilitation facility he had been in ever since. He said he had not taken drugs again, had gone back to school and completed work for his high school equivalency diploma, and was set to enter a twenty-one-month program at the Culinary Institute of America. He had worked in the kitchen in the rehab center and now wanted to be a cook.

After lunch Slotnick began his cross-examination.

"Mr. Canty, in December of 1984, when you were aboard the railroad train, you weren't wearing that nice suit and the tie and the shirt, were you?"

"No, I wasn't."

"And did you have many occasions in December 1984 to wear a nice suit and tie and shirt?"

"No."

In direct examination, Waples made the point that Canty had been shorter and skinnier than his present size of five feet, seven inches and 140 pounds. Slotnick used this as a justification for entering into evidence a black-and-white photo he had of Canty that was to show what he looked like then, enlarged to about three feet by three feet and centered on white poster board, which Slotnick placed on an easel facing the jury box. Later, when asking Canty about Allen, Cabey, and Ramseur, he produced like-sized pictures of them as well and placed them all on easels, all in a row.

There they remained for the next two days, until Canty was dismissed from the stand. The picture of Canty seemed to have been taken in a hallway, and Ramseur's was of him looking at the camera while stepping out of a car onto the curb. Allen's and Cabey's pictures were both facial close-ups. Allen was smiling and looked the least menacing of the four, although we later saw photos of Allen's back that impressed upon me how muscular he was. Cabey and Ramseur looked the most threatening; both were scowling at the camera and seemed to be posturing, trying to look as dangerous as possible.

The photographs didn't have any real impact on me, I should mention; I always felt I was able to keep an open mind. But I do remember thinking what a clever idea this was of Slotnick's, another point scored for the defense's side.

And by the time Slotnick concluded, he'd won another rout. Just as he had succeeded in proving Smithern's testimony unreliable, Slotnick managed to totally discredit Canty's version of events. Although I had believed much of what Canty said happened on the train, and despite the fact that Canty's version coincided with Goetz's in numerous details, Canty appeared to lie so frequently and with such obviousness under cross-examination that his veracity became completely undone.

The major discrepancy between Goetz's version and Canty's had to do with the way in which Canty approached him. Canty said he did not recall speaking to Goetz (saying, "How's your day?") when Goetz entered the train, and he said his intention was to panhandle, not to rob. He remembered having said to Goetz, "Can I have five dollars?" instead of "Give me five dollars," although under cross-examination he admitted it was possible he could be wrong. It was also extremely self-serving for him to say he couldn't see if any of his friends had also stood up to crowd around Goetz. Judging from the way Ramseur was lying next to Canty, it seemed apparent that at least Ramseur was standing next to or behind Canty, perhaps without Canty seeing him, but also perhaps not.

Slotnick set out to undermine Canty's version in two ways: by revealing previous statements he had made that were inconsistent with his current testimony, and through character assassination, spending hour after hour questioning Canty on his criminal past. Canty most often did not deny having made the statements Slotnick attributed to him; instead he simply professed not to remember making them. He also was unable to remember many of the criminal actions Slotnick wanted to reveal he had committed. Canty's memory was so selective, though, that it seemed clear in these cases he was often lying.

It also appeared that these answers were intended to tailor his testimony to his advantage without perjuring himself, and I doubted that this was a strategy Canty had developed alone.

I believed it likely that he'd been coached on what to say and even how to say it. Indeed, on his second day of testimony (a Monday, after he'd had two days to review), he had altered the timbre of his voice when saying that he could not remember. On the first day his voice sounded very mechanical, his answers automatic and rehearsed. The second day, though, he sounded a bit more genuine and would even press a finger to his lips and look at the ceiling as if he were trying really hard to jog his memory, to no avail.

The extent of his forgetfulness to me made Canty's testimony ludicrous, but the effect of his apparent tactics made his confrontation with Slotnick both compelling and bizarre. Here was this extremely slick and experienced trial lawyer face to face with perhaps an equally slick and experienced street person. Slotnick, you could say, had the home-court advantage; Canty was forced to play by Slotnick's rules. But Canty seemed to me to be an intelligent person; I could tell that just by looking at his eyes. He was a sharp, street-smart fellow who was well-schooled for this encounter, either through his previous experiences in court or the advice of counsel or a combination of both. He knew exactly how to answer without elaborating and giving Slotnick ammunition. By saying he could not remember he was closing up areas that Slotnick was hellbent to probe.

Slotnick first asked him a series of questions about statements published in a *National Enquirer* article that was entered as an exhibit by the defense. Canty admitted he had been approached by a reporter and paid $300, which he had split with Barry Allen, and that he and Allen had spoken to the man. But he denied having said virtually every statement attributed to him in the article and said he didn't remember hearing the statements that Allen allegedly had made.

Canty's statements in the article mostly involved the two youths' past criminal behavior, that in addition to robbing video-game machines they also had "learned about taking people's wallets, grabbing gold chains off people's necks and strong-arming people for money." He also was quoted as saying, "The justice system is a joke. If we get caught, we plea-bargain a felony down to a misdemeanor, then walk away."

Canty denied having said this, but Slotnick countered by asking him, "Well, isn't it a matter of fact that you were arrested on many occasions for felonies that were plea-bargained down to misdemeanors, and essentially you walked away?" He specifically brought up Canty's arrest on the theft of merchandise from the WOR-TV office building, pointing out that what was stolen were "toys, tape recorders destined for needy children," and that the value of the merchandise made the theft a felony. Canty admitted this was true.

Slotnick quoted other statements attributed to Canty and asked Canty if he had said them: "The courts are revolving turnstyles, like the ones in the subway. The cops catch us and take us in and the judges let us go right out again."

"We know how to tell anybody anything and make it sound right; we've done it to enough judges."

Both of these statements Canty denied.

Barry Allen's statements involved the Goetz incident itself: "We piled aboard a subway for a day of hassling passengers for money and this nervous-looking guy got aboard at Fourteenth Street and sat right across from us.

"One look in his eyes and we could tell he was scared. We thought we had an easy victim.

"Nudging each other and nodding towards him, we decided to strike. All four of us gathered around him, standing over him threateningly, as he looked up at us from his seat. Troy asked him, 'Mister, can we have five dollars?'"

Canty also denied having said to a police officer who visited his hospital room two days after the incident, on December 24, 1984, "The train started moving and all four of us got up and stood around the white guy," and that he had gone up to Goetz because Goetz "looked soft." Canty said he remembered seeing the face of the officer but that he was heavily sedated and didn't remember speaking to him. And he didn't remember saying to another officer on the train immediately after the shootings, "We were robbing the white guy and he shot us."

"I don't remember saying that to anyone," Canty said.

Slotnick also tried to reveal discrepancies between Canty's grand jury testimony and what he was testifying to here, but I thought the results of these were nebulous. On the one hand his statements made before the grand jury were not nearly as significant as what Canty allegedly had said to police. And even though Slotnick had a written record of what Canty had said in this case, Canty still managed fairly adeptly to sidestep and avoid incriminating admissions. He said in most cases that he didn't remember either the questions or answers.

Slotnick would then follow up by asking Canty whether his alleged answers were the truth. "[I]f you testified [before] the grand jury and you were asked those questions and gave those answers, would they have been false?" Slotnick asked in one such instance. Canty responded, "It would have been what I remembered then."

"Were they true?" Slotnick pressed.

"That's how I saw it then."

"And today you see it quite differently. Is that correct?"

"Yes," Canty said.

Slotnick asked Canty early on in his cross-examination whether he knew two women: one named Tanya Hayes and the other Elizabeth Mays. Canty denied knowing either of them. On Monday, the second day of cross-examination, Slotnick pursued this same area again. "Do you know where Park Avenue and 169th Street is?"

"Yes."

"What's there?"

"Railroad tracks."

"Railroad tracks. And do you remember ever jumping onto the railroad tracks, the Metro North tracks?"

"No, I don't."

"Isn't it a matter of fact that you went behind a woman who was standing on the platform of the Metro North, a woman with a cane. You came up behind her; you knocked her down; you grabbed her pocketbook—you remember? The woman with the cane? And you jumped off [onto] the tracks and ran away. Remember that?"

"No."

"You remember the fact that there was—By the way, over the weekend, have you thought who Tanya Hayes is?"

"No, I don't."

＊　　＊　　＊

"You know that Tanya says she saw you do that, knock

the woman down with the cane, grab her pocketbook and run on the tracks?"

Angry now, Waples stood and objected. "Your Honor—" he began, his tone incredulous.

"The objection is sustained," Justice Crane said.

"Judge, I protest these questions that are so obviously improper no lawyer should ask them," Waples continued.

"Your Honor, I object to that statement. I have a reasonable, fair basis for this testimony," Slotnick countered.

"Yes, but you phrase it in terms of what Tanya *would* say, something this jury is directed to disregard," Justice Crane said, turning his head toward us.

"Let me ask him the following question," Slotnick said, then again addressed Canty. "Don't you know that Tanya saw you mug this woman at 169th Street and . . . Park Avenue, an old black woman with a cane? That you knocked her down, grabbed her pocketbook, and ran on the Metro North tracks, away. Don't you know that she saw that?"

"No, she couldn't have saw it because I never did it before," Canty insisted.

"But you weren't arrested for that, is that correct?"

"I never did it."

"Were you arrested for it?"

"No. I wasn't arrested for it."

"Now, I asked you on Friday whether you ever remembered Elizabeth Mays. Do you remember an Elizabeth Mays?"

"No, I don't."

"Elizabeth Mays had you arrested for threatening her. Do you remember her now?"

"No, I don't," Canty said again.

"Do you know you were arrested for threatening Elizabeth Mays?"

"No, I can't recall the incident."

"You are unable to recall being arrested for threatening Elizabeth Mays, is that what you're telling this jury?"

"Yes."

"Do you remember your brother Carl being arrested for stealing a television set out of somebody's apartment?"

"Your Honor—" Waples leapt up once again.

"I sustain the objection," Justice Crane said.

In a sidebar discussion, as Slotnick continued to probe these subjects, peppering his interrogation with objectionable questions, Slotnick told the judge that Canty's brother Carl had been arrested on the basis of a filed complaint that he had stolen a television set from Elizabeth Mays's apartment; and that subsequently Carl, Troy, and two other youths were arrested for threatening and harassing her. Waples in fact had supplied Slotnick with the arrest report.

"[But h]e denies it," Justice Crane pointed out. "So what good does it do to try to pursue it?"

"He doesn't deny it," Slotnick argued. "He says, 'I don't remember.' I'm trying to refresh his recollection. . . . Are we going to allow this man to say he doesn't know anything about the incident when in fact it's stipulated by the parties he was arrested for that?"

In a great bit of showmanship, Slotnick tried to jog Canty's memory about the two women by producing them in court early on the following day. First Elizabeth Mays was brought in through the rear of the courtroom and walked up to the well of the courtroom.

"Mr. Canty, would you please look at this woman? Does it refresh your recollection that you know her?"

"No, I don't," Canty said with a deadpan expression. The woman looked at Canty incredulously, as if she were stunned.

"Is it your testimony that you never met her, that you never threatened her? Is that correct?"

"Yes."

"And is it also your testimony that she never had you arrested?"

"Objection," Waples said, just as Canty answered, "Yes."

"Sustained on that last question. The answer is stricken," Justice Crane said.

Slotnick then requested a sidebar, and Elizabeth Mays left the courtroom. When Slotnick resumed, he asked Canty, "The last woman that came into court, your testimony is you've never seen her before?"

"Judge, how many times can he ask that same question?" Waples objected.

"I don't think he asked it that same way. Let it be answered. Overruled," said Justice Crane.

"I don't recall seeing her," Canty said.

And so it went as well with Tanya Hayes. She gave Canty a similarly stunned look when he denied knowing her. And Slotnick kept digging at Canty with the little leverage he had.

Waples would get angry as Slotnick seemingly asked the same questions innumerable times so that we would at least hear his accusations of what Canty had done. We were reminded many times by Justice Crane that questions were not evidence, so Canty's lack of memory about an incident meant that we had to disregard it. The cumulative effect, though, of hearing the accusations so often repeated and the absurdity of Canty's negative responses made this virtually impossible for us to do.

"Judge, we're going to be here until Mr. Slotnick's ingenuity is exhausted, not to mention my patience," Waples protested at one point. But Slotnick had a right to explore these areas for as long as he could avoid asking precisely the same questions and could find different ways in which areas could be approached. In a sidebar he complained to Justice Crane that he had legitimate reasons to pursue these areas and said, "Your Honor is cutting me off as if I'm making it up."

"I wouldn't dream of cutting you off," Justice Crane responded.

Nevertheless, Slotnick's tactics infuriated Waples. The most explosive confrontation between the two in this regard involved Canty's inability to recall ever having attended the Bronx-Lebanon Hospital Center's department of psychiatric care. Slotnick wanted to discuss events of Canty's past that were contained in that facility's records, but Canty's assertion that he did not recall ever being there prohibited Slotnick from opening that door. Slotnick repeatedly pressed Canty on this issue on both Friday and Monday, even after Justice Crane had ruled that all questions in that vein had been "asked and answered" and that the subject was closed. To me, though, Slotnick was like a dog that wouldn't let go of a bone. Try to pull it away and he'd snarl and become all the more adamant. And when Slotnick again broached the subject to Canty, Waples finally hit the roof.

"Bronx-Lebanon psychiatric center. Does it refresh your recollection—"

"Your Honor," Waples said as he stood. "This is in flagrant violation of your last ruling."

"That's correct," Justice Crane concurred.

"Just trying to refresh his recollection, Your Honor," Slotnick said. Then, addressing Canty, he relentlessly pressed on.

"My last question: Do you think there is anything in this world that would make you remember the Bronx-Lebanon psychiatric center on the witness stand?"

"I object," Waples said.

"Sustained," said Justice Crane.

"Then one last question. After all of this, do you remember anything about the Bronx-Lebanon psychiatric center?"

"Your Honor, this is misconduct," Waples said angrily.

"Well, let's not—"

"I would doubt that," Slotnick said, cutting off Justice Crane.

"Let's not get excited," Justice Crane offered. "Don't answer any further questions," he said to Canty; "and don't ask any further questions about the Bronx-Lebanon hospital," he warned Slotnick.

"What's my remedy?" Waples pleaded to the judge, looking furious. "What am I supposed to do when he disregards your orders?"

"It's all taken care of by the objections, Mr. Waples. Calm down," Justice Crane said.

"You realize, don't you, that I can't ask you any questions on cross-examination when you just say to an area, 'I don't remember?' You know that?" Slotnick challenged Canty.

"You can still ask, but I don't remember," Canty replied.

There were other touchy moments when Slotnick asked flagrantly objectionable questions. Slotnick kept trying to discuss not only Canty's criminal record but those of the other youths as well. Asking Canty about the day of the shootings, he said, "All four of you, as you alighted to go downtown, . . . had criminal records. Is that correct?"

Waples objected and added, "For the record, Your Honor, I find that unbelievable."

A little later Slotnick asked, "Those were friends of yours that ventured with you downtown on December 22, 1984. Is that correct?"

"Yes."

"Now, you felt somewhat safe with these people, did you not?"

"Somewhat."

"I mean, a couple of weeks before, you know, Darrell Cabey had been arrested for robbing somebody at gunpoint?"

Waples objected, and this time even Justice Crane was irked. He said to Slotnick, "You know full well we have been sustaining objections—"

"I'll withdraw that question," Slotnick offered, cutting him off.

"It's not enough," Justice Crane said. "Don't ask a question like that again."

"Did you ever see Darrell Cabey with a gun?" Slotnick asked Canty.

"No."

"I object," said Waples.

"I sustain the objection. I strike the answer," Justice Crane replied.

Having since read the transcripts of the sidebar discussions that we were not privy to during the trial, I have a stronger feeling now that Waples's indignation over Slotnick's tactics was indeed sincere and his anger real. At the time, though, I was a bit skeptical and considered the possibility that he might also have been posturing before the jury, perhaps that he was even shrewder than Slotnick. I was always aware of Slotnick's efforts at manipulation; I could always see him pulling the strings. Waples's performance, on the other hand, was utterly seamless, and that might have been because it wasn't an act.

Regardless of this, and entertaining as it often was, Canty's cross-examination did become terribly tedious. After a while it became clear that Canty was clever enough to sustain the position he was taking, and that no matter how much Slotnick hammered at him, we were not going to get any testimony from Canty that would tell us precisely what happened on that train. Canty had his own interests to protect, including a $5 million civil suit against Goetz that in itself was a reason why his testimony could not be trusted. The success of his suit would certainly be affected by the outcome of this trial. So it was clearly important to Canty that the shootings be proved here to have been unjustified—enough so that he might have been willing to tailor the truth—despite his disclaimers when Slotnick quizzed him.

"Isn't it in your interest to sue Mr. Goetz and hope that he's convicted here, with regard to a crime against you, so that you could get money from Mr. Goetz?" Slotnick asked.

"It's to my interest that justice is done," Canty replied.

"Who told you to give that answer?" Slotnick said accusingly.

"No one."

"And you just thought of that, is that correct?"

"Yes."

Later, Slotnick pressed Canty on the money involved in the suit. "Don't you think it would be nice if you got some money from Mr. Goetz?"

"I think it would pay for my damages done to me," Canty replied.

* * *

"You're really not that interested in the money. Is that correct?"

"I'm interested, but I'm more interested in justice being done."

"I know that," said Slotnick. "But when we talk about money, tell us about your interest. Would you like to get the money?"

"No, I would like to go to the Culinary."

In Waples's redirect examination, he asked Canty whether he was "proud" of his criminal past and of his drug consumption, then showed Canty the enlarged picture of himself and asked him, "Are you proud of this Troy Canty?"

"No," Canty said to each question. Then, over objections from Slotnick that it was irrelevant, Waples was allowed to elicit from Canty that he felt he was now a different person. Waples asked him what he had learned and how had he changed.

"I changed the way I look at things," Canty said. "I deal with things . . . better. I'm more in control of my emotional feelings. . . . I've learned that life is not peaches and cream,

and some things you have to go through that you don't want
to go through."

Slotnick in recross also showed Canty the enlarged picture
and asked, "In 1984, when you met Bernhard Goetz, were you
this Troy Canty?"

"Yes," Canty said.

"In 1984, when you met Bernhard Goetz, do you think it
was his fault that you were that Troy Canty?"

Waples objected but Justice Crane overruled. "No," Canty
answered. Justice Crane did sustain the resulting objections
when Slotnick then asked Canty if it was Goetz's fault that he
was a "drug addict" and a "criminal."

"You're a different person now than you were then?"

"Yes."

"You were a bad person then?"

"Objection," Waples said.

"Well, for what it's worth, overruled," said Justice Crane.

"I committed crimes," Canty said.

⚖

For what it was worth, Troy Canty's was the only testimony
of the four youths whom Goetz had shot that we were ultimately
allowed to consider. James Ramseur also appeared before us
in the afternoon of the day that Canty's testimony ended, but
with a dramatic gesture he refused to take the stand.

There was some very heated legal wrangling beforehand
over whether we should witness that little scene. Waples alerted
the defense team and Justice Crane in a sidebar just before
the lunch break that he had learned Ramseur would likely
refuse to testify even though Ramseur, like Canty, had been
immunized from prosecution and had testified before the second
grand jury in March 1985. Because he had immunity Ramseur
could not legally invoke Fifth Amendment privileges; he was
therefore "being contumacious," wanting no further involvement in the case. Waples asked that Ramseur be called to the
stand out of our presence, and then for the judge to either
cite him for contempt if he refused to testify, or to call the
jury in if he changed his mind.

Slotnick argued strenuously, though, that it not be done
outside our presence. "I think the jury should be exposed to

the fact he intends not to cooperate with the People," Slotnick said. He talked about how Ramseur was "a major player" in the case and that "there have been major speeches about Mr. Ramseur." Waples said he never promised to call Ramseur as a witness. "And besides," Waples said, "if Mr. Slotnick is suggesting that he would not have commented upon James Ramseur, that's fanciful. He spent half his opening statement talking about a great deal of stuff that may or may not come into evidence."

"I certainly was told he was going to be a witness," Slotnick rebutted, "and if I thought he wasn't going to be a witness, then I suggest—and I charge the district attorney obviously with knowledge that he wasn't going to be a witness—I would have tailored my opening differently. I'm going to look like an absolute living fool."

Justice Crane sympathized with Slotnick's feeling of having been "sandbagged" but was reluctant to call Ramseur in our presence because of the "collateral nature" of his testimony and the "propensity" it might have "to becloud the issues this jury has to decide." The defense would not relent, however. "I think that I have a right to have this jury see this man," Slotnick insisted, adding that Ramseur might change his mind and "may not want to commit contempt in front of a jury. He may decide to become a gentleman in front of a jury, I don't know," Slotnick said.

Slotnick went so far as to say that "unless this man is called, I have a right to a mistrial" and also to plead, "I spent the entire weekend studying this man. I know everything from his date of birth to every member of his family." Then Slotnick pleaded it be done in the interest of fairness. "I'm just saying, in all honesty, Judge, we're attempting to be honest and truthful to this jury."

"I think this pious talk most—I find it disgusting, especially in view of some of the things I've seen in this courtroom the last couple of days," Waples said as the argument wound down.

"Well, I'm going to rise above all that," Justice Crane asserted. "From here on out, I think you're going to see a refreshing atmosphere. I want to keep it on a high plane. This is a tense case. Everybody's emotions are high; blood pressure is rising. I want it to be reduced. What will be done will be done and it will be done fairly. And I want you to have—all three of you, to have the confidence in me that you have previously expressed. And I just want to remind you of that. We'll break for lunch and I'll consider that."

After lunch, Justice Crane told the lawyers at the sidebar of his decision to allow Ramseur to appear before us and told Waples he could avoid that "simply by not calling him." Previous case law gave Justice Crane the discretion to rule either way, and he decided that because the defense "insists that it be done in front of the jury," it was within his power to grant their request.

Waples felt he had no choice but to call Ramseur because, if he didn't, either the defense would call him or the defense could apply to the judge to declare Ramseur a "missing witness" in his predeliberation instructions to the jury, suggesting that the prosecution had something to hide by not calling Ramseur, and that had he been called he might have said something that would have been unfavorable to the prosecution's case. At least by calling Ramseur Waples would be making the good-faith effort to produce him and offer up his testimony, demonstrating both that getting him to testify was not within Waples's control and that the exclusion of his testimony was not part of the prosecution's plan.

"This is a catch-22, Judge," Waples complained.

"No," Justice Crane said, but he admitted, "It's a very difficult situation you are in. I empathize with it. I think that if you don't do it, Mr. Slotnick would call this individual. I do believe there is some persuasiveness to the observation that when he is in front of a jury, with all the people in the audience, he may very well cooperate by answering questions. We don't know in advance."

After a delay of fifteen minutes or so from the time he was called as a witness, Ramseur was brought into the courtroom. He marched up to the witness box and sat down. Robert Hamkalo asked him to stand up, and he did so, but when a court officer approached him and asked him to place his left hand on the Bible, Ramseur pushed the Bible away and said, loudly enough for me to hear, "I'm not taking the stand. I refuse to."

"Sorry, Your Honor, I can't hear the witness," Slotnick said, making the most of the moment.

"I refuse to take the stand!" Ramseur said sharply.

Justice Crane was clearly annoyed and asked Ramseur's attorney to step forward and consult with Ramseur. The two huddled alongside the witness box and had a whispered conversation that lasted about a minute. Ramseur's attorney then told the judge, "My client does not wish to testify in this case."

"It is not his choice . . . ," Justice Crane shot back. "I warn him now, in front of this jury, that if he refuses to take the oath . . . after having been lawfully called, he can be charged and prosecuted for the crime of criminal contempt in the second degree, as well as [be] held in summary contempt before me."

Then Justice Crane addressed Ramseur directly: "Mr. Ramseur, I direct you at this time to stand up and take the oath."

"I refuse," Ramseur said defiantly, his hands in his pockets.

"I cite you to show cause why you should not now be held in summary criminal contempt of this Court. Do you have anything to say?"

"No," said Ramseur.

The judge then cited him for summary contempt, announced to Waples "the possibility of prosecution for criminal contempt," and advised us to "draw no inferences and make no speculations with respect to this matter. This conduct that has occurred in your presence has no bearing on your deliberations and this witness is excused."

"Step down," the court officer ordered, and Ramseur was led away.

"Your Honor, is the witness aware of the fact that he will receive immunity?" Slotnick chimed in, I believe for our benefit.

"Your Honor—," Waples objected.

"Please," said Justice Crane, "no speeches at this time."

May 6

The next day Barry Allen also chose to avoid testifying by invoking his Fifth Amendment right against self-incrimination. This was allowable for Allen because he had not been granted immunity from prosecution for his testimony as Canty and Ramseur had been. Slotnick pressed Waples to offer Allen immunity, thus forcing him to testify, but Waples refused.

Mark Baker said the defense again felt sandbagged by the prosecution. By not offering Allen immunity, the defense was unable to expose the jury to the testimony of another of the four youths, as they had promised in their opening.

"What Mr. Slotnick opened on is his business," Waples countered. "Mr. Slotnick is dreaming, I think, when he's saying he's prejudiced by the fact that he opened by reciting Barry Allen's criminal record, chapter and verse. It's something he obviously wanted to do and whether he proves it or not [it] inures to his advantage."

Legal precedent virtually insisted that this be done outside the jury's presence; nevertheless, Slotnick and Baker fought valiantly to persuade the judge otherwise.

The defense's contention was that Goetz shot the four youths while they were attempting to rob him, while they were in the process of committing a criminal act. "If Barry Allen refuses to testify on the ground that any testimony he gives will tend to incriminate him, I think I have the right to have that seen before the jury," Slotnick argued.

Justice Crane didn't go for it. "In the case of James Ramseur, his refusal to be sworn as a witness was a crime, committed in front of this jury. In the case of Barry Allen, the invocation of a constitutional privilege is something that is not for the jury to speculate about nor for counsel to argue to the jury to speculate about. These proceedings are taken outside of the presence of the jury in the ordinary course."

So during a long stretch that we spent sequestered in the jury room, and unbeknownst to us, Barry Allen was brought into the courtroom and took the Fifth in response to almost every question he was asked by both the prosecution and the defense.

"Mr. Allen, do you know a person by the name of Troy Canty?" Waples began.

"On advice of counsel I serve my constitutional rights against self-incrimination under the Fifth Amendment of the United States Constitution and decline to answer that question," Allen said.

"I would object to that and ask Your Honor to direct him to respond to the question," Slotnick argued.

Justice Crane asked Allen's lawyer, "[H]ow could the acquaintanceship between Troy Canty and this witness possibly incriminate him?"

"I believe it can, Your Honor, based on information I have as Mr. Allen's attorney," the lawyer said.

"Would you offer immunity on that question, Mr. Waples?" Justice Crane asked.

"No, Judge," Waples answered.

"We would move the Court that this man be given immunity so he could testify before the jury," Slotnick said.

Justice Crane refused to do this. "Ask your next question," he said to Waples.

"Mr. Allen, do you know a person by the name of James Ramseur?"

And so on. Waples also asked Allen if on December 22, 1984, he had met with Troy Canty or James Ramseur, and also if he had been shot. Allen refused to answer all questions. Then Slotnick was allowed to cross-examine.

"Mr. Allen, my name is Barry Slotnick and I represent Bernhard Goetz," Slotnick began. "How are you this morning?"

"Feeling fine," Allen answered.

"You got one in there, Mr. Slotnick," Justice Crane said.

Slotnick asked Allen where he was currently living, and over Waples's objections, overruled by Justice Crane, Allen answered, "Rikers Island."

"And is that a prison?"

"Yes," Allen said.

"And are you in prison for a crime that you committed after December 22, 1984?"

That's as far as Slotnick got. He kept fighting, however. For twenty more minutes Slotnick asked questions and Allen refused to answer them, and then Slotnick would ask that immunity be granted and Waples would steadfastly refuse. Though continuing his examination was futile, Slotnick wouldn't give in; wouldn't let go.

"Judge, this is grandstanding. I object to this," Waples said in a sidebar, and he later complained in open court, "We could be here until Mr. Slotnick gets laryngitis."

"That's not going to happen," Slotnick replied.

In hindsight I find this quite amusing. By the time Slotnick gave his closing argument, his laryngitis was so bad he could hardly speak.

I should also mention here that during the trial there were several sidebar discussions concerning whether Darrell Cabey was able to testify. Waples insisted that Cabey was unfit because of the brain damage he had suffered, and Slotnick and Baker reserved the right throughout the prosecution's case to call Cabey as a defense witness. There were legal questions, though, about how much latitude Slotnick would have in an attempt to impeach his own witness, and ultimately Cabey was not called.

Chapter 8

The Eyewitnesses

After Troy Canty was finally off the stand, I remember what a relief it was to hear the testimony of witnesses who didn't answer eighty percent of the questions posed in the negative or by saying, "I don't remember." I also agreed with Justice Crane when he said in several sidebar discussions that the testimony (or lack of testimony) of the youths was ultimately collateral in nature. To me, because of their civil suits against Goetz, their testimony could not be trusted. Several jurors later voiced resentment of Waples for putting Canty and, later, Ramseur on the stand and subjecting us to Slotnick's cross-examinations. The prosecution seemingly had little to gain from their testimony, and because of their crime records their characters were all too easily impeached.

When Waples called Victor Flores, then, I thought, "We're finally getting to the heart of the matter." Flores was the first in a series of people who testified to being in the same car as Goetz at the time of the shootings; and this marked a significant turn in the testimony we heard.

Flores was a fifty-year-old Bronx resident who was a native of Puerto Rico. He'd moved to New York thirty-five years ago and had worked as a cleaner for the New York City Transit Authority for the past twenty-two years. He said he rides the subways "almost every day" and that about twice a week he makes the long trip from the Bronx to Brooklyn where he helps his brother, a building superintendent. He was on his way there on the day of the shootings, after stopping at Macy's at Herald Square.

He reentered the subway system, then, at the Thirty-fourth Street station. He just missed one train then got on the next, which he said came almost immediately. He entered through the middle door and remembered the car was "not too crowded"; about twenty people were in it, he said.

Once seated, he said, "I was aware of noise . . . loud talking and noise" coming from the north end of the car. He looked over and saw "a group of kids," young and black, about fifteen feet from where he sat. Flores said there seemed to be four or five. He then read his newspaper and didn't look over again until he heard a noise that "sounded like a shot" and saw "a man standing with a gun" in his hand "shooting the kids in front of him."

Flores described Goetz as standing erect, holding the gun with two hands and his right arm flexed at the elbow. The gun was pointing in Flores's direction. In fact, when Goetz first shot at and hit Troy Canty, Flores was directly in the line of fire.

"I saw two kids facing me," he said, "and a man just kept shooting at them, and they fell down. Two fell down on the floor. One fell down, but . . . he was not completely on the floor; he was leaning on the seat." Flores said he only saw Goetz shooting at these three persons. It wasn't until after the shooting stopped that he noticed "the fourth one [in] the small seat, by the conductor's cab."

Asked to describe the facial expressions of Goetz and the youths as the shots were fired, Flores said Goetz "looked like he was very mad, like he was angry." The youths' expressions, he said, were indescribable. "I've been trying to find words to express [it], but it's almost imposssible," Flores said.

Flores, meanwhile, was panic-stricken. "I couldn't move. I just—I was just looking," he said, and later added, "I didn't know what was going on, so I was afraid if I get up, this man might shoot me because I didn't know—I didn't know the reason why, what was going on."

After the shooting was over, Flores said he moved to the next car toward the front of the train and there spoke to the train's conductor. Looking back into the car in which the shooting occurred, Flores said he saw Goetz approach Troy Canty and kneel beside him, looking closely at his face. Then, he said, Goetz got up and sat down on the long seat. Flores saw the conductor speaking with Goetz, and the two of them helped up a lady who was lying on the floor. Asked to describe Goetz's expression at this point, Flores said, "He was a different person altogether. He seemed like he was worried. . . . At one time he sat down on his seat and he put his hands on his head in this way for about two or three seconds, and then he got up and paced the train a couple of times. He walked back and forth. And the face from what I saw during the shooting and the face after was a different face altogether."

Meanwhile, the train, which Flores said had not been going fast and had been "moving on and off" because of the train in front of it, had by this time stopped completely. Shortly afterward Flores saw Goetz escape "between cars, down to the tracks."

Flores later reentered the car he'd been riding "to see if I could give any help to the kids that were on the floor. . . . Two of them, they didn't say nothing. They were breathing. I could feel their chests moving. . . . But their eyes, they were like turning, so I think they were unconscious. . . . The one that was not laying—that was almost on the floor, he told me that he did it for nothing. 'He did it for nothing'; 'We were doing nothing.' He repeated that a couple of times."

In cross-examining Flores Slotnick made two important points that were key elements of the defense's contentions. The first concerned the amount of time in which the shots were fired. Flores testified that he heard the first shot, looked up from his newspaper, and that the other shots came "fast . . . one after the other." Slotnick asked Flores, "After the rapid succession of shots, you never heard another shot?"

"Right," Flores said.

❄   ❄   ❄

"Did you ever see [Goetz] turn around and go over to this rear seat and point a gun at somebody sitting in the seat and saying, 'You look good; here's another,' boom?"

"No, sir."

"Did that happen?" Slotnick asked.

"If that happened, I was not there," Flores replied.

"Well, the fact of the matter is, it was your testimony that you heard all the shots in rapid succession. Is that correct?"

"Yes, sir."

"And you stayed in that seat, in that car, for a while. Is that correct?"

"Yes, sir."

"And you didn't leave that car until what happened?"

"Until he put his gun away."

"Until he put his gun away?"

"Yes, sir."

"And you never heard another shot . . . ?"

"No, sir."

The other important detail was that when Flores looked up, he saw three of the youths "bunched together" in front of Goetz, adding credence to Goetz's contention that they had surrounded him before he fired.

Also, a significant development in what would be considered allowable testimony from the eyewitnesses occurred during Flores's direct examination when Waples asked him, concerning the youths' behavior on the train before the shootings, "Were you scared by anything you saw them do?"

"No," Flores said.

Slotnick then objected to the question as irrelevant, and Justice Crane responded by saying, "I think so too." He was in the process of sustaining Slotnick's objection when Slotnick abruptly withdrew it and allowed the answer to stand. He did this so that he would later be able to ask the same question of other eyewitnesses who *had* been afraid. The precedent was set, and thereafter such questions were allowed.

The next witness was the conductor of the subway train on the day of the shootings, a thirty-seven-year-old man named Armando Soler. Soler elicited a big laugh from the audience when Waples asked him at the beginning of his testimony, "What are the duties of a conductor on our subway system?"

"Basically to operate the doors and make sure everybody arrives to their destination safely," Soler answered. The courtroom erupted and Soler looked embarrassed, realizing how ridiculous that sounded under the circumstances.

Soler testified that the express train takes "a good two minutes" to travel from Fourteenth Street to Chambers Street, and so "about a minute and a half" had passed from the time the train left Fourteenth Street until he heard shots being fired. He said the train had just passed the Franklin Street station—the last local station before the Chambers Street stop—and that he was standing outside of the conductor's cab at the front end of the sixth car when he "heard four or five shots in rapid succession" coming from the rear of the seventh car.

"Could you tell how close or how far that sound was away from you?" Waples asked.

"Yes, I could," Soler said.

"Could you tell exactly what car it was coming from?"

"Yes."

"As soon as the shots were fired, the people started running into the car and saying that people were shot," Soler testified. "They were very specific; they said four people were shot." He then immediately got on the public-address system and notified the motorman in code terms that "somebody has a handgun" and to summon ambulances and police.

"After that I made my way back to the seventh car to check out the situation," he continued. "It was mass confusion. Everybody was running for cover. Everybody was running towards the front of the car. . . . [T]here was still a lot of people in the car: half on the floor, half running from the rear of the train. . . . The first thing I did was clear everybody out. And after that I saw six people on the floor and one person seated."

As he was clearing out the car, he encountered Victor Flores. This was especially interesting because the details Soler recounted were significantly different from Flores's version. "I remember he was pressed against the car and he was in shock and I had to shake him to get him out of the car," Soler said.

Goetz was seated by the middle door on the east side of the train. Soler said, "He was just sitting there, very calm."

The other two people on the floor were women. "I went to the first lady. She was a black woman. I looked at her. She was face down. I picked her up, made sure she was all right. . . . She walked away on her own power. She was perfectly all right. She was just a little in shock, I guess.

"Then I made my way to the second lady. She was a white woman. She was also face down and she was—I just sat her down because she wasn't able to make her way out quite yet.

She was still in shock. I just sat her down opposite the seat of Mr. Goetz, to his left. . . .

"After that, as I was picking the lady up, before I even sat her down, I was stooping down and that's when I heard Mr. Goetz say, 'I don't know why I did it. They tried to rob me.' . . . I wasn't sure if he was speaking to me. He was just facing forward; his eyes were straight. And that's when I realized he was the one who did the shooting."

*   *   *

"What was the defendant's demeanor at that time, when he first spoke to you?" Waples asked.

"He was serene; he was calm; he didn't seem too excited," Soler said. "It just seemed he wanted to give himself up. That was the impression I got because he didn't make a move to get away. . . .

"After I sat the lady down, I asked him if he was a police officer. He said no. I asked him, 'You have a permit for the gun?' and he said no. I asked him for the gun. He didn't say anything afterwards."

"Did he give you the gun?" Waples asked.

"No," Soler said.

Soler then went to check on the four youths. Troy Canty was lying "face down . . . directly in front of [Goetz's] feet. . . . I felt his pulse, I looked him in the eyes, made sure he was still with us, and I told him help was on the way, 'hang on.' . . . He didn't say anything. He couldn't move; he couldn't talk; he just seemed stunned." Soler similarly approached James Ramseur, Barry Allen, and finally Darrell Cabey, assessing their condition and trying to reassure them. "None of them spoke at all," he said.

As he finished checking Cabey, Soler looked up and noticed Goetz "making his way through the storm doors" between the sixth and seventh cars. "He opened up the safety gates and climbed down to the tracks."

In cross-examination, Slotnick had Soler reiterate that Goetz had said, "They tried to rob me" and that he had heard a rapid succession of shots. He asked Soler to estimate how quickly the shots were fired; Soler guessed the firing lasted "about a second."

"It almost sounded like a series of firecrackers going off, one next to the other?" Slotnick asked.

"Louder than that, but yeah, that's the series," Soler replied.

* * *

"And did you ever, after that, hear any further shots that day?"

"No," Soler said.

Slotnick also brought up Victor Flores, and Soler clarified that he had found Flores standing up with his back pressed against the middle doors on the east side of the car, a position that Flores never spoke of having been in. Flores originally was sitting on the west side of the car, and had testified that after he'd finally left his seat he'd headed directly to the south exit. This just demonstrated how shook up he had been, and how flawed the eyewitnesses' recollections could be, given the stressfulness of the moment. Soler said Flores "appeared to be in a state of shock" because of the rigid way he was pressed against the door, with Troy Canty lying "right in front of him."

And, I suppose, Slotnick couldn't resist taking a cheap shot when he sensed the opportunity. He asked Soler if while he had been in the witness room waiting to testify he had seen James Ramseur.

"I think—Yeah, I think he was brought in just now. I guess only for a minute or so," Soler answered.

"Did he exchange any pleasantries with you?" Slotnick asked archly.

"No," said Soler.

Waples objected. Justice Crane sustained.

May 6

Despite being relegated to the jury room while Barry Allen was taking the Fifth, we managed to hear from three more eyewitnesses on this day. By this time, though, a pattern had developed that revealed the weaknesses of the eyewitnesses' testimony. Everyone had seen something clearly, but no one had watched the entire incident from beginning to end, nor did anyone have a clear, unobstructed look throughout. They all recalled hearing a rapid succession of shots, and no one had seen an additional, gratuitous shot fired at Darrell Cabey. But once the shots were fired, because of the extreme panic and confusion, all their recollections were proving to be somewhat inaccurate; and they were especially dim about what happened immediately before the shootings. Nobody could without question establish how many of the youths had approached Goetz, and, apparently, no one was watching when Goetz stood up and drew his gun. All they could provide, then, were pieces of a puzzle that we would ultimately have to assemble ourselves.

The first of these next witnesses was Loren Michals, a thirty-three-year-old native New Yorker who worked as a credit manager for a trading company. On that day Michals had been with a friend from California named Christopher Boucher. The two had entered the subway system at Broadway and Ninety-sixth Street and were traveling to Chambers Street, sitting on the long bench on the east side of the train, between the front and middle doors. Michals was the closer of the two to the youths; Boucher was seated to Michals's left.

Michals said the youths had been "a little bit loud. They— There were a bunch of them, four or five, and sitting opposite each other on both sides of the car. And they would get up from time to time—one of them would get up or several of them would get up—and talk to their friends on the other side of the car. . . .

"I only noticed them for a few minutes," Michals added. "They seemed to be kind of laughing and moving around on the seats. And that was all I noticed. Then I went back to my own thoughts and didn't really notice them."

"Were you, Loren Michals, frightened by any of their behavior?" Waples asked.

Again, though, Slotnick objected to this question, as he had at first when Waples asked Flores. Waples requested a sidebar, in which Slotnick said to Justice Crane, "I don't want— if I have the occasion to ask people the same question— [Waples's objection] to be sustained."

Justice Crane was opposed to this line of questioning of the eyewitnesses. "It's a subjective state of mind," he said, that "wouldn't necessarily be probative of Bernhard Goetz's reaction when they allegedly surrounded him." Also, he said, "it doesn't relate in time to when the shots were fired and to the reasonableness of the situation as it was presented at that moment. It relates to a time prior to that when these witnesses were removed geographically from the kids."

"I think it bears upon the question of how a reasonable person perceives circumstances," Waples argued.

"How do we know this individual and Mr. Flores are reasonable persons rather than frightened individuals that . . . exceed the bounds of what a reasonable person would be?" Justice Crane asked.

"The jury does not have to accept their assessment of whether there was real danger," Waples said. "But they can consider whether an individual who they know something about, because that person has appeared as a witness, did or did not react in a fearful way to a set of circumstances."

"I have difficulties with it," Justice Crane commented, adding, "I understand that you're both approaching it from certain strategic standpoints." He warned Waples, "It does open up for Mr. Slotnick an avenue with other witnesses to state that they were afraid," and then he said, "I implore you to think about it."

"I've thought about it, Judge," Waples replied.

"Okay," Justice Crane said.

Back in open court Waples asked Michals if he had seen the youths approach any of the other passengers in the car, or if he had seen anyone moving to get away from them. Michaels said no.

When the shots were fired, "I was kind of just half-dozing," Michals said, and he said that the first sound "seemed to come from outside the car." The subsequent shots clearly came from the back of the car, though. "I tried to look down at that end of the car. Right at that moment, a woman to my right was holding a baby and started to get up, so I didn't have a clear view instantly. . . . She got past me and I could see down the center of the car. . . . I saw someone slumping to the floor in a kind of fetal position near the bench that was directly across from me. . . . I [saw] someone who happened to be slumping in a seat. . . . It's a little vague to me now. There were other people I thought were perhaps part of the group, and I saw a young man—I don't know, in his twenties or so, blond hair—standing there. And I started at the same moment to move to the front doors to get out of the car with my friend."

The two moved forward through the train cars "as did pretty much everyone else," according to Michals. Then, after they got off the train and out of the station, they "stood on the corner of, I guess, West Broadway and Chambers. . . . [W]e could hear that ambulances and police cars were rushing to the scene. I wanted to see if they brought, you know, anyone out on stretchers or [in] handcuffs, but after a minute or two Christopher really seemed shaken up, so we went uptown and went to a bar and had a quick drink."

"Did you feel better?" Waples asked.

"Yes," Michals said. "We then went Christmas shopping."

"Did there come a time when you spoke to police on December 22?"

"Yeah. We still didn't really understand what happened. It was just something crazy in the subway, and we actually bought a few things in SoHo. I saw a police car just sitting by the curb somewhere and thought just in case they were still looking for people, I could give my name and address, whatever. And when I explained to them we had been there, they asked if we could come downtown and they took us in the police car."

"Referring to you and Mr. Boucher?"

"Yes."

"And were you interviewed by a detective later?"

"Yes."

In cross-examination, Michals estimated he and Boucher were seated forty feet from the end of the subway car where the shootings took place.

"But even at that distance you found [the youths] noisy and rude?" Slotnick asked.

"I didn't say rude particularly," Michals replied; but Slotnick then produced transcripts from Michals's grand jury appearance where he had said the youths had been "a bit noisy and rude."

"And isn't it also a matter of fact that you were concerned about your friend Christopher? In fact, you were nervous on his behalf?"

"Yes," Michals admitted.

"And isn't it also a matter of fact that while you sat . . . in the subway car, looking at that group of four, you tried to make sure that it wasn't going to be unpleasant for your friend Christopher in any way?"

"Well, I assured myself that it wasn't going to be any disturbance that would bother us."

"Quite clearly you understood that there might be a disturbance that would bother others. Isn't that correct?" Slotnick pressed him.

Waples objected. Justice Crane overruled.

"That's a possibility every time you ride the subway, you know."

"How about on this occasion, Mr. Michals?"

"I counted it as a possibility," Michals said.

Michals also concurred he had heard a series of "four or five shots" (the precise number "has faded with time," he said), that the shots had been fired in rapid succession, and that he did not recall hearing any later shots. That Michals's memory was affected by the trauma of the moment was evident, though, when Slotnick asked, "[A]fter hearing those four or five shots in rapid succession, things seemed to move rather slowly in terms of what was happening around you. Is that correct?"

"Yeah, people started moving, but nobody seemed to get hysterical or anything," Michals said.

We knew better from Armando Soler's account.

After lunch we heard from Garth Reid, a twenty-six-year-old computer operator born in Jamaica, West Indies, who had been living in New York for about five years. In December 1984 he was living in the Bronx with his wife and one-year-old child and was attending the Borough of Manhattan Community College, located at Chambers Street. The day of the shootings he was traveling there with his wife and child in a baby carriage. The trip to his school from his stop in the Bronx takes an hour and fifteen minutes, he said. As they neared their destination, Reid said he was sitting on the long seat in the middle of the east side of the car with his wife seated just to his left (and, clearly, with Michals and Boucher farther to his left) and his child in his arms.

Reid didn't notice the youths until the train was in Manhattan and said when he saw them, "They were laughing a little out of the ordinary, [and] just moved back and forth, sitting on the chairs, swinging on the—holding the handles of the train, et cetera. . . .

"I didn't want to be too obvious," he added. "I occasionally was peeping over in that direction." He remembered noticing Goetz sitting to his right before the shootings. He also remembered one of the youths "saying, maybe, 'What's up?' or 'How are you doing?' " but he didn't know to whom the statement had been directed.

Between Fourteenth and Chambers streets, Reid said, "I saw one guy was up and I basically saw two guys standing around him, in his vicinity. . . . Their backs were towards me. And I remember he shot those two and he turned and shot the other two in the opposite direction, basically."

"What exactly were you doing when the shooting began?" Waples asked.

"Well, I had my kid in my arms, as I said before," Reid stated. "I bent over, but I was looking over my shoulder at the incident while it was taking place." Reid was a little uncertain whether he watched the incident from the time he heard the first shot or if his attention had been drawn to it before that. "I'm trying to remember exactly. I'm not too sure," he said, but then said, "I remember when the guy was up," meaning Goetz. "Maybe that was what drew my attention. I don't know if I saw when he got up or when he was up, but I saw him up."

Reid said he remembered hearing two shots before Goetz pivoted ninety degrees to his right and two more shots were fired. He saw one person that Goetz was then shooting at "going towards the . . . end of the car." Waples asked if the person was "moving away from the defendant," and Reid answered, "Yes, maybe." He did not see a fourth person shot.

"The incident took place very rapidly," Reid said. "After the incident [was] finished, my wife grabbed the kid and ran. I followed behind her a bit at a slower pace."

Waples asked Reid, in conclusion, if he had seen any of the four youths with any kind of weapon or making a threatening gesture at Goetz. He also asked if Reid had seen all four of the youths surrounding Goetz. To each of these questions, Reid answered, "No."

Slotnick began his cross-examination by pointing out that Reid had seen two of the youths in front of Goetz, and that the third individual Reid had seen shot could have also been standing just to Goetz's right. Reid admitted this was possible. Then Slotnick asked Reid whether a fourth youth might have been there, blocked from his view, and Reid answered, "Well, I didn't see, but maybe it's possible." Waples objected to the answer as speculation, though, and Justice Crane sustained the objection. So Reid's testimony was that he saw two youths around Goetz, or possibly three.

In exploring whether Reid had felt afraid of the youths, Slotnick also exposed us to a potentially damning hearsay statement that infuriated the judge when Slotnick first mentioned it. This was the only time in trial that Justice Crane really blew his cool.

"Isn't it a matter of fact you were seated there with your wife and your baby and you saw these men and were a little concerned and a little frightened?" Slotnick asked.

"I don't know if you want to use such strong adjectives to describe it," Reid replied. "I would say I was more alerted than before."

"And you were alerted [to] the fact that perhaps they could spell trouble if you brought their attention to you?"

Waples objected to this, but Justice Crane overruled.

"Should I answer that?" Reid asked the judge.

"Yes, please," Justice Crane answered.

"Maybe," Reid said.

"And, as a matter of fact," Slotnick went on, "isn't it true that the reason you took notice of these four individuals is because someone said, 'Look at those four punks bothering that man'?"

This was what Justice Crane blew up about. Waples objected and the judge told Slotnick, "Please don't include something that's not evidence in your question."

"Your Honor," Slotnick persisted, "I'm asking for an utterance that was made that caused him—"

"I object to this," Waples cut him off.

"Let's have a sidebar," Justice Crane said; then, to Slotnick, he said, "Next time please call for a sidebar before you spread another question like that in front of the jury."

At the sidebar, Justice Crane was visibly angry. "I thought we had an understanding this would not happen again, Mr. Slotnick."

"What would happen again?" Slotnick asked.

"That you would spread upon the record, in front of the jury, in open court, something that's not in evidence on your cross-examination. Your questioning has been admonished on several occasions."

"Judge, you can speak a little louder and the jury can hear you," Slotnick said.

"I'm upset with your conduct," Justice Crane said, livid.

"I'm upset with *your* conduct," Slotnick replied.

"You know where you can go with that," Justice Crane answered back.

"That was an appropriate question," Slotnick argued, and said he offered it "not for the truth of the utterance but the fact the utterance was made."

"The utterance is totally irrelevant," Waples countered and complained that Slotnick's improper conduct was "persistent" and "highly prejudicial to me."

As the judge's temper calmed, though, he accepted the defense's argument that Slotnick had had a right to ask the question. The door had been opened to explore the eyewitnesses' states of mind concerning the youths before the shootings occurred on the train, and so while the statement, "Look at those four punks bothering that man," was hearsay and therefore not appropriate as evidence, it was allowable inasmuch as it might have affected Reid's perception of the youths. In this case, then, Waples had dug his own grave.

Still in the sidebar, Justice Crane said he would give us a curative instruction about the statement's being hearsay and to be considered only in the context of Reid's state of mind.

"I would ask Your Honor not only to give a curative instruction, but to indicate to the jury sometimes judges make mistakes when they yell at lawyers," Slotnick said to Justice Crane.

Justice Crane refused to go that far. He said to Slotnick, "When you spring something like that, even if you're right . . . I didn't know what the devil of a statement was you were eliciting; he [Waples] was on his feet objecting. I implore you, I direct you not to do it if you know it's going to create that kind of reaction."

Waples continued his own complaint. "I don't want to hear hearsay and then it's too late to jump up," he said. "It's happened before."

"Both of you," Justice Crane addressed Waples and Slotnick. "I know the strain we're all under. We're all under it. This is the kind of situation that calls for me treading very carefully so as not to precipitate a motion for a mistrial, either way."

Waples also argued against the judge's overruling his objection, but Justice Crane's mind was made up. "He's entitled to establish that Mr. Reid had a state of mind bordering on alarm," Justice Crane said of Slotnick. "He's entitled to show it circumstantially as well as to get it out from the statement . . . I didn't call for the subject being opened in the first place. I rather urged you both to consider not doing it and you chided me for trying your cases for you. Now it's open and he's going into it."

So Slotnick was allowed to elicit from Reid that he first became alerted to the youths when someone said to him, "Look at those four punks bothering that guy by himself" and that he then looked over and witnessed their "irregular" behavior. (We learned much later, when she finally came to testify, that the person who made the statement was Garth Reid's wife, Andrea Reid.) He also concurred that the four shots he'd heard were fired in rapid succession, and that he hadn't seen Goetz walk over to any place and fire another shot.

Waples countered in redirect by asking, "Mr. Reid, you never saw four punks picking on a white guy, did you?"

"No, I didn't," Garth Reid said.

In recross, Slotnick asked Reid again about what he saw just before the shots were fired. Reid reiterated that he had seen two youths standing in the aisle in Goetz's vicinity; but when pressed about just how close they were, Reid said he wasn't sure.

In re-redirect, Reid explained that he was confused about what had happened in the moments surrounding the shootings because it was "a panic situation." He remembered seeing two youths about three feet from Goetz but, he said, "It's hard to remember if it was after the shooting or just before the shooting, because it was a snap of time."

Outside our presence, Reid was also quizzed by Slotnick about his failure to testify before either grand jury, this having to do with the defense's motion to dismiss the case that was based in part on the fact that Reid's testimony had not been heard when the grand juries made their decision to indict. Reid admitted in this examination that he had been evasive about what he'd seen in the subway car when he'd originally talked to Assistant District Attorney Susan Braver. "Maybe I was reluctant in opening up to her about everything that I saw," Reid said. "I was trying to keep out of the case as much as possible."

A week later, Braver took the stand also outside our presence regarding this matter. She testified that after interviewing Reid she "ultimately decided it was not going to be necessary" to make him appear before the first grand jury. "He was very reluctant to participate in the proceedings at all and he had indicated great fear for his wife and child," Braver said. "It didn't seem as though he could offer the grand jury any information that would be useful to them in making their decision or at least over and above other witnesses that were going to be called . . . who seemed to have observed more."

In his cross-examination, Slotnick challenged Braver's judgment that Reid was not an important witness; but given Reid's evasiveness and the fact that Waples had later persuaded Reid to testify, the judge ultimately denied the defense's motion to dismiss.

The day ended with the testimony of Mary Gant, who was the white woman Armando Soler, the conductor, had helped up from the floor of the subway car after all the shots had been fired. She was an actress who also did temp work to support herself. Originally from Wisconsin, she had been living in New York since 1976.

Gant had entered the subway system that day at the local station near Eighty-sixth Street and Broadway, switched to the express train at Seventy-second Street, and was intending to get off at Fulton Street to visit the South Street Seaport. She said she was sitting at the end of the northern long bench, next to the middle doors on the east side of the car, and that she was the only person on that bench when she first sat down. To her left, then, on the long bench on the other side of the doors, were Garth and Andrea Reid, their child and their baby carriage, and also Loren Michals and Christopher Boucher. Across from her, she said, was another group of people that would have included Victor Flores. And to her right were the four youths, about fifteen feet away.

Gant observed Canty lying on the long bench near the rear door on the side opposite hers, and she said the others were "sitting and lounging" and "looking about." She began reading her book and at some point looked up to glance again at the youths. They were still seated in the same area, but this time, she said, "They were looking at me." She returned to her book, and after that avoided looking directly at the youths again.

"[A]t some point," she said, she was aware of the train car doors opening and "someone got on and I did sense some movement." Shortly afterward, she looked up and "saw one of the black men standing in front of a man in a blue jacket with his hand hanging on a strap, on the subway bar." This was taking place at the other end of the long bench she was sitting on, just to her right. "It looked as though they were conversing," Gant explained. She could tell the two men were talking, but she could not hear what was said over the screeching of the train.

Gant said Canty was not brandishing a weapon. She saw him simply standing in front of Goetz, holding onto the strap with one hand and speaking to him, and Goetz looking up at Canty, speaking back. She did not see Canty "make any kind of menacing gesture," nor did he ever raise his voice. However, when Waples asked her where the other youths were when this conversation was going on, Gant responded, "They were nearby."

In addition to Canty, Gant said, "To the best of my recollection . . . [t]here was another man near to him or next to him. A third man was maybe in the middle of the aisle. And it is my impression that the fourth was still seated at that point."

Gant then again returned to her book, and hearing shots being fired was the next thing she recalled. "I thought to myself, this is the loudest noise I ever heard," Gant related. "And I said to myself, these are gunshots. And at some point someone shoved me to the floor."

*   *   *

"Did you look in that direction when you heard the shots?" Waples asked.

"No," she said. "Someone pushed me—Someone either fell on me or pushed me to the floor in front of the door on my left. . . . I heard everyone run out, or I assume everyone ran out. And I decided to remain still because I didn't know who was shooting and I thought perhaps they would continue to shoot if I moved. . . . Then I looked to my right and I saw a young black man on his stomach with his head towards me and his eyes open and we looked at each other. And then someone came up behind me and said, 'Miss, are you all right? Did I hurt you? Did I hit you?' and I thought it was the guy that knocked me down. Then someone came to help me up, someone in dark clothes. And I got up, picked up my bag, my book, my hat, turned around and saw a man in a blue jacket and three other wounded young men behind me. And then I left the train."

In further questioning by Waples, Gant said she remembered hearing four shots, and that when she saw Goetz after the shootings, when she was exiting the car, "He seemed agitated, . . . [n]ervous, upset. . . . He was wringing his hands."

Slotnick asked Gant in his cross-examination if she knew how much time had elapsed between the time she saw Canty standing over Goetz and the time she heard the shots.

"It could have been a minute or two," she said.

"And during that minute or two, do you know whether the other three men walked to positions to surround the man in the blue jacket?"

"I don't know."

"Because you weren't going to look over there, were you?"

"No," she admitted.

"At that point, when you saw that man hanging onto that strap, standing over the man in the blue jacket, you were afraid, weren't you?"

"I was concerned. I was afraid," Gant said.

Slotnick suggested to Gant that she had been concerned about the youths "even at the first glance" and that she had kept glancing over at them and returning to her book because she had been "a little fearful." Gant also admitted that this was true.

"Did there ever come a time prior to the shooting that you had decided, in your own mind, you were going to get out of that subway car because of the behavior of those four men?" Slotnick asked.

"Yes," she said.

In redirect, Waples asked Gant if, because of some prior experience she had, she was "more apprehensive" of the youths "than the objective facts warranted."

"Perhaps," she replied.

Slotnick then recrossed, asking her again about the youths' behavior on the train. "I would have to say their posture and attitude was—"

"Menacing?" Slotnick offered.

"Defiant," Gant chose instead.

"So it was those four men that made you apprehensive, not any other experience you may have had in your mind?"

"Not consciously," Gant said.

May 7

The next day—a short one for us before a three-day weekend—we heard from two more eyewitnesses and were kept out of court while another person testified who was also on the train.

Her name was Arnetha Gilbert, and she had been sitting one car ahead of where the shots were fired, the same car that Armando Soler was in. She did not say she heard the shots as

Soler had; she said she became alerted because there was "a lot of commotion—people running from the car behind me. . . . One person came running through and fell right at my feet where I was reading my newspaper and ran to the front of the train."

Gilbert got up and went into the car behind her to try to assist the people she heard had been shot. The first person she approached—presumably James Ramseur—was, she said, "unconscious. His eyes was like rolling back in his head." Then, "when I was there, the second person to the right of me said, 'Miss, I've been shot through the heart and I'm dying.' So I went and checked him and I told him, 'If you were shot through the heart, I don't think you would be talking to me.' And then he said that 'He shot me for nothing. I didn't do anything. I only asked him for five dollars.' "

A few moments later Gilbert approached Darrell Cabey, who was slumped in the short seat by the conductor's cab. "He was like leaning over. He was conscious. And he said to me, 'I didn't do anything. He shot me for nothing.' "

Slotnick grilled Gilbert about the lucidity of Canty and Cabey when they made these statements to her, insisting that Canty had in fact been "semiconscious, his eyelids were drooped," rather than "coherent" and "alert" as she claimed. Slotnick then said of Cabey, "He wasn't speaking clearly; he was slurring his words. . . . He really didn't know what he was saying to you." But Gilbert refuted this. "His words were . . . not slurring," she said. "I understood every word completely and fully."

Gilbert was then excused while the attorneys debated whether the statements she had heard from the youths were allowable for our consideration. If the statements could be considered "excited utterances"—those made in the heat of the moment, before the person had had time to reflect—they would be admissible as evidence under New York State law. Justice Crane ruled, however, that "[e]nough time elapsed here, though it was very short, to permit the inference that reflection had set in."

⚖

We were then brought into the courtroom and Waples called his next witness, Josephine Holt. Holt was a black woman, a native of Gastonia, North Carolina, who had lived in upper Manhattan for about seven years. In December 1984 she was working six days a week as a chambermaid in Fort Lee, New Jersey. In the early afternoon on December 22 she had left her job and returned to Manhattan and was taking the subway to do some shopping downtown.

Holt said the youths were seated "much further down" from where she was seated, but that she noticed them shortly after she got on the express train at Ninety-sixth Street because they were "laughing loud and talking loud amongst themselves." She described them as "teenagers, average kids." A few moments later, she said, "I was reading my newspaper and one of the teenagers came over and asked me did I have a match and I says, 'No, I don't.' And he went on and said something to another lady passenger . . ." After that "he went on back down to his friends."

"Now, when this individual spoke to you, where was he in relation to you?" Waples asked her.

"He was standing over me," Holt replied.

"Were you sitting down?"

"Yes."

* * *

"When you say standing over you, what do you mean?"

"He was holding the strap handle."

"What tone of voice did he address you in?"

"A casual voice," Holt said. "It wasn't—He said, 'Miss, do you have a match?' That's all."

After the train stopped at Fourteenth Street, Holt said she noticed Goetz "getting on and several more people getting on and off, and I went on back to reading my paper. And when I looked down again, I seen two . . . of the kids standing over him and what they were saying, I cannot say."

* * *

"Tell us, in your words, what happened next," Waples said.

"Well, like I said, I was reading my paper. I didn't give nothing of a thought of anything of what was going on at the other end of the subway. As the train . . . got like into Franklin

. . . and then it slowed up, I heard like a firecracker. It sound like a firecracker to me; I would take it to be a firecracker. And I didn't look up; I did not look up. And the train slowed down and when it got into Chambers Street, somebody holler, 'Oh, my God.' And the doors open and I run out.''

Slotnick had his work cut out for him in cross-examination, and it even seemed at times that he had finally met his match. Holt got in a huff whenever she felt Slotnick was questioning the veracity of her testimony, and Slotnick, who needed to be somewhat on her side, would back down a little, though he wouldn't give up. The version Holt had told to the two grand juries was more favorable to the defense than her testimony here, and Slotnick was bound to point out all the inconsistencies he could. By the end, though, Slotnick seemed to have done not only this; he'd even seemed to have invented some that didn't exist.

Holt had said to the first grand jury that the youths were "harassing" and "bothering" people on the train. Confronted with this previous testimony, Holt responded, "I wouldn't say like they were going from [passenger to passenger] harassing people, but they were harassing and they were talking loud.''

"So they were talking loud," Slotnick said, and then pointed out another inconsistency: she'd said to the grand jury the youths were "not too loud."

Holt had also told the grand jury the youths had been saying dirty words, and Slotnick asked her whether she'd been telling the truth.

"Yes I was," she said indignantly. "To the best of my ability that I can remember it to get it right, sir, yes. But dirty words were said," she admitted now. "One of them said something dirty to the lady passenger. . . . He did say something out of line to her.''

"Remember telling the grand jury that you didn't want to stare at them because you were a little afraid?" Slotnick later asked.

"Yes," Holt said.

"And remember telling the grand jury that you just sat there and tried to look at your newspaper because you were afraid of them?"

"Yes, I did.''

In addition to Canty, Slotnick asked Holt, "Did you tell the grand jury that you thereafter saw the rest of the fellows come over and they also were standing around the white man?"

"Yes, I did," she also admitted.

* * *

"And these were the same three people that you saw and noticed to be loud, boisterous, harassing, and menacing?"

"Yes."

"The ones you were afraid of?"

"I'm not afraid of anyone," Holt then said.

It was somewhat unclear, however, whether Slotnick merely had Holt flustered at this point, in getting her to state that she had seen three youths in front of Goetz instead of two. In redirect, Waples read directly from Holt's testimony before the first grand jury.

"Question: Okay. What happened when you noticed the man who originally asked you for the match speak to the white person?

"Answer: Well, he was over there speaking to him, and then another one came up, like I just said. Then the white man stood up. He stood up, and when he stood up, that's when he went off. Somebody said he had a gun and the next thing we heard was pop."

"Objection, Your Honor," Slotnick said after Waples had read this. "Is he trying to impeach his own witness?"

"No, I think he's trying to flush out an avenue that you opened up," Justice Crane said. "I'll give you recross on it."

"So, you were saying there you'd seen two people in front of the white man?" Waples continued.

"Yes," Holt answered.

* * *

"Incidentally," Waples asked, "when this person was standing in front of you asking for a match, holding onto the strap, looking down at you, were you afraid of him?"

"No," Holt said.

In recross, Slotnick, I believe, purposely twisted Holt's words to the grand jury to make her contradict herself on this issue again. "When you told the grand jury . . .—this is a question—that there was one person talking to the white man where he was and there was another person coming towards these two—toward the white man and this guy—and you said, 'Right.' That adds up to three, right? In January you said three. Do you remember that?"

"It was two standing over him," Holt insisted. "I know I said that, but it was two I seen standing over him."

"And in January, before the grand jury?"

"I said three. I was wrong."

"You were insistent that it was three."

"But I was wrong. It was two that I seen."

"And now, today, your memory is better about what happened than it was—"

"It's not only today," Holt cut him off.

"Miss Holt, please respond to my question."

"Yes, it's not only today that my memory is better. It came to me."

"I see," said Slotnick, giving us one of his "Can-you-believe-this?" looks.

†

Slotnick did an even more effective hatchet job on the credibility of the next eyewitness, Solitaire MacFoy. MacFoy was a computer programmer for an investment brokerage firm in midtown, born in West Africa, educated in England, who had come to the United States in 1981. He was living in Brooklyn and testified that on the day in question had come into Manhattan to buy some pieces of Plexiglas. He said he boarded the subway at Forty-second Street and stood on the east side of the car, in front of the middle set of doors.

MacFoy's version of the shootings was drastically different from the others we had heard. "Shortly after the train took off from Fourteenth Street, in a position somewhat diagonally across from myself, suddenly, a man took out a gun and started to shoot at some people who were on the train. . . . He was standing, and he motioned with the gun out of some of his clothes with his right hand, and made a step towards his left, and pointed, and started shooting at some people who appeared to me might have been sitting on the seats."

MacFoy described Goetz's facial expression as he pulled out his gun and shot at the youths as "calm and bland" and also "somewhat calculating," and Goetz's manner of firing as "deliberate."

"After he took the step he continued to fire in a somewhat regular pattern, some few shots, and at this time pandemonium broke out in the train. Everybody sort of scattered, and people were screaming and making a lot of noise and going in every direction. He continued shooting at these people and then, when he had finished, he left the train in the direction opposite to that which the train was going." MacFoy recalled hearing "four or five shots" in all.

"When you saw the man firing, did you see what, if anything, he was firing at?" Waples asked.

"I wasn't really sure what he was firing at or the people he was firing at," MacFoy said. "All I know was that there were people there on the seat."

* * *

"And what was the general position of his arm when he was firing the gun?"

"He was standing and pointing down towards where somebody would be sitting on the seat."

"What were you doing when this was going on?"

"Well, all this time I was very terrified, standing with my parcel and remaining motionless."

"What did you do after the firing was over?"

"I went to the opposite direction to which he was."

MacFoy said that prior to the shootings he had not seen Goetz being "surrounded" and that he "had not noticed anybody threatening anybody." He said of the shootings, "The whole motion when he started was very swift and . . . it was over very quickly." But in demonstrating the motion of Goetz's arm and the pattern of fire, MacFoy, like Sally Smithern, remembered it being in the opposite direction as Goetz and the other eyewitnesses: right to left instead of left to right.

Slotnick began his cross-examination by asking, "Mr. MacFoy, the incident occurred . . . on December 22, 1984. Do you remember where you were that Christmas season, 1984?"

"Where I was?" MacFoy responded.

"Were you in New York?" Slotnick asked. "Or perhaps somewhere else?"

As with Sally Smithern, Slotnick's contention was that MacFoy was never on the train that day. He quizzed MacFoy about when he first contacted police about what he had seen, asking, "[I]sn't it a matter of fact that the first time you came forward and identified yourself . . . was in March of 1985?"

"No, no, that's not true," MacFoy answered. "I called in on a hotline number." Slotnick then asked three successive questions that all discussed the police's having no record of MacFoy's call. To each question Waples objected and Justice Crane sustained.

Slotnick also questioned MacFoy about his relationship with William Kunstler, the renowned leftist defense attorney who was representing Darrell Cabey in his $50 million civil suit against Goetz. MacFoy admitted having spoken to Kunstler before contacting the district attorney's office in time to testify before the second grand jury, but denied he was acting in collusion with Kunstler.

"I have some friends who had been urging me constantly to contact the police," MacFoy explained. "One of these friends has a friend who knew Mr. Kunstler, and then Mr. Kunstler spoke with me and urged me to come and speak with him. . . . I thought before speaking to Mr. Kunstler I should go speak to the DA. It seemed like the proper way to proceed to me."

Besides the right-to-left motion of Goetz's arm that MacFoy described in his direct examination, Slotnick revealed several other major discrepancies between MacFoy's account of the shootings and the testimonies of other witnesses. MacFoy had not seen any conversation take place before the shootings between Goetz and Canty. After the shootings he could not recall if he had seen anyone on the floor of the car and he had not seen anyone come to the aid of the people who were shot before he fled the scene. He also said that Goetz fled from the car via the north (rather than the south) storm door right after the shooting ceased.

"And you went south and ran to the front of the car?" Slotnick asked.

"Yes," MacFoy said.

"I guess Mr. Goetz ran before you ran?"

"Yes."

Slotnick took some cheap shots toward the end of MacFoy's testimony. He ended his cross-examination by asking him, "Did [Detective] Clark ever tell you that your version of the events was inconsistent with virtually every known fact?" Then, when Waples began his redirect, "Mr. MacFoy, on the evening of December 22, 1984, after you left the subway train—," Slotnick jumped up and interrupted, "Objection. Pursuing a state of facts that hasn't been proven." Slotnick withdrew his objection a moment later.

In an effort to restore MacFoy's credibility after Slotnick's attempt to impeach it, Justice Crane allowed Waples to then call two witnesses who testified that MacFoy had told them what he'd seen on the subway on the same day the incident occurred. The first was Ruth Chasek, MacFoy's girlfriend, who said she saw him in the early evening, before she'd heard any other report about the incident, "and he said, 'I just had a very bad day. I just saw some man shoot some people in the subway.'" The second was another friend, David Gilfix, whom MacFoy had called even earlier—around 3:30 or 4:00 p.m., Gilfix said—and described what he had seen.

The appearances of these two witnesses did not alter my opinion of MacFoy's testimony, however. The contradictions between MacFoy's version of the shootings and those of the other eyewitnesses, along with the revelation of the Kunstler connection, convinced me that his testimony was unreliable. Slotnick had successfully won me over in this instance, and had succeeded in discrediting MacFoy's account.

Chapter 9

The "Myra" Guns

May 11-12

In the thirteen-count indictment against Goetz, two of the charges we had to consider stemmed from an incident separate from the shootings on December 22, 1984. These charges involved two guns that Goetz had bought out of state that were alleged to have been in his possession in New York City around the time that the shootings occurred. Neither of these guns was the one he used on the subway that day, but the mere possession of an unlicensed handgun in New York is a misdemeanor, punishable by a maximum sentence of six months to a year in jail.

Toward the end of the following Monday and then continuing Tuesday morning, we heard Myra Friedman's testimony concerning these guns. Friedman was a neighbor of Goetz, living in the apartment directly below his in a co-op apartment building on West Fourteenth Street. The two had several conversations in the days following the shootings, before Goetz finally gave himself up.

I found Friedman to be a very strange woman, like a character Lily Tomlin or Carol Burnett might invent. Part of this, I learned later, was because she had a speech impediment brought on in part by the stress of having to testify in this trial. Her chin seemed drooped and her tongue too thick; she slurred her words and slightly lisped. She made a passing reference to it right at the beginning of her testimony, and after the trial I learned that Waples had considered making some more specific announcement to us about it but ultimately had opted not to. I think that was a mistake, though, because I definitely feel that Friedman's voice negatively affected my impression of her testimony. Its bizarreness only heightened the strangeness of her story.

Friedman testified that eight days after the shootings, in the early afternoon on December 30, Goetz came to her apartment with a brown paper package. She said she had been aware that Goetz owned and possessed guns, but that she wasn't certain of the package's contents.

"He walked into my apartment and said, 'Can I leave this with you for a few days?'" Friedman explained. "And I let out some kind of yell and said, 'What is that?' And he said, 'This is not the weapon that was used.' . . . [H]e walked very fast towards my bedroom. And I said, 'No, not there. There.' And I pointed to my hallway walk-in closet. . . . As he walked over to the closet, I said, 'Will that explode?' And he said, 'There are no bullets in there.' I said, 'Do you have a license for that or those?'—I am unclear as to whether there was singular or plural in my own language. I'm not sure; there may have been a reference to a plural. But I said, 'Do you have a license?' And he said, 'This or these'—once again, I'm not sure as to the plural or singular—'were or was purchased legally.'"

Goetz stayed a maximum of five minutes, according to Friedman. After he left, she "went upstairs to Mr. Goetz's apartment to knock on the door with the intention of asking him to take the package back." There was no answer.

The next day—the day that Goetz surrendered himself to the police in New Hampshire—Friedman said she took the package to her lawyer's office. And then two days later, on January 2, she was present when some law-enforcement officials came to her attorney's office and took the package away.

The major point of contention about Friedman's testimony was her relationship with Goetz at the time this occurred. Friedman said she had known him for nine years, but "only as a consequence of us living in the same building."

"Do you consider yourself a friend of him . . . ?" Waples asked her.

Friedman replied, "No, absolutely not."

"Have you ever considered yourself a friend of the defendant?"

"Absolutely not."

"How do you characterize your acquaintance with him?"

"Mr. Goetz was and is a distant acquaintance," she insisted emphatically. "I had nothing to do with him. Nothing."

Slotnick's cross-examination also probed their relationship, suggesting that the two were closer than Friedman would admit. His reason for pursuing this, we learned later, was that if we decided in our deliberations that Friedman had been an accomplice rather than an unwilling victim in the possession of those guns, her testimony of how she came to possess the guns by law would require some form of corroboration, opening a door for Goetz's possible aquittal on those counts.

Slotnick first brought up a phone conversation the two of them had had on December 29, the day before Goetz came to her apartment with the package. They talked on that occasion for over a half an hour, in the course of which Goetz revealed he was the subway gunman being sought by police. Friedman, meanwhile, recorded the conversation by switching on her phone machine.

Slotnick asked her if after the conversation she had immediately called the police to tell them she knew who the subway gunman was. Friedman answered that she had not.

"[W]ere you aware of the fact that on December 29, 1984, other than Mr. Goetz, you were the only other person that knew who the tall, blond man on the train was?" Slotnick asked.

Waples objected, saying, "How could she possibly know that?" But Justice Crane overruled, allowing Slotnick to question her about her "belief at the time."

"I wondered if anyone else knew about that but thought that I was the only one that knew," Friedman replied.

* * *

"[Y]ou were aware, after the phone conversation, that Mr. Goetz had not turned himself in?"

"Yes, I was aware of that."

"And you did nothing to alert the authorities who the . . . person on the subway was?"

"No, I did not."

"As a matter of fact, were you—When Mr. Goetz called, did he call you Myra or Miss Friedman?"

"He—He—He called me Myra."

"And did you call him Mr. Goetz or Bernie?"

"I called him Bernie."

"As a matter of fact, during the phone conversation, . . . you not only asked him what happened, but you rendered advice to him: 'Bernie, this is what you should do,' things of that sort?"

"I most certainly suggested that he turn himself in," Friedman said.

* * *

"And did you tell Bernie, 'I'm not going to tell a soul'? Did you tell him that?"

"Sure, yeah."

"And did you also say, 'Bernie, when you get in tomorrow, give me a call?' "

"Yeah, something like that."

* * *

"In other words, did you express to Mr. Goetz sympathy, concern, and care?"

"Of some nature, yes, I did," Friedman said.

Waples had been objecting to this whole line of questioning, but Justice Crane often overruled. "I've been allowing this line over objection except when the line starts to reveal the contents of the conversations," Justice Crane explained to the attorneys in a sidebar. "I have been allowing it in order for Mr. Slotnick to undermine Miss Friedman's statements that she was . . . barely on speaking terms with him. I have given him latitude for that purpose, but not for the purpose of putting the contents in."

Slotnick, however, wanted to discuss the specific contents of their conversation, both to "show how friendly and chummy they were," and because apparently Friedman had said to Goetz that she felt he was innocent, which was something that Slotnick clearly wanted us to know. He and Baker asked the judge to allow them to enter into evidence the tape of the conversation for this end, but the judge steadfastly refused. Left with no proper course to continue, then, Slotnick resorted to his old tricks again.

"Miss Friedman, when you had this phone conversation on December 29, 1984, the first one you taped, you expressed the feeling that Mr. Goetz was innocent of any wrongdoing. Why did you have that impression?"

"Your Honor, I object," Waples said, genuinely furious.

"Objection sustained," Justice Crane said. "The jury is to disregard questions that don't have answers."

"This is outrageous," Waples declared.

"Mr. Slotnick," Justice Crane continued, "please don't reveal any contents of any conversations between the witness and your client."

"Without going into words," Slotnick then began to ask Friedman, "did you have an impression as to Mr. Goetz's culpability—"

"Your Honor—" Waples cut him off.

"Objection sustained," said Justice Crane.

"Would Your Honor direct Mr. Slotnick to please cease and desist from this line which you have already ordered him not to pursue?" Waples asked, exasperated.

"Mr. Slotnick, please don't ask any further questions about the communications at all and go on to another subject. I think you have had enough on this line."

The reason such subjects were not allowable, of course, is that Friedman's impressions were not evidence of anything. For the same reason, Waples was not allowed to ask Friedman about the basis for her dislike of Goetz, which stemmed in part from a remark she heard Goetz make during a meeting of the Fourteenth Street Block Association, to the effect that, "The only way we're going to clean up this street is to get rid of the spics and niggers." I mention this statement, having learned of it after the trial, to illustrate how unfairly prejudicial Slotnick's tactics were when he disregarded instructions and offered up self-serving statements within objectionable questions, knowing full well that it's difficult to remain objective and just wipe things out of your mind once you've heard them. Waples, I suppose, could have used the same tactics to get us to hear Goetz's "spics and niggers" line, but by not playing the same game as Slotnick, Waples did gain some favor in my mind. In my diary entry that night, I supposed that part of Waples's exasperation with Slotnick was "part of his style and technique in dealing with this case," and I found it "to an extent . . . quite effective."

"I find myself feeling bad for the guy," I commented, "as it seems he's trying to play it straight and Slotnick is breaking every rule in the book, or at least bending them as far as they can go."

⚖

Reluctantly, then, Slotnick moved on to the day after Goetz and Friedman's first phone conversation. Goetz came to her apartment and Friedman admitted that the visit was not unexpected. He stayed for about twenty minutes, then left and returned less than an hour later, this time with the package in hand.

"Now, between the time he left your apartment and the time he returned, did you happen to call the police and the authorities and say, 'The man you are looking for has just been in my apartment'?"

"No, I did not."

"And when he left your apartment, it was still Bernie and Myra, was it not?"

"Well, yeah."

"Now, he came back, and when he came back he came back with a package, is that correct?"

"That's correct."

❋   ❋   ❋

"And you let him in?"

"Yes."

"And it was *still* Bernie and Myra, was it not?"

"I don't remember. I don't remember if he said 'Myra' or just 'you,' " she responded, becoming a little agitated. "I mean, I don't remember. I mean, do you mean did he call me Miss Friedman, the answer is no."

"Of course not," Slotnick offered, attempting to calm her a bit.

Slotnick then pointed out that although she could infer the contents of the package, she allowed Goetz to leave the guns with her. "You kept them in your closet?"

"Yes."

"And you didn't say, 'Oh, no, Bernie, don't put them in my closet'?"

"To be a little less humorous about it, this was a very unexpected visit," Friedman replied.

"Please answer my question. Did you tell him not to put them in your closet?"

"No, I did not tell him that."

"You were and you are and you were then a mature adult?"

"At that moment I was kind of in a state of shock, but I am a mature adult, yes," Friedman said.

"That was the thirtieth, is that correct?"

"Yes."

"Isn't it a matter of fact you kept the package in your closet the entire day?"

"Yeah, uh-huh."

"You didn't call police?"

"No."

*   *   *

"And you still, on the thirtieth, maintained this concern, sympathy, as you expressed before, about Mr. Goetz? Is that correct, yes or no?"

"Objection," Waples said.

"Sustained," said Justice Crane.

Slotnick then discussed with Friedman her second telephone conversation with Goetz, which took place the following day, on December 31, and which she also taped. Here he was clearly trying to establish that she was an accomplice.

"Isn't it correct you told him you were very concerned because you thought you may be committing a crime?" he asked.

"Yes, indeed," she said. "That I—Yes, I was very frightened."

*   *   *

"And did you ever say to him, 'Well, can I drop them in the river'?"

"Yes, I said that."

"That was a good way of getting rid of them?"

"Yeah."

"By the way, that was your idea, not his?"

"That's correct. It was my remark."

*   *   *

"As a matter of fact, at that point really what was going on is that you and your neighbor, Bernie, were somewhat conspiratorial with regard to what was in your closet?"

"I did not feel conspiratorial, Mr. Slotnick. I felt scared," Friedman said.

"But the essence of it was you and he were discussing how you would dispose with what was in your closet?"

"I was extremely concerned about being in the position I was put in."

"Why didn't you call the police?"

"I did not—contrary to the turmoil that later developed, and got out of hand—I did not want to end up in the headlines."

"You did not want to end up in the headlines?"

"No, I did not."

From then on, Slotnick grilled her on the cover article with her byline on it that had later appeared in *New York* magazine, entitled "My Neighbor, Bernie Goetz." The article largely consisted of the transcripts of the two phone conversations she had taped, unbeknownst to Bernie. Friedman argued that she never wrote the article because she had been unable to meet the magazine's deadline, but she admitted during questioning that she had been paid by the magazine, and that she did not ever call the magazine to complain about what they'd published.

Friedman was a writer by trade but denied she had approached *New York* magazine with the story idea for money or fame. "[W]riters write," she said. "That's what they do. The reasons are manifold." She said she'd originally envisioned the article focusing on her reaction to Goetz's having phoned her and told her about the shootings, and that she'd wanted to write it in a way that she "would be able to say things that I wanted to say."

Slotnick asked Friedman if sometime after the article was published she had tried to apologize to Goetz for having taped their conversation without his knowledge or consent.

"I don't recall it, but it certainly is a possibility, yeah," Friedman replied, adding that, "I don't think there was anything wrong with that . . . but other people were saying there was something wrong with it."

"As a matter of fact," Slotnick said, "these people had indicated to you that you had broken a confidence in taping his phone call."

"Who said that? Well, a whole bunch of silly people felt that," Friedman said.

In order to establish the complete chain of possession of the "Myra" guns, Waples next called Detective Michael Clark of the New York City Police Department, who from the beginning had been in charge of the Goetz investigation, to testify that he, Susan Braver, and two other detectives had gone to the office of Myra Friedman's attorney on January 2 and there obtained custody of the brown paper package. He said the package contained two guns: a nine-millimeter semiautomatic pistol and a .38-caliber revolver. Both were unloaded. Clark took them to the ballistics section of the New York City Police Department to be examined.

Waples then called John Campbell and Kenneth Ditchfield, the owners of the stores where Goetz originally bought the guns. Campbell's store was in New London, Connecticut, and Campbell testified that Goetz legally bought the revolver in August 1970; Goetz was a Connecticut resident at that time. Ditchfield's store was in Orlando, Florida; Goetz had had a Florida driver's license at the time he purchased the semiautomatic, in September 1984.

Finally, Waples called Detective Frank Nicolosi, a ballistics expert who ostensibly was testifying that he'd tested the two guns and they were operable. Waples had other questions about ballistics that he wanted to ask Nicolosi, though, and he did this over some heated objections by Slotnick, who wanted to hurry Nicolosi off the stand.

Slotnick first tried to cut Waples off while he was asking Nicolosi about his stellar credentials as an expert in firearms and ballistics examination. Nicolosi had testified as such in over three hundred and fifty trials. Slotnick told Justice Crane he was willing to stipulate that Nicolosi was an expert without Waples's having to go over his credentials. But Waples wanted us to hear them and so refused. Slotnick then wanted to concede that the guns were operable, once again to cut Waples off. Again, however, Waples preferred to "go through" Nicolosi's testimony rather than to accept a stipulation. Once this was done, Waples began asking questions about "basic ballistics information" so that Nicolosi could "explain the evidence that was recovered at the crime scene" to us: information regarding "cartridges and bullets and so forth."

"But he seems to be referring to those guns," Slotnick objected in a sidebar, arguing that Nicolosi's testimony was irrelevant because neither of these guns had been used in the shootings. "I think that Detective Nicolosi is here just to wave the guns in front of the jury and cause them some prejudice by it," Slotnick continued, complaining that Waples was "picking [the guns] up and moving them around and holding them in the air" while he was questioning Nicolosi. He said to Waples, "I mean, you're having a nice show by a ballistics expert, and as long as we're standing up here, those guns are sticking in front of the jury."

"Mr. Slotnick kept pictures of the four people Mr. Goetz shot on an easel for two days in front of the jury," Waples argued. "I think it's inappropriate to say now he's being prejudiced by the retention of a witness on the stand."

Justice Crane ruled that Waples could proceed but instructed him to leave the guns on the prosecution table. "[C]ontinue your examination and when you're finished, we can have them shown to the jury by a court officer," Justice Crane said to Waples. "Let's move it along."

"I do resent the Court's imputation that I am wasting time," Waples replied testily.

"I didn't impute that in the slightest," Justice Crane answered.

"That, I think, is the way the record is to be read."

"The record should be corrected, if that's the implication arising from the record," Justice Crane offered. "Mr. Waples has been more—much more than cooperative, expeditious, and thorough in his preparation. This case is moving along faster than I expected. I commend Mr. Waples for it, and if he read anything to the contrary in my remarks, I apologize to him and I certainly—"

"I don't need an apology," Waples said. "It just seems to me that you're getting short-tempered with me when—"

"Oh, no," Justice Crane interjected.

"When you listened to two days of petty cross-examination of Troy Canty and the Court would not intercede to curtail it," Waples went on.

"You wound me. You wound me deeply," Justice Crane said. "I am not short-tempered with you. I have been and I apologized to Mr. Slotnick for that one time that I was short-tempered. I'm not short-tempered at all, really."

"That was a poor choice of words and I apologize for that. I didn't mean to imply that," Waples said.

"Okay," Justice Crane replied. "Let's take our time."

Slotnick interjected at this point, "Now that we've all apologized to each other, can we continue on?"

Waples asked Nicolosi a series of questions about different types of bullets that exist, those that have standard velocity charge as opposed to high velocity charge, and those that have hollow points that "expand upon impact . . . to increase in caliber" and therefore have "greater damaging potential." In his audiotaped statement Goetz said that he had used hollow-point bullets, and that the first two bullets were standard velocity, while the latter three were more highly charged.

Waples produced several photographs of bullets, both intact and after detonation, revealing the differences between the effect of regular bullets and those with hollow points. He wanted Nicolosi to come down off the stand and explain the photographs in front of us, but Slotnick objected to this and called for a sidebar yet again.

This time Waples explained that there was case law in which "the nature of the bullets used bears upon the question of intent." Baker argued that Waples "has to prove intent to use that specific weapon at a specific time, in furtherance of a specific moment. I don't think this testimony is going to prove that."

"Bullets are bullets, sir," Slotnick added to Justice Crane, calling Nicolosi's "demonstration and lecture on hollow-point . . . insignificant and prejudicial."

"If Mr. Waples fails in his effort, I think that's something you're going to be most gleeful about," Justice Crane answered. "I think he's entitled to try."

Nicolosi showed us the photographs then, and Waples concluded by asking him whether he had been able to tell by examining the physical evidence what types of bullets had been used in the shootings. Nicolosi said he couldn't, explaining that the recovered bullets had been too deformed to be identifiable in this regard.

"I tried to make that determination, but there is not enough there to make it," Nicolosi testified. "I can't say for sure whether they were hollow point or not."

Chapter 10

⚖️

Christopher Boucher and the Videotape

That night I remarked in my diary:

A lot went on today that we were not privy to once again. I can only assume that there are arguments before—or perhaps not before—the general court as to what the jury will be allowed to see and hear. We have not seen the videotape of Goetz that was made in New Hampshire, and I don't know if we will. We still haven't seen any of the other shooting victims. We saw Canty come up and lie to us for a few days, but that was it. The only other one we might see, I guess, is Barry Allen, since we've already seen Ramseur come in and refuse to testify. Maybe Allen was actually in court and they didn't want us to see him, and that was one of the long periods that we were playing poker.

We also still haven't seen anybody who can definitely corroborate one way or another what happened on the train. If we had to go into deliberations today, based on what we've seen so far, I still couldn't tell you what the ruling would be. I know you'd have twelve people scratching their heads wondering what actually happened. I'm certainly hoping that things become more clear for us, but I realize that the defense benefits if things remain unclear, because our instructions are to rule for the defendant unless we think he has been proven guilty beyond a reasonable doubt.

The following day, though, was a big one for the prosecution. In grand theatrical style, Waples seemed to have saved the best for last. With the testimony of Christopher Boucher, we finally heard from an eyewitness who claimed to have clearly seen Goetz shoot Darrell Cabey at point-blank range when

Cabey was sitting in the seat by the conductor's cab. Of course, we'd heard from no other witnesses who also saw this, and Boucher's account of the shootings differed from those of other witnesses in certain details. But Boucher's account corroborated what Goetz himself had said in his audiotaped statement, and what we saw and heard him say again on the videotape, which was played later in the day. I felt that having even one eyewitness to substantiate Goetz's version, which had proved to be reliable in so many other details, was enough to solidify the manner of the Cabey shooting as a fact. And by the end of the day I declared in my diary,

> "I don't think I'm prejudiced against Goetz at this point, but I am just now beginning to form a more solid opinion of the events on the train as I believe they happened; and today for the first time I find myself perhaps leaning against Goetz."

May 13

Christopher Boucher, if you recall, was Loren Michals's friend who was visiting from San Francisco. A thirty-three-year-old display artist for a department store, Boucher had moved to San Francisco from New York in 1982 and was originally from Ohio. He and Michals were taking the subway that day from Ninety-sixth Street to Chambers Street to do some Christmas shopping in SoHo.

Boucher said he noticed the youths immediately as he entered the car through the middle door at Ninety-sixth Street. They were "talking loud and joking," he said, and as a result he and Michals "just veered off and went to the front of the car." He had not noticed precisely how many in the group there were, just that they were "young males, late teens," all seated on both sides in the back end of the car.

The two sat together, with Michals to his right, on the end of the long bench in the southeast part of the car. During the ride downtown he and Michals conversed until the train noise grew too loud. They stopped talking then, and "were pretty much sitting waiting to get to Chambers Street," Boucher said, when "the first thing I noticed a woman jumped up and had fallen over Loren."

The woman had been sitting in the middle of the bench, Boucher explained. "At this point I had no idea what was going on, I didn't know why. I heard popping and my immediate thoughts were the kids at the other end were shooting off firecrackers. And Loren helped the woman up with the baby and was heading her towards the door. At this time other people were running by. And I was sitting there. And as he helped her up, my vision became clear to the end of the car and I was looking down to see what was going on. And the immediate thing I saw was the man standing with the gun at the end of the car."

"What happened next?" Waples asked.

"He shot someone sitting in a seat," Boucher answered.

"You saw that?"

"Yes."

Boucher said he heard two pops initially, but that he couldn't see to the back end of the car because his vision was blocked. He was still seated when the aisle cleared and he "saw a man that appeared to be in his late twenties, early thirties, blondish, standing at the end of the car, in the middle of the aisle, about two or three feet from a young black man sitting on a bench, at the end of the car, near the conductor's cab, on the right side. . . . One of the men I had noticed earlier was lying on the floor, in the aisle, face down," said Boucher. "His head was up, looking to the . . . front end of the car.

"In your direction?" Waples asked.

"Yes. One of the other men was slumped in the doorway, on the left side, and those are the only two I'm really positive about. My eyes went directly to the action."

Goetz, he said, was "standing, looking down" at Darrell Cabey, who was "[s]itting back with his hands like grasping the bench and a frightened look on his face. When it caught my vision, his hand was already up with the gun. . . . He was standing, holding the gun pointed at this individual and in just a matter of seconds he fired . . ."

"And what did the person who was sitting down do at the moment the shot was fired?" Waples asked.

"Well, he was sitting, grasping the bench, and he just tightened," said Boucher.

"Did you ever see that person try to get out of that seat?"

"No."

"Did you ever see him threatening Mr. Goetz?"

"No."

"Did he have anything in his hand that you saw?"

"No."

"After you heard that shot, did you hear any additional shots?"

"At that point I looked up and saw Loren at the doorway motioning to me to get the hell out of my seat. And at that point I just turned my back and I went, and I don't remember hearing anything after that."

"How many shots did you hear altogether?" Waples asked a few moments later.

"Three. I'm positive," Boucher said.

Waples concluded his direct examination by asking Boucher if immediately before the shootings he'd heard any commotion emanating from the back end of the car, or if he had seen the youths surrounding Goetz. Boucher said no.

"Is there any doubt in your own mind that you saw a person sitting in that seat when that shot was fired?"

"No, no doubt," Boucher asserted.

"And how is your eyesight?"

"It's perfect."

"That's all, Judge," Waples announced to Justice Crane.

Slotnick opened his cross-examination by asking Boucher if he'd followed the Goetz case in the media. Boucher said he hadn't but was kept somewhat informed by his friends and family. When asked if he had watched any television programs on the case, Boucher said, "I do not watch television."

"You don't watch television?" Slotnick asked incredulously. Boucher answered, "No."

*　　*　　*

"Now, Mr. Boucher, you testified that you heard what you believed to be firecrackers, is that correct?"

"Yes."

"You've never heard a gun before, have you?"

"No, I haven't."

"And you've heard firecrackers before?"

"Oh, yeah."

"And did what you hear[d] appear to be a string of fire-crackers in rapid succession?"

"No."

"In other words, there was separation between the times that you heard the pops, is that correct?"

"Yes."

"It would be 'pop' and . . . then 'pop' again. . . . And then some more time passed by and there would be another 'pop'?"

"Yes."

"So, when you said firecrackers, if I were to assume that it was in rapid succession, that would be totally wrong?"

"That would be wrong," Boucher replied.

Slotnick also pointed out that in his grand jury testimony Boucher had said he first heard the popping noises *before* the woman with the baby had fallen over Michals, not afterward. "I don't remember that now," Boucher said.

Slotnick then questioned Boucher about his emotional state at the time the shootings occurred. Michals had testified that Boucher had been "shaken up" by the incident. Boucher denied that he'd become "traumatized" or seriously disturbed by the incident, but he admitted that immediately afterward, while on the subway platform, he "was quite shaken" and "emotionally upset."

What Slotnick meant to establish, though, was that Boucher was already upset before he saw Goetz.

"Now, what actually happened was that, if I may refresh your recollection, you heard some popping sounds. Sounded to you like firecrackers or cap pistols or something like that?"

"Yes."

"Loud noises?"

"Yes."

"And this woman fell—I'm sorry—You were gazing ahead, then this woman fell . . . Is that correct?"

"Yes."

The woman was presumably Andrea Reid. Boucher accurately described her as "a young black woman . . . normally built, thin." He said, though, that Michals "helped her up and *walked* her towards the door." [Italics mine.]

"And then, after all that happened," Slotnick continued, "you then looked to the right and saw a profile of a tall, blond man, is that correct?"

"Yes, that is."

"But the first thing you saw, before you even saw that tall, blond man—and I think you testified to this earlier—the first thing that you saw when you looked to your right was a man lying on the floor."

"Yes."

"Before you even saw the blond man?"

"Yes."

"And you saw this man lying on the floor, and that, obviously, had some emotional effect on you. You knew that there was something wrong at this point."

"Well, I had no idea what was going on," Boucher responded. "I thought they were kidding around or—I had no idea."

"Well, you saw this man lying on the floor with his eyes rolling around a little bit?"

"He was staring straight ahead," Boucher said.

Slotnick then switched his questioning to Boucher's recollection of the way Cabey was shot. Boucher said Goetz fired while standing directly in front of Cabey, pointing the gun in a downward direction, holding it waist-high with his elbow bent.

"Now when you saw this, did you see the man's head jerk at all?" Slotnick asked, referring to Goetz.

"No," Boucher said.

"Or his foot jerk or hand jerk or anything of that sort?"

"No."

"Nothing? You saw no jerks from the body of this person whatsoever?"

"No."

Boucher likewise did not see Cabey so much as flinch when he was shot.

"He was just seated, holding on almost in a paralyzed state?" Slotnick asked.

"Seemed to be," Boucher replied.

"In fact, he *was* in a paralyzed state at that point, wouldn't you say?"

"He seemed to be," repeated Boucher.

Slotnick also brought up some discrepancies between Boucher's testimony here and what was written on a police report based on his statements to a detective four hours after the incident. According to the detective's report, Boucher said he'd first noticed five or six youths in the back of the car at the Forty-second Street station, which contradicted his current testimony that he remembered positively seeing only three, and that he'd noticed them immediately when he got on at Ninety-sixth Street. The report also stated that Boucher saw two youths lying on the floor of the train, a third "crouched down near the exit door," and Goetz shooting at *two* youths seated by the conductor's cab. Boucher admitted he had told the detective about having seen three felled youths instead of one but denied that he had ever said two youths were seated where only Cabey was. In fact, Boucher said, he had until recently been under the mistaken impression that that short seat could hold only one person. He was now aware that it was big enough for two, but he said it had looked like a one-seater because he "saw the seat in profile" from his perspective, forty feet away.

A more significant flaw in Boucher's recollections, I thought, was his insistence that he had not felt stressed and traumatized while the shootings were occurring despite his obviously distorted sense of the speed of people's movements and the sounds going on around him. Slotnick asked Boucher, "[T]here were also things that were distracting you, were there not? There were noises, people screaming, people moving?"

"No one screamed," Boucher replied.

"No one screamed at all?"

"No."

"Very quiet?"

"Yes, it was."

"People were moving?"

"It was strange. People moved very orderly off the train. No one ran; no one screamed; no one fought to get off. People helped each other. That's why it was so odd."

"Your adrenaline was flowing?" Slotnick continued.

"No," Boucher insisted. "At the time that was occurring, I didn't realize it was a shooting. I didn't know. I thought they were kidding around. I had nothing to be scared of. I had ridden that train for four years to and from work. I felt very safe."

After Slotnick finished his cross-examination, Waples in redirect merely asked Boucher again, "Is there any doubt in your mind that on December 22, 1984, you saw this tall, blond man firing a gun [at] a person who was sitting in that seat?"

"I have no doubt about it, no," Boucher replied; and to me, when I heard it, that was really the bottom line. There were admittedly quite a few contradictions and inaccuracies in Boucher's testimony, but I felt they were all very tangential, that they did not alter the substance of his testimony, and that they could all be easily explained. So much of what happened occurred so quickly, and what happened in the car before the shootings were things a person might not take special notice of to begin with, much less recall with precision two-and-a-half years later. In my mind, therefore, there was with all the eyewitnesses a great deal of room for certain types of discrepancies because so much time had elapsed since the incident. And I felt that the crucial aspect of Boucher's testimony— seeing Goetz shoot Cabey while Cabey was seated—was the kind of image that would stick with a person, not something a witness would likely forget. Boucher seemed very clear and confident on this fact and it corroborated what Goetz said and I believed him. It would take a lot to make me think that it hadn't occurred.

Next on the stand was Detective Clark, who had testified the day before about the "Myra" guns, to lay the foundation for the admission into evidence of the videotape. Clark testified that he and two other New York City detectives flew to New Hampshire after learning from the Concord police that they had Goetz in custody. They arrived at the police station at 7:45 p.m., and were met there by Susan Braver, who had driven in from Stowe, Vermont, where she'd been vacationing. Goetz had already given two statements by this time, first orally to Officer Foote and then on audiotape to Detective Domian. Nevertheless, at 9:40 p.m., Goetz went through it all again, submitting to another two-hour interview that was videotaped.

Present in the room were Goetz, Braver, Clark, Detective Dan Hattendorf of the New York City Transit Police, and a Concord police detective who ran the videorecording equipment.

The videotape was played in court after we'd recessed for lunch. We wore the same wireless headphones with which we'd listened to the audiotapes, and again each of us was provided with a written transcript. This time, though, the judge discouraged us from referring to it while the tape was played. "[U]nlike when we were hearing the audiotapes, don't concentrate on the transcript. Concentrate on the exhibit," Justice Crane said. He reminded us as he had with the audiotape that the transcript was not evidence, but simply a guide to understanding the audio portion of the exhibit. Furthermore, he said, the lights in the courtroom were going to be dimmed, and he didn't want us "rummaging through" the transcript and missing what was happening on the video screen before us. "I urge you to watch the video because that's what it's for. Put your attention there," Justice Crane said.

We watched the video on a twenty-seven-inch Sony TV monitor that was placed before the jury box on a large, wheeled, metal stand. Two similar monitors were set up for the audience, another for Goetz and the attorneys, and a fifth one for the judge. On the screen we saw Goetz sitting at the far end of a rectangular table. The camera angle remained fixed, but occasionally we'd see either Detective Clark, who was sitting to Goetz's left, or Braver, who was across from Goetz, enter the frame.

Goetz's mood had changed perceptibly in the five-and-a-half hours since he'd completed his audiotaped statement. At first he was unwilling to discuss the incident with Braver and the New York detectives; he said several times to them, "I don't want to talk to you," and, "I have nothing to say." But eventually he relented and agreed to be interviewed. "I'll go through this thing again," he said, "but this exhausts me to go through this. I hate it. What I've been trying to do by talking to the people of New Hampshire is to try to forget about this. I've been trying to forget about it and it's fading away, thank God, in my mind."

Besides his exhaustion, Goetz was now confronted with New York City law-enforcement officials against whom as a group he bore a bitter grudge. He made it clear that he did not trust them for this reason and that he knew that all they wanted to do was get his statement and extradite him to New York as quickly as possible. It was New Year's Eve, and he could probably sense that they didn't want to be there; he didn't feel they sympathized with what he was going through.

Because of this he wavered between feeling angry and resentful and then contrite and compliant, and he would even apologize. His words at times were laced with sarcasm, as when Braver tried to begin the interview with, "Okay, I'm an assistant district attorney from Manhattan." "Congratulations," Goetz shot back, then said, "I'm—I'm sorry. Excuse me."

In another exchange, Goetz said, "I would just like to get out of this room." Braver replied, "We'd like to resolve this also, Mr. Goetz."

"Okay, good," Goetz said testily. "You would like to resolve it. I know you would like to."

"And I know you would," Braver said.

"Oh, yeah, yeah. Isn't that great. I—I apologize. I know I'm not being civil," Goetz said. A moment later he added, "Because—Because for you this is all business. That's what it is for you. It's just all business, you know?"

Most of Goetz's hostility was aimed toward Susan Braver. He became immediately disturbed by her accent, which seemed to grate on his nerves. She was talking to him and he interrupted her in mid-sentence: "Oh, God, you know, just when I hear New Yorkers speak, I don't even want to—" Later he complained again about her voice. "I can't stand it," he said. "Just, just the sound. It's—It's, uh—It's all, you know—"

For that reason Detective Clark ended up conducting most of the interview. Occasionally, though, Braver would interject a question that more often than not would incite Goetz's anger and bring out the viciousness in him. In my opinion Braver didn't handle the interview well. Her questions were often inflammatory, such as when she asked Goetz, concerning why he had shot the youths, "Mr. Goetz, why these four?"

"Oh, oh, isn't that beautiful," Goetz responded, his voice filled with sarcasm. "You asked the question in an intellectual way. 'Why these four?' . . . I didn't pick out these four. I never met those guys."

"Why these four, though?" Braver asked again.

"Because—Because I saw what they were going to do with me, Miss. Miss, they were intending to play with me, like a cat plays with a mouse. Now, you're not familiar with these things because you're not familiar with violence. They shouldn't have sent you up here. . . . They should have sent people—I'm sure there are people in the New York City government who are familiar with violence, who know violence, okay? Because it's a realm of reality that you are not familiar with, and—and—and so—so you speak of these things in an . . . intellectual way and I am going to be judged on, 'Oh, oh this was not displayed' or 'That was not displayed' or 'How could you possibly have known what would have happened?' I mean, it's the way how I look at the bureaucracy of New York. It makes me sick."

In several tirades Goetz berated the New York City legal system, calling it a "self-serving bureaucracy" that was a "joke," a "sham," and a "disgrace." He called New York City "lawless" and the subway system "an atrocity" and, speaking of all the publicity that the shootings had received, he stated, "The subway system itself is a disaster. The school system is a disaster. The crime system is a disaster. And this is getting all this attention and you're somehow—you're going to have to prove that the system works somehow. But if you don't know it's a joke, then you have your head buried in the sand.

"The situation is so bad in New York it's unbearable for the people," Goetz went on, adding that "New York City doesn't give a damn about violence. Otherwise this never would have happened. And there is violence all over New York. . . . People have said the response was—was out of proportion. . . . I wish that they were sitting there in that seat instead of me. That would have been beautiful. That would—I wish I was never there and they were there. That would have been great. . . . But all this is—it's like a dam and water is building up behind that dam and this is just a crack in the dam or a little hole that's in the dam and eventually something, you know—The city—There are basic things that people must have. People can't—It's unbearable for people to live in fear. People must have police protection. The problem—The problem isn't the police. The problem is you. It's your legal system. . . . Oh, if you knew how sick your legal system makes me."

Clearly, much of Goetz's rage against New York City was in response to the media reports of the shootings, which Goetz was well-versed in and had obviously followed closely. As he had in his audiotaped statement, he made it clear that he had been shocked and overwhelmed by the extent of the media coverage and felt it was an overreaction. He had said on the audiotapes, "[T]o me it's just one more crime," but the media had been calling it the act of a madman and the most violent crime of the year. As a result he felt he would not be treated justly, and he stated that, by allowing himself to be extradited, "I consider what I'm doing as just throwing myself to a bunch of wolves, because that's what I look at you as being." He mentioned in particular having heard some statements made by Mayor Koch. "The thing that hurt is I respected that guy," Goetz commented, saying he felt pained "to hear him say the things that he said about me. . . .

"[The] New York City government is acting hysterically," Goetz insisted. "New York is going to have a need to show . . . that I'm a nut or . . . that this act was not correct, was inappropriate." Later he added, "If you say this wasn't wrong, it means people have to carry guns . . . in New York and the city will never admit that. The city . . . doesn't have the guts to admit that. . . . If you don't wipe the floor with me, . . . it's going to be a statement that something is very wrong and rotten in New York."

Goetz's major gripe against New York's legal system— that it was based on "technicalities"—was also connected with his belief that he would not be treated justly under it. On the audiotapes he had often stated that he did not want to be acquitted on technicalities such as whether a robbery was in progress or whether he had been afraid for his life. This time, though, it was clear that he felt the city would use just such technicalities to define his guilt. "You're gonna wipe my ass. You're gonna wipe the floor with me. I know it, okay? You— You have to. And the reason you have to is so many rules have been broken," Goetz asserted. "But," Goetz had stated earlier, "to survive in this city you have to break rules."

He spoke again about wanting the incident to be judged holistically, on some ultimate sense of right and wrong. He seemed to be feeling quite a bit guiltier, though, than he had earlier that day. "The truth has to come out," he said; then he added, "The truth is so ugly that you don't want to know the truth." Later he commented, "I turned into a vicious animal, and that's what I was. . . . And if there's a God, God knows what was in my heart. And it was . . . sadistic and savage. . . . That was me."

Goetz called himself a "cold-blooded murderer" and a "monster" but stated, "I wasn't a monster until several years ago in New York." Again he told the story of his previous mugging, this time in more graphic detail: "Several years ago I got jumped . . . on Canal Street. Two-thirty in the afternoon. . . . I was jumped by three guys. Now, they deliberately went after my knee and they got it. Like I got kicked in the knee and then what hurts you—They didn't have weapons, and people—you don't have to be maimed with a weapon. What— What really hurts you is the sidewalk. They tried to push me through a plate-glass door also, you know? . . . I pushed as hard as I could when I—when I hit that door, with my hands. I still hit that door so hard, the glass hard. The glass didn't break, thank God, you know, because I—that would've been it. . . . But the handle—yeah, yeah—the handle hit my chest, and it—afterwards now, I was a wreck."

Goetz said that his chest injury took six months to heal and that his knee was permanently damaged. He was saved from an even more severe beating when an off-duty cop came to his rescue and nabbed one of the three muggers while the other two ran away. The man who was caught was arrested but could not be charged with attempted robbery because the crime had been thwarted before it went that far. Goetz was enraged by this and on the audiotapes explained that he even offered to fabricate a story so that the man could be charged with a more serious crime. "I said, 'Look . . . whatever you want me to say, I'll say. If you want me to lie, I'll lie. I'll say whatever it takes to, you know, arrest these guys or whatever it is.' And someone's immediate response in victim's aid was, 'Don't you say that; don't you ever say that.' You see, I had completely . . .—According to the rules and the technicalities,

I had completely disqualified myself, whatever I was gonna say."

The man who had been caught was charged with a series of lesser crimes related to the assault. He was released on his own recognizance but later did serve six months in jail. As far as Goetz was concerned, though, the legal system had failed him. On both the audiotapes and the videotape he mentioned that the man was charged and released after two hours and thirty-five minutes, while he spent six hours and five minutes at the police station while the charges were being processed.

He had also been deeply affected by the trauma of the mugging and the injuries he had suffered. "When my kneecap gave in, it didn't even hurt," he said. "It was like, if you take a Rice Krispie that's a little bit mushy and you squish it between your fingers. That's exactly what my knee felt like when it happened." Goetz said of the experience, "It taught me that there were vicious people out there. It taught me that anything can happen." And he reiterated, as he had said on the audio-tapes, that "it taught me the worst thing about violence is not even what happens . . . , it's not knowing what will happen next."

As a result, Goetz then applied for a license to carry a handgun, and again the system failed him. After spending much effort and approximately $2,000, his application was rejected by a detective who told him, " 'We can't go giving anybody a gun permit who wants it in New York. . . . That would be irresponsible.' " So Goetz began carrying a gun illegally and purchasing guns legally in other states. He also encouraged others to arm themselves, and he confessed to having sold people guns at cost.

Goetz also described two incidents prior to the subway shootings when he had drawn his gun without resorting to firing, because showing the gun proved effective enough. The first occurred while he was walking along Central Park North. "By accident I was up there," he said. "I got on the wrong train. I was up there and I—I quickly wanted to get back to, uh, a more civilized section, if that's what you want to call it. People use the word 'civilized' section. Two fellows, uh, . . . one ran up from behind me and one ran up in front of me. And . . . the guy in front of me whipped out a cane and shouted, 'Okay, motherfucker, give it up.' What I did is, I pulled out my gun and I was scared. He was scared. I was so scared I was shaking. I thought I was going to shoot him. He thought I was going to shoot him. I—I just didn't know, but he—his knees buckled. He—He could hardly walk . . . And people have said, 'Well, showing the gun is enough.' But this was an—this was a—"

In the second incident Goetz drew his weapon with far less provocation: "A fellow on the street, this was just a crazy kid on drugs. He . . . asked me for some money or something, and I just kept on walking. He was walking behind me and this was on Sixth Avenue at about 8:00 p.m. . . . . He threatened me, okay? He said—He said, 'I hope I catch up with you 'cause I'm gonna—you know, you know— . . . because when I do' and whatever and stuff like that. And I got pissed off and pulled out the gun. And that was stupid, because I didn't have to pull the gun, and showing it was enough to make him run away."

"Why did you pull out the gun?" Detective Clark asked.

"I just—Okay, okay, it's true; I was pissed. But I didn't shoot him. He deserved to die. I—I—I—I—I told him something like, 'I'm gonna blow you away,' or something like that. He got scared shitless and that was it."

Goetz's version of the events that led up to the subway shooting was substantially the same as on the audiotapes. What Goetz made clearer on the videotape, however, after having detailed his previous experiences where he had drawn his gun but had not fired, was when and why he made his decision to shoot. The key, he insisted, was the look Troy Canty gave him when he asked for or demanded five dollars. "The threat, when I was surrounded—At that point pulling the gun would've been enough," Goetz explained. But when I saw this one fellow, when I saw the gleam in his eye and the smile on his face . . . What happened is I snapped."

When Canty first asked him, "How're you doing?," Goetz said, "It wasn't even a warning signal. . . . These were just kids kidding around. . . . But then two of them stood up, okay? And they walked over to my left, okay? . . . The situation, when the two move on my left and the two are on my right—Now that is a real fucking threat. . . . I knew at that point I would have to pull the gun. I'll—I'm gonna say this: At that—At that time I was gonna pull the gun, but I wasn't gonna kill them. . . . [W]hat my intention was at this time was to follow the situation as closely as I could."

Again Goetz asserted that although one youth showed a "bulge in his pocket," he did not fear that the youths were armed. And he said that "robbery had nothing to do with it": "[Canty's] exact words were, 'Give me five dollars.' He said it with a smile and his eyes were bright. The words meant bullshit. Five dollars to me is bullshit. . . . I knew I had to pull the gun, but it was the look and—now, you cannot understand this—it was his eyes were shiny. He had a smile on his face. He'll claim it was all a joke. If you believe that, I accept that. When I saw the—the smile on his face and the shine—and the shine in his eyes, that he was enjoying this, I knew what they were going to do. You understand? . . . And it was at that point I decided I was going to kill 'em all, murder 'em all, do anything."

"What did you think they were going to do?" Braver asked, again inciting Goetz's wrath.

"How can you ask a question like that?" Goetz retorted indignantly. "They were going to—They were going to have fun with me, Miss."

"What do you mean by that?" Braver continued. "What is your interpretation of that? I can't get inside your head."

"Beat the shit out of you," Goetz said.

"You thought they were going to beat you up? . . . Is that what you're saying?"

"You just use such a casual phrase. What are *you* saying, Miss? Miss, your attitude—your attitude. You are so far removed from reality, and yet they send you here as a professional, as a *professional*, to investigate this. It's beyond belief. . . . Look, they—what they were going to do is enjoy me for awhile. They were going to beat the fucking shit out of me, okay?"

"Did you feel trapped?" Braver asked Goetz a few minutes later.

"Did I feel—What do you think?" Goetz snapped back sarcastically. "Oh, no, no, no. I felt free. I felt—I felt great. I was enjoying Fun City. You know, I was gonna—"

"I'm trying to see what you felt at the time," Braver offered.
"I was just whistling Dixie, okay?" Goetz said.

Goetz's animosity toward Braver was so profound that he became like a different person during these exchanges. There was a marked change in the tone of his voice and particularly in his body language. Throughout much of the interview Goetz sat sideways in his seat with his left leg crossed over his right and his back hunched, as if he were withdrawing into himself and away from the camera and the people seated around him. Responding to Braver's questions, though, his body would uncoil as he lashed out at her: his back stiffening, his torso twisting in his seat as he turned to face her, and often a pointed finger thrusting at her emphatically. I also remember Goetz using his arm as if it were a mallet (the four fingers pointed straight out and locked together, thumb curled), hammering downward to emphasize his words when he told Braver and the detectives, "I wanted to kill those guys; I wanted to maim those guys; I wanted to make them suffer in any way I could."

It was at such times during his videotaped statement that we had our only glimpse of the dangerous nature of Goetz's wrath. Otherwise we would have never seen evidence of how the meek-looking, mild-mannered individual sitting across from us in the courtroom had been capable of committing the violent acts he had.

Goetz's description of the actual shootings also reiterated what he'd said in his audiotaped statement: that he'd planned his "pattern of fire" while still seated; and that he'd then got up, made a step to his right, drew his gun and then wheeled around to face Canty, fired one shot each into the two youths who had been standing in front of him, then pivoted to his right and fired at the other two.

"Speed is everything," he said again. "You just think of speed and the count. He gave me verification when he said, uh, 'Give me five dollars.' I pulled out the piece. I just started firing. As I told the fellow in there, it's unimportant to look at what you're firing at. You just target images in your mind.

You fire. It is—to use his expression—you—you—you aim for the center of the mass. You run. You keep moving. All you have to do is be, uh, faster than they are. Now, perhaps they're —But you don't know what is happening on your right-hand side, but it doesn't matter. You do what you have to do as quickly as possible. You don't think. You live from the fraction of a moment to the fraction of a moment. The—The, uh— You—You just react. You forget everything that happened an instant before. You—You sight—You don't understand; I'm explaining what happened. You sight—listen; listen—You sight your target. That was number one. I got rid of number one. Got number two. They—They say I shot him in the back. It doesn't matter. I wasn't even aiming—I wasn't aiming for their backs. You aim for the center."

Goetz said of the third youth he shot, "I don't know if he was facing from the front or from the back or whatever; it seemed as if he was trying to get through the steel wall of the subway car. But he couldn't. And I let him have it.

"And I let one of the other guys have it, the guy who was pre—the guy who was, uh, pretending he wasn't with them," Goetz continued, speaking now of Cabey. "And I—I ran up to the first two to check them—who were on the ground, the first two that I had shot—and they were taken care of. It was all very cold-blooded, Miss, and this is going to offend everyone. I went back to the other two to check on them and the fellow who was standing up, I was sure I had shot him. . . . I wanted to know if I missed. But I—I went—I went to him a second time and I looked at him—and he can't verify this because he was probably out of it by then, if I shot him or if I wasn't; I don't know. And I said, 'You look all right; here's another.' I was gonna shoot him, but he—didn't matter—he—Again, I thought—I was sure I had shot him. Maybe I didn't. He jerked his arm and I just—The trigger pulls on reflex."

Goetz then went back to where Canty was lying, and, he said, "I was gonna—I was gonna gouge . . . the guy's eyes out with my keys. . . . You—You—You—You can't understand this," he went on. "I know you can't understand this. That's fine. The reas—The only reason I didn't do it was because he had changed his look. . . . I saw his eyes twitching and I saw the fear in his eyes and then I just—and then I just—and then you just—Suddenly, you know, things started dissipating."

As clear as all of this was in his mind, though, Goetz was still very confused about his escape from the train. He explained that he had run on an empty set of tracks to the Chambers Street station platform, but he was unsettled about why those tracks were there. The detectives explained to him that they were the tracks for the local train.

"I've been trying to understand that for a week," Goetz said, acting relieved. "I've been trying to understand this— this whole week, where—where—where would—where did those tracks come from? But it was the local tracks."

After Braver and the detectives had finished their questions, Goetz again complained about just wanting to live a normal life and made a number of requests. First, he said he was not going to fight extradition, but he didn't want to return to New York immediately. "I'll come back, but you have this statement and you have all the information. And—And, you just—you just take it back to New York and think about it for one or two days." He explained to Braver, Clark, and Hattendorf, "You're not familiar with this reality and you're gonna be involved in passing judgment."

"No we're not. We're not the jury," Clark said.

"The jury," Goetz said reflectively.

"We're not a judge."

"The jury," Goetz repeated. "I don't have the strength to go through this again."

He also reiterated his wish to be allowed to visit his apartment when he returned with them to New York. "I just need a few hours in my apartment to straight—to straighten up things," he said. "I'll open it up . . . for you. I have the keys. I'll show you around. You can—You need no search warrant or anything like that. . . . You can do anything you want and you're gonna find plenty of dirt. You're gonna find— uh, I have marijuana in my apartment. I haven't smoked it for perhaps forty days, by the way. And drugs have nothing to do with this. . . .

"I've always lived a very organized life," he pleaded. "My life is probably ruined. . . . If you'll just let me do some paperwork. I'm—I'm not gonna abuse your trust. I'm not gonna jump out of the window."

Finally, Goetz asked, "I know this sounds ridiculous . . . , is it possible that my name and address not be rereleased to—to—publicly? That—That this thing be taken care of and that—and that—Is it possible? If you can't do it, you can't do it."

"We haven't lied to you up to now. We're not gonna start lying to you now. That's highly unlikely," Clark responded.

"Oh, shit. Oh, shit," Goetz said. "I can just—You see what this means? It means I'll never—You know what it means to live a normal life? This shit—I'll never escape this shit. If you do that, I'll never escape this shit. People are looking for a hero or they're looking for a villian and neither is—nothing is the truth."

In a calmer moment near the end of the interview, Goetz changed his tune, accepting that there would be no way to avoid going through the legal process in this case, and no escaping the notoriety he'd gained. "What happens to me at this . . . point is un—is unimportant. I'm just one person. This at least raised—has raised issues in New York. Fine," Goetz said.

Chapter 11

Andrea Reid and Ramseur
(Round 2)

May 19

After five days off, the trial resumed the following Tuesday, with the prosecution's case nearing its end. We heard from a final eyewitness, Andrea Reid, who had not testified earlier because of scheduling conflicts with her classes at school; and then—surprise, surprise—James Ramseur reappeared, having decided to testify after all, in order to purge himself of the contempt citations Justice Crane had previously charged him with.

Andrea Reid was the wife of Garth Reid, who had already testified that they and their baby were seated together on the long bench on the east side of the subway car, south of the middle doors. Garth Reid was holding the baby in his lap. The Reids' testimonies contradicted each other, however, about which of them was sitting closer to the youths.

They were traveling from their home in the Bronx to Garth Reid's school near the Chambers Street station, and she said she noticed the youths immediately as they entered the train. "I don't ride the subway that often, and [am] very afraid at all times, [so] I am aware of the people around me," she said.

Because of her fear, she monitored the youths' actions very closely and could have proved to be an important witness. Such was not the case, though. Her testimony was riddled with inconsistencies and ultimately lacked credibility. Like Garth Reid when he was first interviewed in January 1985 by Susan

Braver, Andrea Reid knew more about what had really happened than apparently she was willing to tell.

Reid testified in direct examination that she saw one of the youths, while seated, say, "How you doing?" or "What's happening?" to a white man sitting across from him. She said the white man in response "shook his head and said, 'Fine,' and he put his head . . . back down." At this point Reid said she became afraid that there was going to be trouble on the train, and she turned to her husband and said, "Look at those four punks messing with that white man." But she also testified that she wasn't sure where the train was when this all took place. She said she knew it was "somewhere in Manhattan . . . I guess Fourteenth Street, or maybe further down, further up." And she said that she believed the white man in question was not the same white man she saw shooting the youths shortly afterward; that the first man had gotten up and exited the train.

Although she said she spent the majority of the train ride observing the youths, Reid testified that during the moments before the first shot was fired she was talking to her husband and therefore was looking away. Then, she said, "I heard a gunshot. I turned my head and I saw a white man standing, and he was continuing shooting. I saw maybe one male in the middle—one male, one male standing up. I saw two others, two others sitting. I turned around very fast to grab my baby, and it was like I was fighting, because my husband was telling me to sit down before I get shot myself. And it was like, I really wanted to get out of there. So I grabbed my baby, and I grabbed her, and I walked towards the door, and I turned back, and I saw Goetz—I saw the last—I'm sorry—I saw the last shot, and I just called my husband. And that's when he came behind me and the rest of the passengers did too."

Reid contradicted her own account of what she saw and what happened when several times during her direct examination. For instance, although she first said she saw only one of the youths standing, she later explained that she had seen two youths "running" from Goetz and that immediately afterward she saw them fall. She did consistently say, however, that she had seen the other two youths sitting in the short seat by the conductor's cab when she heard the first shot and looked that way. "The aisle was very clear," she said. "I saw two sitting, and after I turned my head, after that I don't—I have no idea what they did after that."

She remembered hearing five shots in all, with a slight pause between the first two and another pause between shots four and five. The middle three were very rapid, perhaps a quarter of a second apart. According to her testimony, between shots one and five she had been able to look to see what was happening, then wrestle her baby away from her husband, move to the storm door, and look back again. She did not recall falling over Loren Michals, as Christopher Boucher had testified.

Reid also seemed confused about what she'd seen when she looked back just before exiting the car. "I went to the door, I ran to the door, and I looked back to see if my husband was behind me," she said.

"What exactly did you see at that point?" Waples asked.

"I heard the last shot."

"What did you see? Did you see any of the young men at that point?"

"No," she said.

"Where were the young men the last time you saw them?"

"On the floor."

"When did you see them on the floor?"

"When I looked back."

"How many did you see on the floor?"

"Three."

* * *

"Miss Reid, before you heard the first shot did you see any of the four young men approach the defendant?" Waples asked, concluding his questioning.

"No," she replied.

"Before you heard the first shot did you hear any of those four men say anything to the defendant?"

"No."

"Before you heard the shot did you see those four young men surrounding the defendant?"

"No."

"That's all, Judge," Waples said.

Throughout her time on the stand, Andrea Reid was clearly nervous; her body was tense and she was wringing her hands. Her anxiety increased, though, during cross-examination, when

Slotnick took her to task for having given, according to him, a substantially different account of what had happened to two of his investigators one week before.

On the previous Wednesday these two investigators had spoken with Reid at her home and secretly recorded their conversation. Although the tape was not played in open court, Slotnick had Reid listen to specific parts through an earphone to see if it would "help her recall" what she had said. Reid did not admit to the contradictions Slotnick was trying to assert, however. She insisted that she did not remember what she had told the investigators, and she would not confirm the dialogue that Slotnick said was on the tape. Apparently the tape was difficult to decipher; its audibility was poor because the microphone had been concealed and because of the amount of background noise.

"Were you asked the following question by either Investigator Barna or Newsome on May 13, in your apartment: 'Goetz got on the train at Fourteenth Street and there was nobody sitting around him and he sat there. Did you see the four of them go over to him, or did you see two of them go over to him?' And did you respond and say, 'Yeah, at least—or it was like two of them went over to him.' Do you remember being asked that question and giving that answer?" Slotnick asked.

"I don't remember," Reid said. "I really don't. At that time my kids was crying. I was—I don't remember those— Maybe I said it; I don't know. I can't tell you because I don't remember."

"Were you asked this question or these questions, and did you give these answers, on Wednesday, May 13? Question: 'When you seen the four people go over to him, or the two people, were they this close to him?' Answer: 'They were next to him. They asked him a question. They asked him a question.' Question: 'Were they right in his face; he's sitting down?' Answer: 'They were standing right over him.' . . . Did you ever give those answers to those questions last Wednesday night, to my investigators in your apartment?"

"No, I never—I said I never saw anyone stand over him," Reid replied.

Slotnick also pressed Reid on other issues: that the shots had been fired more quickly than she had testified; and also that she was fully aware that the "white man" whom she'd seen the "four punks" were "messing with" was in fact Goetz. Reid vigorously denied having told the investigators she had heard the fifth shot before she left her seat; but she did admit telling them the "hassling" incident occurred after Fourteenth Street. Still, she insisted, "It could have been Bernhard Goetz. I'm not sure."

What Slotnick did elicit from Reid was a statement she had made to her husband on the day of the shootings, that the youths "got what they deserved." At first Reid denied telling the investigators this, but after listening to the tape she admitted she had.

Slotnick also questioned her about her extreme reluctance to testify in this trial. "I never did want to get in this whole situation," Reid stated. She admitted having asked her husband not to get involved and having said to people that if she were subpoenaed she would testify that she didn't remember anything. She also admitted that at some point Waples had promised if Garth Reid testified she wouldn't have to, and Slotnick asked her if Waples was forcing her to testify. She was on the waiting list to enter the police academy, and she and Waples had previously discussed her desire to become a cop. Reid said she was aware that a memorandum from the district attorney's office against her application could ruin her chances of being accepted, but she stated, "I choose to come to court because I feel that I should, not because he forced me."

Reid admitted that she had met Darrell Cabey's mother since the shootings, but in cross-examination she denied having told the investigators, "That's why I don't want to get involved." In redirect she explained that they had met at a "crystal party." Waples asked her if she and Shirley Cabey had spoken at all. "About crystal, yes," Reid said.

"Did you talk to her about the case at all?" Waples followed.

"No."

"Did you indicate to her you were on the train when her son was shot?"

"No."

"Has the fact that you met that woman influenced your testimony under oath in this court today in any way?"

"No."

Waples should never have brought it up, though, because in Slotnick's recross-examination Reid turned around and contradicted herself again.

"Miss Reid, am I correct that you admitted that on Wednesday, May 13, you told my investigators, who you now know were taping you, that the reason you didn't want to get involved in this case is because you met Shirley Cabey?" Slotnick asked.

"Yes," Reid answered, even after having previously denied it when listening to the tape.

"Thank you very much," Slotnick said. "I have no further questions."

"I'd like to clarify that," Waples said to the judge.

"Why did that concern you, the fact that you had met Shirley Cabey or one of the mothers of the persons who were shot?" Waples asked Reid, in re-redirect.

"Because I was afraid because she brought one of her sons at the crystals party and that frightened me," she stated.

"You wanted to stay out of the case?"

"Yes."

"I have no further questions," Waples said, deadpan. "Thank you very much."

After lunch Ramseur's testimony began. The day ended early, though, due to the suffocating conditions in the courtroom. New York was having a heat wave with extremely high humidity, and the air was hot, stuffy, and close, as though there were not enough oxygen mixed in with the steam. As a result some of the jurors were having a hard time remaining alert while listening to testimony. The heat aggravated the tendency of minds to wander and even to doze.

Ramseur's testimony under direct examination was exactly what you might expect, and I also got a little restless while listening to it. I might not have minded so much if Ramseur had testified when he was originally called, right after Troy Canty, but now his appearance seemed totally irrelevant. Ramseur was an extremely bitter young man who was in the process of serving an eight-and-a-third to twenty-five-year jail term and who had every reason to offer a self-serving version of the events surrounding the shootings. He also was suing Goetz—his suit was reportedly for $9.5 million—and that fact by itself made his testimony suspect in my eyes. He had a vested interest in the trial's outcome and an awfully big incentive to hedge the truth or to lie.

As he had with Troy Canty, Waples made the point that Ramseur was smaller in December 1984 than he was now. Ramseur said he had grown from five feet, nine inches and 129 pounds to five feet, eleven inches and 139 pounds. Ramseur maintained that he was being currently incarcerated "for a rape charge I never committed," having been convicted of "supposedly acting in concert to rape, robbery, sodomy, and assault."

Ramseur also, like Canty, was a high school dropout, and he admitted he had supported himself primarily by shoplifting and breaking into video-game machines. He said he had known Canty and Barry Allen for many years and Darrell Cabey for a year or so prior to the shootings. "We weren't tight friends, but we were, you know, friends," he said. Before December 22, 1984, he said he had acted as a blocker for Canty and Barry Allen "about three times, four times . . . at the most." He also testified that his longest previous stretch in jail had been sixty days for a ninety-day sentence, and that he smoked marijuana but took no other drugs.

On the day of the shootings he said he ran into the other three youths at the bus stop at 169th Street and Third Avenue in the Bronx and that he agreed to go with them to rob video-game machines in Manhattan. The four boarded the bus through the back door without paying their fare, and on the bus Ramseur passed the screwdriver he had in his pocket to one of the others. Darrell Cabey also had two screwdrivers, and Ramseur indicated that they all were passing the screwdrivers around.

At 149th Street they exited the bus and entered the subway system, taking the IRT number 2 train into Manhattan. Ramseur said they entered through the middle doors and then walked down to the north end of the car, as Andrea Reid had testified. During the ride he said he talked mostly with Darrell Cabey. The four stood up to get off the train at Forty-second Street, Ramseur said, but then Canty decided they should go to Chambers Street instead.

Ramseur's recollection of where he, Darrell Cabey, and Barry Allen were seated at the time the train stopped at Fourteenth Street diametrically contradicted what Goetz, Canty, and others had said. He recalled sitting next to Darrell Cabey on the short bench just to the left of the doors Goetz entered, rather than across the aisle in the short seat by the conductor's cab. According to Ramseur, that was where Allen sat. His recollection of Canty's position (lying on the long bench to the right of the doors Goetz entered) conformed with previous testimony, however, as did his memory of where Goetz sat.

Ramseur said he noticed Goetz boarding the train through the doors on his right and sitting down on the long bench across from Canty. Then, Ramseur said, "After the door closed, a little while later, I turned my head to look towards where Troy Canty was sitting and he was up in Bernhard Goetz's face."

He described Canty as being directly in front of Goetz, bending over with his hands on his knees, their faces about a foot apart. He said he heard Canty say something to Goetz but thought Canty was asking him for the time. He described Goetz's face as being expressionless: "He was looking at him. That's about it." After seeing this, Ramseur said, he turned away and was looking toward Cabey, seated to his left.

"I was facing Darrell Cabey and I seen Darrell Cabey was looking—His eyes were more wider, looking towards them. When I turned around, I guess the gun already went off, and I heard, you know, the shot, and he fell. Darrell—Troy Canty was on the floor. . . .

"Barry Allen jumped up and yelled out—If I may curse, I'll say it," Ramseur offered demurely.

"Just tell us what you heard," Waples said.

"He yelled out Troy's name. He yelled out, 'Oh, shit, Troy,' and went over to try to get to him, whatever." Ramseur said he heard the second shot as he and Cabey leapt out of their seats and sprang for the storm door to exit the car.

"He jump up—He was trying to get out the door, but I had my back pressing [against] his. He couldn't get out the door," Ramseur said, referring to Cabey.

"What happened then?" Waples asked.

"Goetz shot me."

"What was your position when you were shot?"

"When I was shot, I seen him—you know, the gun aiming towards me. Looked like it was towards my chest. So I turned to the side and I just felt it, and I felt the bullet go in my chest. . . . [It] went through my arm and into my chest, but I didn't feel it go through my arm."

Ramseur then heard "another shot," and afterward, he said, "Darrell Cabey was yelling, 'I didn't do nothing.'" He then saw Goetz "going towards Darrell Cabey" from where he was lying on the subway car floor. "Next thing I heard was him saying that 'they tried to rob me,'" Ramseur said.

Besides the discrepancies between Ramseur's account and all the others we had heard concerning where he, Cabey, and Allen were seated when Goetz entered the car, the other major flaw in Ramseur's version involved the distance from where he said he and Cabey were when Goetz shot them and where their bodies ended up. Ramseur said he was shot while standing in front of the short bench where he and Cabey had previously been sitting, and that he then "dived" forward so that his head wound up by Troy Canty's feet, his body fully on the other side of the double doors. And even more unlikely was how Cabey could have wound up in the seat by the conductor's cab from the position where Ramseur last saw him, pressed against the north storm door.

Ultimately, though, none of this mattered because in his lengthy cross-examination Slotnick made little effort to discredit Ramseur's testimony about the events surrounding the shootings. Indeed, the incident itself seemed almost beside the point. Slotnick's goal appeared to be strictly that of character assassination, and to this end he limited his questioning to Ramseur's criminal past and prior inconsistent statements. By doing this he also was fueling Ramseur's anger, and it became clear to me that if Slotnick kept it up long enough, Ramseur would be certain to self-destruct.

Slotnick spent the remainder of the afternoon questioning Ramseur primarily about his rape conviction, his civil suit against Goetz, and about an incident after the shootings in which Ramseur falsified his own kidnapping. Ramseur steadfastly denied that he had committed the rape; and although he admitted that he had staged the bogus kidnapping, Ramseur said he had done so in an effort to thwart a plot by two housing detectives who had told him they were going to set him up for having testified in the Goetz case. The rape conviction, Ramseur contended, was the result of that plot.

Here are the facts that Slotnick imparted through his questioning: On March 25, 1985—the same month in which he had testified under the grant of immunity before the second grand jury—Ramseur called New York's emergency 911 number, said his name was Darryl Thompson, and reported that he had seen two men grab James Ramseur off the street, force him into a blue Lincoln, and drive away. Later that same day Ramseur walked into his mother's house while police were questioning her and gave them a complete description of what had happened and what the men looked like, claiming that one had put a gun to his head. The police brought in a sketch artist to draw pictures of the men Ramseur described, and the investigation went so far as to involve New York City's police commissioner and its chief of detectives. Manhattan District Attorney Robert Morganthau was also notified, Slotnick said.

As Slotnick went through these questions, Ramseur kept talking back, asking to be allowed to elaborate, declaring, "There was a reason" he had done this, and asking, "Can I tell the jurors why?" Later he said again to Slotnick, "You got your point. Let me explain to the jurors the real deal." He then related that the two men he described to the police and of whom the artist made sketches were real people, not fabrications. He said they were housing detectives and that they had in fact tried to kidnap him.

"They approached me, asked me questions about my case, and they actually told me that I was going to be set up," Ramseur said.

"Well, did they put you in a car?" Slotnick asked.

"They asked me to get in a car," Ramseur said, "and I twisted around."

"Did you go into the car?"

"Nope."

Slotnick made a big point that the police didn't prosecute Ramseur for his phony kidnapping report because he was a witness in the Goetz case. He also related that Ramseur was being sought for not returning to court on four separate pending cases when he was shot by Goetz on December 22, and that the jail term he got for all of these was a total of ninety days. Slotnick had made the same point when questioning Troy Canty about the fact that Morganthau had intervened on Canty's behalf and enabled him to get into a drug rehabilitation center in lieu of a jail term. Slotnick's suggestion was that Ramseur and Canty felt that because they were getting special treatment from New York's most powerful law-enforcement officials, they were free to testify before the grand jury and in this trial without fear of prosecution for perjury. He inferred that they felt they had a "license to lie."

Ramseur's conspiracy theories, meanwhile, went beyond an attempted kidnapping and a "setup" on a rape conviction. While questioning Ramseur about his civil suit, Slotnick argued, "[Y]ou knew that in order to get Mr. Goetz's money you would have to be able to show you weren't part of a robbery."

"Is that why you all set me up?" Ramseur replied.

"Did you know that in order for you to get Mr. Goetz's money you have to prove you weren't part of a robbery?"

"Of course," Ramseur said. "I never was until this—until after this Goetz case."

"And, as a matter of fact, you knew quite clearly that in order for you to prevail you would have to maintain a story that you were innocent of attempting to rob Mr. Goetz?"

"Yes, and that's exactly why I got set up, right? You, Goetz, are in on it."

"As a matter of fact, Mr. Ramseur, you knew, did you not, as far as Mr. Goetz went, that if in any way whatsoever he were to be found not guilty of shooting you, you wouldn't get any money, is that correct?"

"He's going to be found not guilty anyway," Ramseur stated. "I know what time it is."

⚖️

May 20

Ramseur's cross-examination continued the next day but not until about 2:30 p.m. One of the alternate jurors, Augie

Ayala, had experienced some chest pains in the morning, so he notified the court and went to the Bellevue Hospital emergency room to make sure he was all right. The attorneys decided to wait for a report rather than to proceed without him. "I would rather lose a day than an alternate," Slotnick said.

When cross-examination did resume, after Augie had received a clean bill of health, the tension between Ramseur and Slotnick that had risen throughout the previous day's session steadily worsened as the interrogation wore on. Slotnick questioned Ramseur about various statements he'd made to the police and to the grand jury, accusing him of lying and covering up the truth. Ramseur, meanwhile, denied having made many of the statements and accused both the police and Slotnick of "putting words in my mouth" and "twisting" them around. When Slotnick asked Ramseur to look at pages of his grand jury testimony to see if it would refresh his recollection, Ramseur at first refused.

"I don't want to see them," he said to Slotnick. "You could have just made those up."

"No, give it a try, Mr. Ramseur," Justice Crane intervened. "It might jog your memory. If, after you've read it, you decide it doesn't help, then you can say so."

A court officer then handed Ramseur the document. He studied it briefly, then said, "Nope."

As Slotnick continued to press him, Ramseur became more and more upset. "Why are you trying to twist my head up?" he responded at one point. Then, when asked again about the court summonses he had not honored on the four outstanding cases against him at the time of the shootings, he responded, "[W]hat's that got anything to do about him shooting me, huh?"

Then, I thought, Slotnick became cruel, asking him what year he would be up for parole. Ramseur said it would be 1993.

"And if they don't release you in 1993, how long can they keep you?" Slotnick asked.

"Up to twenty-five years for a crime I never committed," Ramseur answered. "You know that."

* * *

"And didn't that judge say to you that you were a vicious,

brutal criminal and he was going to give you the maximum sentence?"

"Objection," Waples said. Justice Crane sustained.

*   *   *

"Did your lawyer tell you that the judge could have given you a significantly lesser sentence than eight and a third to twenty-five? Yes or no?"

Waples again objected, but this time Justice Crane overruled.

"Yes," Ramseur answered.

"You know you could have gotten a sentence of three to nine?"

"Yes," he said.

Slotnick again brought up statements Ramseur had made to police while in the hospital after the shootings. I thought the discrepancies were relatively trivial. Apparently Ramseur had said to the officers that he had seen Canty go up to a white woman and ask her for the time, and that Canty had been asking Goetz for the time when Goetz pulled his gun and fired. Ramseur later testified to the second grand jury that he didn't hear what had been said. "I could hear him talking. I couldn't hear exactly what he was saying," Ramseur stated now; and as for whether Canty had approached a white woman first, Ramseur now said that he couldn't remember. Slotnick suggested Ramseur had invented that story to cover up that the youths were robbing Goetz. Ramseur argued that the statements had been taken while he was "half dead" in the hospital, "going through hell," and further suggested that the police might be lying.

Ramseur was asked to look at the police reports, and again he resisted. "I don't want to read it because I know what happened, and I know what I told people," Ramseur said. "I told the truth," he insisted. "I've got nothing to hide."

Once again then Justice Crane had to direct Ramseur to read the reports as Slotnick had requested. "I need you to do that so you can answer the next question," Justice Crane said, exhibiting a great deal of patience. "If you have any difficulty reading, Mr. Ramseur, we will have it read to you silently," Justice Crane added.

"No, I'm reading it to myself," Ramseur said.

"All right," Justice Crane said. Then, after a pause, "Mr. Slotnick, we're ready for your next question."

"Does that refresh your recollection?"

"Nope."

"Well, if you would, would you please tell the jury how your day started on December 22, 1984?"

"Yes. I slept . . . with a girlfriend. Left the next day, afternoon, whatever. I don't remember exactly what time it was."

Ramseur's answer, however, was said much too softly. Throughout his testimony, he often spoke too quietly and while shifting in his seat or nervously rubbing his hand over his mouth. Justice Crane frequently had to ask him to speak louder and to move closer to the microphone. He did so again at this point. "The jurors can't hear," Justice Crane explained.

"Do you want me to put the microphone into my mouth?" Ramseur answered testily. He was becoming more and more intolerant and unresponsive to Slotnick's questioning, but he also seemed sensitive about having to talk about a girlfriend.

Ramseur went over again how he had run into Canty, Cabey, and Allen that day, and Slotnick reiterated that the four of them had all "stolen and robbed" with each other before.

"We never stole and robbed nobody. We broke into machines. Why you putting robbing in? We never robbed anybody together. . . . Don't try to convince the jurors that I'm a robber."

"Well, let me ask you a question, Mr. Ramseur. Weren't you convicted of robbing from [the woman] on the day that she was raped and sodomized? Yes or no?"

"Yes, I was. I never committed that crime."

"I guess the jury believed that when you were on trial, didn't they? Yes or no?"

"I guess they did. They was paid to. I was set up."

"How many jurors were paid?"

"All of them. You probably paying the jurors now."

"I pay the jurors?" Slotnick said, looking toward us and smiling wryly.

"This could be a setup," Ramseur scowled. "I don't . . . fuckin' know."

"Mr. Ramseur, have we ever met?"

"No, we never ever met, but I heard about you," Ramseur said.

"I hope it was nothing unpleasant," Slotnick said.

"It *was* unpleasant," Ramseur shot back. "I know about you, baby."

The final blowup occurred a few minutes later, when Slotnick asked Ramseur again to discuss what he had done on the day before the shootings. This time Ramseur refused to answer. "What I did before then does not have anything to do with this case," he said.

"Well, the judge will make that determination," Slotnick responded. "Tell us what you did the day before."

"No."

"Your Honor, I would ask for a direction," Slotnick then said to Justice Crane.

"Do you remember, Mr. Ramseur, what you did on December 20?" Justice Crane asked.

"No," Ramseur said.

"You don't remember?" Justice Crane asked again and Ramseur nodded. "Your answer then is you don't remember."

"Didn't you just tell this jury two minutes ago that you remembered what you did the day before?" Slotnick asked.

"I remember, but I'm not going to tell you. It's none of your business," Ramseur said defiantly.

"Your Honor, I don't have to take this abuse, and I ask the Court to intercede," Slotnick said, getting hot himself now. Justice Crane very calmly explained to Ramseur that he was obligated to answer Slotnick's question. "It's something that you promised you would do when you took the oath," Justice Crane said. "Would you please answer the question, please? To the best of your recollection."

"What I'm doing with my girlfriend doesn't have nothing to do with this case," Ramseur answered.

Justice Crane persisted in trying to get Ramseur to answer, and then Slotnick offered, "I'm not going to ask you what you did with anybody. . . . I'm going to ask you what you did that day."

"Regardless, I'm not going to tell you," Ramseur said; then, a few minutes later, he stated, "Judge, you better take me out of here."

"Just cool it," Justice Crane responded. "If you want a break, I think maybe we can take a few minutes."

"If Mr. Ramseur needs the time, certainly, Your Honor," Slotnick said, and Justice Crane then excused us from the courtroom.

While we sat in the jury room Justice Crane asked Ramseur's lawyer to come forward and consult with him. "Tell him he's not on trial," Justice Crane said. "I'm taking the testimony of your client as a purge, and I want to purge him of his contempt, and I know he wants to purge himself. Please talk with him."

Their efforts were to no avail, though. Justice Crane advised Ramseur, "Now, we're almost finished with cross-examination, and that means you're almost finished with being a witness here. I simply remind you to listen to the questions of the cross-examiner. There are a few remaining. Be attentive to them. Answer them as shortly as you can, with as few . . . words as you can, and we'll be finished with this in no time flat. Okay? Are you with me?"

"Yes, sir, Judge," Ramseur answered, but then he added, "I'm tired of him playing games with me. We not talking about this case. I'm ready to get out of here. . . . He's playing games with me. This is a serious case. He playing games. He going to ask me about some old bullshit. Take me out of here."

Justice Crane again tried to reason with him, but Ramseur would have none of it. "Let me tell you something, Judge. I think this all bullshit. They all fuckin' together. Just take me out of here."

"Okay," Justice Crane said then. "Let's just finish this up, and let's bring the jury out."

"Judge, get me for contempt. I'm not going to answer the questions."

"You want to cooperate?" Justice Crane asked.

"I'm ready to cooperate, but he playing fuckin' games."

"James, why don't you shut up?" Waples interjected.

"Just answer the questions, Mr. Ramseur," Justice Crane said firmly. "Don't volunteer anything and don't put on a show."

We reentered the courtroom at this point, and Slotnick continued cross-examination by asking Ramseur what he'd done two days before the shootings. "[Y]ou said you spent that time and those days with your girlfriend, is that correct?" he asked.

"I'm not answering your questions. You're playing fuckin' games," Ramseur responded.

Justice Crane was unable to sway him, so he instructed Slotnick to move on to his next question: "And the day before that day— the day before the nineteenth, on the eighteenth— did you spend time with your girlfriend during that day also?"

It was all so ludicrous. Slotnick was only trying to establish that Ramseur had not spent any time during the week prior to the shootings "working, fixing windows," which was the reason he had told police while he was in the hospital that he'd had the screwdriver in his pocket. At worst that was a minor lie, but Ramseur would not relent.

"I'm not going to answer this question," he said to Justice Crane. "If you are going to get me for contempt, go ahead. I'm in jail for something I didn't do. Time isn't going to hurt me."

Justice Crane again had us leave the courtroom and made one last plea. "James, I cannot understand how you can come down the home stretch, be almost finished testifying, and then refuse to answer a couple of lousy questions at the end. What prompts you to put up your back again after you promised me you would purge your contempt?"

"Judge, take me back. I am tired of this bullshit."

"I'm about to take you back because Mr. Slotnick is almost finished."

"I'm not going to answer any fuckin' questions," Ramseur answered. "The decision is already made, already."

"The decision *hasn't* been made," Justice Crane responded.

"The decision is made already."

"I'm sorry you believe that, but it hasn't been made."

"Yeah, all right."

"Your testimony is important," Justice Crane said. "I don't want to strike it out because Mr. Slotnick hasn't been able to cross-examine you. And that's the next application I'm going to get. . . . I don't want to give you contempt because I want you to answer the last questions. Can't you do that last little bit?"

"No," Ramseur said.

"Do you think tomorrow morning, after you talk to whoever you are with at Rikers Island, you might feel better if you came back tomorrow?"

"No."

"Your Honor, respectfully, I appreciate the concern of the Court for this person, but I don't like to see the Court humbling itself to the point it has and I would respectfully ask the Court to deal with this witness accordingly," Slotnick interjected a few moments later. "How dare he use the language that he has used in this courtroom, and I'm sure the district attorney joins with me, how dare he use and abuse the majesty of this Court."

"You would do the same thing if you were in my predicament," Ramseur said to Slotnick.

"But I didn't rape and sodomize a woman," Slotnick answered; to which Ramseur replied, "You know damn well you committed that crime."

"The very essence of fairness and justice requires that this witness be completed on the witness stand and not that his entire testimony be stricken—which you and I both know is the consequence of his refusal to complete his testimony— especially after this jury has heard all that it's heard. Unless you're not going to make that application and are going to terminate your cross-examination now," Justice Crane said to Slotnick. "The majesty of this Court is not terribly much involved more than the fairness to the parties in this proceeding."

"I appreciate that, Your Honor, and I'm just concerned; and perhaps my anger has to do with the reactions of the witness. . . . If I insulted the Court, I apologize," Slotnick said. He added, though, "I would like to finish my cross-examination."

"See what he's doing?" Ramseur said to the judge. "If it wasn't for those charges—That's all he can use is those charges. He's not talking about the Goetz case; he's talking about some other charges. He's trying to come up with some other bullshit."

"You don't understand, Mr. Ramseur," the judge replied. "Whatever he says to this jury about those charges is under my strict control, and I'm not a partisan here, I'm a neutral. And I'd like to see what is required in this case be done. You are almost finished. You are so close to the end and you are walking at the very finish line, if I can borrow an analogy to the Preakness. Don't you understand that you are almost there?"

We returned then into the courtroom to witness the final five-minute segment of what I called in my diary "The James Ramseur Comedy Hour." Slotnick asked another series of questions, and Ramseur remained mute and unresponsive, except to hurl a few more insults.

"Prior to December 22, 1984, when was the last time you had been with Darrell Cabey, Barry Allen, and Troy Canty together? Answer the question, please," Slotnick said.

"When was the last time you and Roy Innes and Goetz and [the woman] were together?" Ramseur replied.

"I never met [the woman]," Slotnick answered.

"Yeah, please."

"Don't answer the witness's questions, Mr. Slotnick," Justice Crane warned.

One question later, Slotnick asked, "When was the last time prior to December 22, 1984, that you, together with Darrell Cabey, Troy Canty, and Barry Allen, committed a crime against another human being?"

"When was the last time you got a drug deal off—"

"Your Honor, I ask the jury to disregard this man's statement," Slotnick protested.

"That is nonresponsive, ladies and gentlemen of the jury. The answer is stricken," the judge said.

For each nonanswer Justice Crane cited Ramseur for contempt, until Slotnick finally hung it up, saying to the judge, "I think it's a waste of time and effort. I don't want to waste the jury's time, the Court's time, nor Mr. Goetz's time."

"Thank you very much," Justice Crane said. "Unless the DA has any redirect of Mr. Ramseur—"

"I'll waive, Judge," Waples said.

"Thank you very much, Mr. Waples. The witness is excused. . . . Let the witness be removed from the courtroom."

"Excuse me, Judge," Robert Hamkalo said. "May we have a date for him to reappear?"

"Friday, this week. Fingerprint him," said Justice Crane.

Ramseur was then ushered out of the courtroom by the half-dozen or so armed court officers who closed in around him as the scene reached its climax. In fact I should mention that throughout Ramseur's second day of testimony there had been several extra officers in the courtroom, and as Ramseur became more upset they drew closer to him. Four officers stood behind the witness stand—two on either side—and by the end they were right at his shoulders. There were also several other officers scattered around the room, lining the walls. I was surprised when I learned after the trial that some of the jurors had become fearful of Ramseur toward the end of his testimony even though he was surrounded by these officers, all of whom were armed with guns. There really wasn't anything to be worried about. If Ramseur had tried to escape he would have never made it out of the witness stand.

I also learned about the media reports that Ramseur had moved to take off his shoe to throw it at Slotnick toward the end of his cross-examination. Those reports were simply inaccurate. I talked to one of the court officers who had stood around Ramseur while he testified, and the court officer said that Ramseur merely had needed to scratch his foot.

That Friday Justice Crane sentenced Ramseur to the maximum jail sentence, 180 days, for the six contempt citations he had incurred. He castigated Ramseur for having played right into Slotnick's hands with his behavior, which Justice Crane said had conveyed "viciousness and selfishness more eloquently than words could." He said that Slotnick "owes you a vote of thanks."

"The jurors saw your contemptuous conduct," Justice Crane remarked. "That can never be erased from their minds."

To us, however, during the proceedings the following week, Justice Crane announced simply, "A motion has been made . . . which has been granted in your absence, having to do with the testimony of a witness . . . you have heard, named James Ramseur. The entire testimony of James Ramseur has been stricken and it is not for your consideration in this case. You're not to speculate as to why the testimony has been stricken. All you need to know is it's no longer any proof in this case for your consideration."

I can say with some assurance that I was not unduly biased by Ramseur's sad performance. I did not feel frightened or intimidated by him, and I had felt from the onset that his testimony was irrelevent to finding out the facts in the case. The major damage Ramseur—and, for that matter, Andrea Reid—did to the prosecution, in my opinion, was to steal some of the luster and momentum that Waples had created through the playing of the videotape and the testimony of Boucher. Instead of closing out his case with a bang, then, Waples's case ended, well, not with a whimper, but with an explosiveness of a different kind.

Meanwhile, although we jurors of course did not talk about the case among ourselves, I noted in my diary that I was picking up certain vibes at this point—whether by people's expressions, little cryptic comments made, whatever—that several of my fellow jury members had not been impressed with the prosecution's case. Why this was so may have been for a number of reasons ranging from the preponderance of witnesses whose testimony seemed irrelevant or contradictory to the testimony of witnesses whose credibility was so bad that it was downright offensive. To these jurors, the picture Waples had drawn was of too grand a scale and tended to obscure the truth.

I believed I had my focus intact, however, and for me the truth about the shootings was best found in Goetz's own statements. Goetz said in his taped statements exactly what he had done, under no coercion, and Boucher corroborated the essential aspects of Goetz's testimony. Several of the other eyewitnesses corroborated different aspects of it, while others did in fact contradict it. I wrote off a lot of the contradictions, though, as owing to the amount of time that had elapsed since the incident, and others because people had not been paying much attention before the shooting started and afterwards everything happened quickly and amidst mass confusion. Because of this, the picture the prosecution drew to me had been necessarily abstract. I was eager, though, to get on to the defense's case and to see what Slotnick would have to add.

Chapter 12

The Defense's Case

May 21

The defense's first witness was Charles Cozza, the off-duty cop who had helped Goetz when he was mugged in January 1981. Cozza was a sanitation cop, which Waples explained in cross-examination is a peace officer responsible for enforcing the environmental laws of New York City: "illegal dumping, things like that." Cozza testified that he was in a restaurant near the corner of Canal and Varick streets at 1:30 p.m. when he saw Goetz run by the window with three men in pursuit. He went outside and saw one of the men, Fred Clark, "repeatedly punching and kicking Mr. Goetz." Goetz "stumbled to the ground" and the punching and kicking continued until Cozza grabbed and handcuffed Clark, whose back was toward Cozza, while the other two men ran away.

As a result of the beating, Cozza said Goetz had a red welt on his face and his jacket was torn. Slotnick asked him whether he had noticed Goetz limping after the attack, and Cozza answered, "No." Goetz was then driven in one police car to the local precinct while Cozza went to "central booking" in a separate car with Clark. Cozza had not witnessed the attempted robbery that Goetz asserted was the motive behind the mugging, so he signed a complaint charging Clark with third-degree assault, criminal mischief, and harrassment. In cross-examination, Waples asked Cozza if he was aware that Goetz was dissatisfied that Clark was not charged with attempted robbery.

"Well, as I say, he wasn't with me when the charges were drawn up," Cozza replied. "I don't know what happened to Mr. Goetz after I left the incident on Canal Street."

The next witness was Dr. Murray Burton, an orthopedist who treated Goetz for the knee injury he had sustained in the mugging. Goetz first came to Burton complaining of pain in his right knee over a year after the incident happened and said then that the knee had been bothering him for a month. Burton's diagnosis was "chondromalacia, which means a softening of the undersurface of the kneecap . . . characterized by crunching or pain with activity."

Waples pointed out in his cross-examination that chondromalacia is a "rather common knee ailment" that can be caused by simple overuse.

"For instance, runners suffer from chondromalacia?" Waples asked.

"They can," Burton admitted. He testified, however, that Goetz's description of how his knee had been injured—when he and Clark fell and his knee struck the pavement with Clark's weight on top of him—was consistent with the damage he found. Burton prescribed exercises for Goetz's knee and reexamined him three months later, by which time the pain had vanished and Burton determined that the knee was sound.

I found the testimony of Cozza and Burton very interesting because the points both sides were trying to make concerning Goetz's prior mugging, I believed, were conceivably valid. On the one hand it was clear that the experience had been very frightening and painful for him, and therefore it could explain why Goetz felt he needed a gun to protect himself afterward. The mugging could also be construed, however, as an experience that turned Goetz into "an emotional powderkeg," to use the words of Waples in his opening. The question was which of these was closer to the motive behind why Goetz chose to shoot the youths.

Slotnick next called Vincent Palumbo, a stenographer who'd recorded portions of Troy Canty's grand jury testimony, in order to prove certain inconsistent statements Slotnick was asserting that Canty had made. In some cases I didn't find the statements contradictory at all; several had to do with where the other youths were when Canty approached Goetz, and in all of these Canty maintained that he thought they were seated but couldn't be sure because he didn't look behind himself to see. He did tell the grand jury that he was the leader of the group, a fact he denied when he testified here, but I felt that was a rather minor point.

The only statement Canty made to the grand jury that I did think could be considered consequential involved how close to Goetz Canty said he stood. In describing how Goetz "took a couple of steps" away before drawing his gun and firing, Canty said Goetz did this because "he was too close." Canty was then asked how close he was to Goetz. He answered, "I walked up to him like that. If he pulled it out, I could have jumped on him, so he had to get up and back off so I wouldn't jump on him."

What we learned through this testimony about what Canty had said before the grand jury, however, was not allowable as "evidence-in-chief," meaning evidence bearing upon Goetz's guilt or innocence. The judge told us we could consider it only as evidence impeaching Canty's testimony. Canty had testified to us that when he stood before Goetz he had been "three or four feet" away. Again, then, the discrepancy was relatively minor; we'd already heard several versions of the incident that placed Canty in Goetz's face when he asked for five dollars. We were not free to consider the more substantive point, which was Canty's belief that if Goetz hadn't moved away, he would have been able to prevent Goetz from shooting. I suppose that Slotnick just wanted us to hear it, and so he offered it the only way he could.

⚖️

May 26

After four days off for the Memorial Day weekend, the defense's case continued with the testimony of Officer Peter Smith. A young, handsome guy who several jurors mentioned looked a little like Robert Chambers of the Jennifer Levin murder case, Smith and his partner, Dennis Driscoll, were the first cops at the scene after the shootings occurred. On the subway platform they met the conductor, Armando Soler, who, Smith said, "gave us a brief statement about four males that were shot and a brief description of the person that did shoot them. And he told us where they were, and . . . we ran down a few cars until we reached the [car] where the four men were shot."

Smith had been called by the defense specifically to relate a conversation he said he had with one of the youths he found lying on the floor of the train, who, we understood, must have been Troy Canty.

"I asked him if he was all right, and he said, 'No, I am shot,' " Smith testified. "I said, 'Where are you shot?' He said, 'In the chest.' I said, 'What happened?' and he said, 'We were going to rob him but he shot us first.' And I asked him what the person looked like and he described the person to me."

When Canty made this statement, Smith said he was kneeling beside him. He said Officer Driscoll was "in front of me . . . between five and ten feet" away. Minutes later Smith and a third officer who arrived on the scene then searched the tracks for Goetz while Driscoll remained behind. They went uptown as far as the Franklin Street station and then downtown to the World Trade Center before returning to the train. By that time several detectives as well as paramedics were present; the youths were being treated and taken away.

Smith's testimony provided Waples with his first challenge as a cross-examiner in this case, and he made a thorough attack on Smith's credibility. Slotnick's direct examination lasted about three minutes; Smith stayed on the stand all that afternoon and was finally excused at lunchtime the next day.

Waples's contention was that Smith never heard Canty make that statement, and he attempted to discredit Smith's story in a number of ways. First he pointed out that Smith had been an extremely green cop at the time of the incident, only one year out of the police academy and with only six months' experience as a patrolman on a beat. Smith admitted that he had been extremely nervous and under stress from the moment he and Driscoll spoke to the conductor. "We assumed [Goetz] was still on the train," Smith said, and so as he and Driscoll went through the cars toward the youths, they were also on the lookout for someone who fit Goetz's description.

Waples suggested this must have been "an unnerving experience" and said to Smith, "[Y]ou were obviously concerned with your personal safety because as far as you knew there was a person with a gun and an inclination to use that gun aboard the subway in which you were entering, is that right?"

"Yes," Smith said.

Smith also admitted to Waples that the situation was still stressful when he heard Canty's statement.

"Now, at this point, you were excited, Officer Smith, were you not?" Waples asked.

"Yes," Smith said.

"I mean, you found four persons who had actually been shot lying in a subway car, right?"

"Yes."

"And you were a new police officer; you'd never seen actually one shooting victim before, had you? Before December 22, 1984?"

"No," Smith replied.

"And you certainly hadn't seen four, right?"

"No."

"Especially in the close confines of a subway car, right?"

"No."

"You were excited, right?" he repeated.

"Yes," Smith said.

"On the other hand, you had a person who was lying in front of you with a gunshot wound in his chest, near his heart. You knew that, right?"

"Yes."

"Let me ask you this, Officer Smith. Is there any possibility in all honesty that you misunderstood or miscommunicated with this individual who [was] lying on the floor in front of you with the wound in his chest?"

"No."

"Well, let me ask you this. Is it possible that he said . . ., 'The white guy must have thought we were trying to rob him and that is why he shot us' or words to that effect?"

"No."

"That is not at all possible?"

"That is not what I heard," Smith replied.

* * *

"And are you saying that it's impossible that he said, '*I* tried to rob the white guy,' as opposed to, '*We* tried to rob him'?"

"No," Smith insisted. "I remember specifically."

"Those words ring clear in your head today, two-and-a-half years later. Isn't that right?"

"Yes."

Waples also suggested that Smith might be remembering something the conductor had said to him on the platform, before he and Driscoll entered the train. Perhaps Armando Soler had mentioned to Smith what Goetz had said to him, "I don't know why I did it. They tried to rob me." Smith denied this possibility as well, asserting that he was absolutely sure of what had been said between himself and Canty, and that Canty was "pretty coherent" at the time that they spoke.

Waples's attack on Smith then became more personal, suggesting that Smith had been negligent in not following correct police procedure. Smith remained outwardly calm throughout the questioning, but he sat so stiffly and spoke with such reserve that it was clear he was also quite tense.

Smith had no written record of Canty's statement because, Waples pointed out, he had not made *any* entry in his memo book about the incident; and Waples explained that the memo book is an activity log—a daily diary of on-duty events—that every police officer is required to keep. Waples also read from the New York City Police Department's "Patrol Guide" concerning an officer's duties when arriving at a crime scene: to "remove unauthorized persons" and secure the area; to "detain witnesses"; and to record in his activity log observations, the identities of suspects and witnesses, and "any relevent statements made whether casually or as a formal statement." From our understanding of the events within the subway car after the shootings as well as from Smith's own testimony, it was clear that Smith had not properly secured the crime scene, that important eyewitnesses (for instance, Garth and Andrea Reid) were not detained nor were their identities recorded;

and that this extremely relevant statement was not recorded in either Smith's or Driscoll's log.

Smith also failed to inform any of the detectives at the crime scene about the statement. In fact, Waples's assertion was that Smith didn't tell anyone of authority about the statement until he volunteered the information to two detectives and an assistant district attorney almost a year later, in November 1985.

Smith, on the other hand, asserted that he had told Detective Clark at the precinct later in the afternoon on December 22 that he had obtained a statement from one of the youths.

"Well, isn't it a fact that on November 27, 1985, you said to Detective Parr and Detective Harvey that one of the kids had said something to you, and that they in turn asked you, 'Who did you tell this to?' and you said, 'No one'?" Waples asked.

"I believe I said I was never interviewed," Smith replied.

"Do you deny making a statement, 'I told no one,' to Detective Parr?"

"I don't deny it."

"So, it's possible you said that?"

"It's possible," Smith admitted, but he claimed that if he had said this it was because he had understood the detective's question to mean whether he had told anyone *after* the day the incident happened. He insisted that *on* the day of the incident, he had spoken to Detective Clark.

In redirect, Slotnick brought out that in Smith's memo book he had made an entry at 11:30 a.m. on December 22, 1984, that read, "See Police Officer Driscoll." Smith testified that at that time he and Driscoll "switched positions," with Smith becoming the driver of their patrol car and Driscoll the "recorder" who kept his log for the both of them. "It's a common practice," Smith said. "I'm not sure if it's against the rules."

Smith also was questioned in greater detail about what he had told Clark that afternoon. "I remember going upstairs to the second floor [of the precinct] to tell the detectives that a statement was made to me," Smith said. "When I got up to the second floor I saw Detective Clark talking with one or two individuals out in the hall. . . . . I told him that statements were made to me by one of the perps—or one of the victims."

"And what did he say to you?" Slotnick asked.

" 'Don't worry about it. I will get back to you.' "

"And did he ever get back to you?"

"Later," Smith said.

"And when you say 'later,' how much later?"

"About eight months."

Slotnick asked Smith if he had told anyone else connected with the police department, other than Detective Clark, about the statement shortly after the date of the shootings. Waples objected to the question as irrelevant, but Justice Crane overruled.

"I told my partner; I told my sergeant; and I told the police department chaplain," Smith said.

May 27

Court recessed for the day with Slotnick still pursuing his redirect examination, and with me believing, despite Waples's efforts to undermine his testimony, that Smith had heard what he claimed Canty had said. Overnight, though, a very unusual thing happened. As a result of Smith's appearance on the stand, WNBC-TV dredged up from their files and aired on their eleven o'clock news program a brief videotaped interview with Smith on the day of the shootings. On the videotape, which was not played before the jury, Smith was in uniform, seated in the driver's seat of his patrol car. It was approximately 3:30 p.m., after Smith had already returned to the precinct to wash himself off, and about the time he went off duty. A female reporter held a microphone out to him and asked, "What did the victims have to say?"

"They just gave me a quick description," Smith answered. "He said that they were involved in—They said they were just fooling around with the guy, so I would assume that that would be possibly harrassment. I'm not sure. It's hard to say. It all happened so quick. We were only there a couple of seconds."

As a result of this new information, Waples, in an open-court discussion out of our presence, asked to be allowed to reopen his cross-examination. His application was granted, and the lawyers then agreed that this would be done after Slotnick had finished his redirect. Meanwhile, Slotnick argued vigorously with the judge that he be allowed to bring out the fact that Smith had passed a lie-detector test on this matter. Waples cited case law, however, that held the results of polygraph exams inadmissible as evidence in New York courts because they are considered unreliable, and Crane denied Slotnick's request.

Once his reopened cross-examination began, Waples asked Smith if he had told the reporter the truth.

"In substance," Smith said.

"'In substance,'" Waples commented. "That's an interesting word. . . . Was your testimony yesterday . . . the truth in substance?"

"My testimony was the truth," Smith insisted.

"Just the way your account to the news reporter was the truth?"

"That was different."

"Well, are there degrees of truth in your own mind?"

"No."

"Did you lie to that reporter, Officer Smith?"

"Somewhat," Smith said.

Waples ended his reopened cross by pressing Smith to admit Canty's statement had never been made.

"[Y]ou had forgotten about that little interview until late last night when your wife called it to your attention, isn't that right?" Waples asked.

"Yes," Smith admitted.

"And isn't it a fact, sir, that . . . on December 22, when you walked into that car and kneeled down to the person who was shot in the chest, he didn't say anything about trying to rob the white guy, did he?"

"Yes, he did."

"He did? You stand by your testimony?"

"Yes, sir."

"Isn't it a fact, sir, he never said anything at all about a robbery?"

"No."

"You know, as a police officer—even a relatively inexperienced police officer, Officer Smith—you know there is all the difference in the world between someone fooling around with a guy and someone robbing him, right?"

"Yes, sir," Smith said.

In re-redirect, Slotnick asked, "Now, why did you say that to the TV reporter?"

"I was nervous and had never been interviewed before," Smith explained. "And I had what I thought was a very important statement that had to be made. . . . And I wasn't about to put it over national TV or what might have been on national TV before I told the detective or someone in charge of the investigation."

"Isn't it correct that you almost did give away the statement when you said, 'He said they were involved in—' and then you went on to say, 'They were just fooling around with the guy'?"

"Objection," Waples said, but Crane overruled.

"It appears that way," Smith answered.

Despite this explanation, though, the seeds of doubt about Smith's credibility that Waples had planted the day before finally took root and blossomed in my mind. Smith obviously had made several mistakes in this matter, and we even learned on this second day of testimony that there was an internal affairs investigation of Smith's conduct, which, Waples told Justice Crane in a sidebar, was "awaiting the disposition of this case to proceed." By the time Smith was excused from the stand, I no longer felt I could trust his testimony. I wasn't discounting the possibility that Smith was correct about what Canty had said, but I now believed it was also possible that Smith had gotten the statement wrong.

That afternoon the defense called three more witnesses, and in each case the testimony was relatively brief. The first of the three was by far the most important. Dr. Bernard Yudwitz, a Massachusetts neuropsychiatrist who was board-certified in psychiatry, neurology, and forensic psychiatry, was presented as an expert witness concerning human biological responses to fear.

Dr. Yudwitz had served at various times in his career as the director of psychiatry for the Massachusetts Corrections Department, as director of legal medicine in Massachusetts, and as a consultant to various police departments and state police and correctional offices in Massachusetts. In these capacities, he stated that he had consulted with and analyzed many individuals who had discharged firearms in fearful and traumatic circumstances and could testify with authority about "the adrenaline response."

"There's a part of our nervous system called the autonomic nervous system," Yudwitz explained. "The autonomic nervous system is a basic system to life. What it does, it works automatically without any conscious control of our minds. It controls our respiration—we breathe without thinking of breathing—it controls our heart so our hearts beat without missing a beat, and so forth.

"[W]hen we are put in a fearful situation, the autonomic nervous system stimulates the outpouring of adrenalin and, as I say, that adrenalin is a substance that flows through the body and empowers us to do certain things. It enables the heart to beat faster; blood pressure goes up; the lungs expand . . . ; the blood flows more to our muscles; our muscles tense up and get us to respond. It is done on an automatic basis, so we're ready to meet the emergency situation."

"Assume the circumstances were [that] an individual fears the serious threat to his physical safety and in response . . . discharges a weapon. How would the body react at that point?" Slotnick asked.

"Well, if that individual was in a fearful situation and discharging a weapon, the body goes on what we call 'automatic pilot.' Once started . . . , that action continues until completion. In other words, one keeps on going automatically. It is the body in control at that time rather than the mind . . ."

"Once the threshold of fear is crossed, does the brain shut off completely?"

"Well, when you have the adrenal response, what happens —there's no conscious control over what is happening . . . The mechanism . . . in the body is working on its automatic self, in order to protect oneself or someone else in this type of life-threatening situation. It is the body that is in control rather than the mind being in control under those circumstances.''

"No further questions," Slotnick said.

Before Waples began cross-examination, however, he called for a sidebar. Yudwitz's testimony had gone a little beyond the scope of what Waples had expected, and rather than challenge his testimony with a lengthy cross-examination that he said he had not prepared for, he worked out a deal with Slotnick to amend the doctor's testimony instead.

The agreement they reached was for Slotnick to withdraw his last question and therefore remove Yudwitz's answer from our consideration. Slotnick then asked, "Doctor, you testified that in fearful situations, the brain goes on automatic pilot. That's something that may or may not occur depending upon the individual. Am I correct?"

"Yes, depending on the circumstances of the individual. Yes," Yudwitz replied.

Waples then cross-examined. "Doctor, just so I understand your testimony, you're acknowledging, are you not, that each individual response to stress is unique. Is that correct?"

"Within a certain threshold, yes," Yudwitz said.

"It depends upon the individual and it depends upon the circumstances . . . Correct?"

"Yes."

"And to ascertain how an individual would respond to particular stress, you would have to acquaint yourself both with the individual and the stress-inducing event. Is that correct?"

"Yes."

"And you have not examined the defendant in this case?"

"I have not."

"So, your testimony should not be construed by this jury as reflecting in any way an assessment of how this individual defendant responded to stress on December 22, 1984, or on any other date?"

"He hasn't been presented for that purpose, Your Honor," Slotnick piped up.

"So, your answer is your testimony should not be so understood?" Waples continued.

"That is correct," Yudwitz said.

"Thank you," Waples said. "Nothing else."

Because the doctor had not personally examined Goetz, my impression when I heard this testimony was that it was inconclusive and certainly did not prove that Goetz was not in conscious control of his actions when he was shooting. The subject of Goetz's adrenalin and how it altered his state of mind at the time was one that Goetz had spoken about at length in both his audiotaped and videotaped statements, though, so that added some credence to the defense's theory. And, most significantly, Yudwitz's testimony provided us with an argument for why, perhaps, Goetz would have continued firing at the youths after the physical threat had been thwarted. It proved to be an important consideration in our deliberations about whether Goetz's actions could be legally justified, especially in shooting the last shot at Darrell Cabey, who had been apparently the least threatening of the youths.

Next up was John Barna, the investigator who secretly taped Andrea Reid when he went to speak to her on behalf of the defense before she testified. As with Vincent Palumbo, the court stenographer who had recorded Troy Canty's grand jury testimony, Barna was called solely to try to prove that Reid had made certain inconsistent statements between her conversation with him and her testimony here. He testified to the circumstances surrounding the interview, and then we were allowed to listen to four excerpts from the tape. Once again we were provided with headphones and a transcript that was particularly necessary because the audibility of the tape was so poor.

Slotnick's principal contention concerned what Reid saw before the shooting started. She had testified that she had not seen any of the youths standing over Goetz, and that after she had heard the first shot she had seen two of the youths in the aisle "running" and the other two still sitting down. In the third excerpt, however, we heard her say, in response to Barna's suggestion that the youths were "right in [Goetz's] face," "They were just standing over him like this." After the excerpts were played, Barna demonstrated how Reid was standing when she said that, leaning forward from the waist.

The other issue was how many youths Reid meant when she said "they" were standing over Goetz. It seemed pretty conclusive that Reid saw at least two, but whether she saw more than two was nebulous. She said in the fourth excerpt, according to the transcript, "It was about two of them and that's my—unintelligible—[it] was about two or three of them in that direction."

Slotnick was allowed to ask if Barna remembered what Reid had said that was marked as unintelligible on the transcript. "She said it was two or three of them. Then she said—I believe she said four, and then she went back to two or three of them again," Barna stated.

Waples then began his cross-examination: "She never said anything about four of them."

"Pardon me?" said Barna.

"She never said anything about four of them," Waples repeated.

"Yes, she did," Barna replied.

"Sir, would you point out on this transcript where she says four persons were standing over this individual?"

"Where it's crossed out," Barna asserted. "I believe she said at least four."

After some arguing about what could be heard on the tape and what Barna contended he remembered, Waples asserted, "I am content with the jury's recollection." The truth, I suppose, had been lost in the space between Andrea Reid and the microphone, obscured by the fabric of John Barna's clothes.

Finally, we heard once again from Detective Michael Clark, who had testified twice previously for the prosecution and now was called by the defense to discuss what had happened to the subway car in which the shootings occurred. Clark stated that the car had not been impounded and had since been gutted for use as a work train, so it was not useful as evidence in this case. Slotnick pointed out that it was Clark's "duty and obligation" as the detective in charge of the Goetz investigation "to see to it that evidence is preserved," and he also asked him what had happened to the steel panel by the conductor's cab that Detective Haase had testified had been dented by a bullet. Clark admitted that he did not know.

Chapter 13

Bullet Wounds, Trajectories, X rays, Etc.

The one part of the prosecution's case that I omitted until now was the testimony of three doctors on May 11—the first day Myra Friedman testified—concerning the injuries and medical treatment of the youths.

First, Dr. Harry Adler, who in 1984 had been a staff surgeon at Bellevue Hospital, testified to having treated James Ramseur and Barry Allen on the day they were admitted. He said that Allen arrived "in stable condition, awake and alert, with a gunshot wound—single gunshot wound, it appeared—to his back. . . . He had X-ray evidence of fluid in the chest. He had a chest tube placed for drainage. He had several other X-ray studies done to rule out any other injuries. He was treated for drainage of the pleural cavity for three or four days and then discharged."

Adler stated that the bullet stuck Allen "between his spine and scapula, on the left side." When asked what had been "the course direction" of the bullet, he answered, "I couldn't say anything more except that the X ray showed several fragments spread out along the left side in that area." The bullet "[a]ppeared to fragment and spread along the left shoulder," Adler stated, and he said that the bullet was not removed.

Ramseur's wounds also appeared to have been caused by a single bullet that entered the outside of his left forearm, just above the elbow, exited the inside of his arm and then entered the left side of his chest, according to Adler. He said that

Ramseur's condition also was stable and that an "exploratory laparotomy . . . an operation where the abdomen is opened and injuries repaired" was performed on him. The "laparotomy showed a hole in the stomach, a laceration of the spleen, and a hole in the diaphragm through which the bullet had entered the abdomen from the chest," Adler said. Ramseur's "spleen was removed, the hole in the stomach was repaired, the hole in the diaphragm was repaired and that concluded the operation." The bullet, Adler stated, was neither found nor removed; he said that "[i]ndirectly from the X-ray evidence, it appeared to be lodged [near] his left adrenal gland."

A few days after the operation Ramseur suffered a partial collapse of the left lung that was "treated with suctioning of the lung and a bronchoscopy." Ramseur left the hospital without having been discharged on January 8, but then returned later that day complaining of abdominal pain. Further X rays revealed a "small bowel obstruction," and Ramseur received a second operation to repair this problem. He left Bellevue again on his own on January 13.

In cross-examination Slotnick asked Adler if the trail of metallic fragments that traveled from the entrance wound "toward the left shoulder" of Barry Allen "could be consistent with the flight of the bullet," since the bullet had not broken any bones. Adler answered that that was possible. In Waples's redirect, though, Adler said the bullet "presumably . . . hit some bone . . . and then bullet fragments distributed themselves along the way." Then in recross, Adler clarified that although "there's no evidence, on X-ray examination" that the bullet struck bone, "to have the bullet in twenty pieces, it presumably stuck something hard."

"That's your guess at this point, is that correct?" Slotnick asked.

"That's my guess," Adler said.

*　　*　　*

"Now, in terms of your expertise, which is surgery, there are other individuals who have greater expertise in terms of gunshot wounds and [the] travel, and locomotion, and path[s] of bullets. Is that correct?"

"That's correct."

"For example, could there be a finer expert than a medical examiner who deals with gunshot wounds on almost a daily basis?"

"I suppose that person would be fairly expert," Alder said.

"Doctor . . . , you are not—and I say this respectfully—you are not an expert in ballistics, are you?" Slotnick added, in re-recross.

"No, I'm not."

*   *   *

"If it turned out that . . . the bullet was one in which it would fragment upon touching soft tissue, would it not be reasonable to believe that the force continued the bullet in one direction, and fragmented as it continued on?"

"That could be," Adler replied.

Next up was Dr. Peter Adams, a surgeon at St. Vincent's Hospital who treated Troy Canty and Darrell Cabey upon their arrival. He stated that Canty's wound was just below the left nipple, and that the bullet "traversed the lung and lodged in the skin of the back." An operation was performed to place "a tube into the [left] chest cavity to drain out the contents of blood and fluid and to reexpand the lung." Adams said that "drainage suction" was maintained for several days, and then the bullet was extracted from Canty's back ten days after the incident, on December 31. He was discharged on January 2, 1985.

"Mr. Cabey had suffered a gunshot wound to the lower chest and back," Adams said. "From X-ray determination, apparently the bullet went from the left side of the lower rear chest area, across the spine, to the right side. . . . [B]oth left and right lungs were injured by the course of the bullet fragments and the spinal cord was . . . essentially severed," leaving Cabey completely and permanently paralyzed "from the level of the ribs or the diaphragm down."

Tubes were placed in both of Cabey's chest cavities to drain them of both blood and fluid and to re-expand Cabey's "partially collapsed" lungs. Cabey's ability to breathe was complicated by his paralysis, however, because, Adams explained, the paralysis "[a]ffects the ability of the muscles around the ribs to contract normally—expanding the chest to allow air in—to allow the patient to breathe deeply and also to allow the patient to expectorate or cough and clear his own secretion. The paralysis prevented this to a certain degree."

As a result, Adams said, Cabey "went on to develop significant pneumonia in both lungs." Then—inexplicably, according to Adams—on January 8, 1985, Cabey "suffered a respiratory arrest in which he stopped breathing altogether." Cabey's heart and lung functions were restored, but his brain had been deprived of oxygen and he became comatose. He remained in a deep coma, sustained by a respirator, for several days.

"Did you expect him to live?" Waples asked Adams.

"I did not, no," Adams said.

On a chart Adams marked the trajectories of the bullets as they passed through the bodies of Canty and Cabey. He showed Canty's bullet as having angled slightly from right to left, "toward the middle of the chest." The bullet that struck Cabey entered below his left armpit and traveled laterally, "roughly" in a straight line across his back, according to the path of metal fragments that the shattered bullet left. There was no piece of the bullet large enough for doctors to remove.

During Adams's testimony Slotnick called for a sidebar to offer to stipulate that Cabey had "suffered life-threatening injuries" and claimed that Waples was "attempting to prejudice the jury with blood and gore." He reiterated his protest, this time in open court, when Waples next called Dr. Claude Macaluso, a neurologist who took over the care of Darrell Cabey after he went into his coma.

"Your Honor, we would object again to the cumulative nature of this testimony. It's irrelevant, and I don't think we can go on with five thousand doctors. I think I have been very good in not cross-examining," Slotnick declared.

"I appreciate your spirit of moving the case along, and I think that's healthy," Justice Crane responded. "But on this subject the people have the burden of proof beyond a reasonable doubt, and they are entitled to call what witnesses they think are necessary to establish their burden, if they can do so."

Waples had two issues to prove through the testimony of Adams and Macaluso: one, that deadly force had been used against Darrell Cabey and the other youths; and, two, that the brain damage Cabey had suffered as a result of his coma made him unfit to testify. In order to establish the second point, Macaluso discussed the details of Cabey's coma and the nature and extent of his brain damage. I could understand why Slotnick would protest this, because the details were gory indeed.

Macaluso testified that Cabey's "deep coma," where "he was responsive only to deep, painful stimuli," lasted several days. "Shortly thereafter, the patient was able to open his eyes spontaneously," and "it was determined that he was in what was called persistent vegetative state." His "eyes were open and roving in response to threat," but his "upper extremities were tight, rigid, spastic. There was no response to the external world . . . There was no speech production." Macaluso explained that "persistent vegetative state . . . signifies damage to the cortical level of the brain—the cortex—which is . . . the most vulnerable area to . . . lack of oxygen." The damage, he said, was not reversible, and "in recent studies, being in a persistent vegetative state for over two weeks carries a very poor prognosis for recovery and for life." Cabey remained in a persistent vegetative state for six weeks, Macaluso said.

Sometime in March 1985, then, Cabey emerged from his coma and began a slow recovery. He went through eleven months of physical therapy in the hospital to restore his motor coordination and "to assess the amount of intellectual damage, cognitive damage, and work with whatever is there, whatever is left." At the time Cabey was finally discharged from the hospital, February 1986, Macaluso said that he "was able to speak, but with slurred speech . . . He was able to use a wheelchair, propel his own wheelchair," but he had a "lack of coordination" in his arms and upper body, "plus, obviously, he was paraplegic from the original wound." He said Cabey's memory was significantly impaired.

In cross-examination Slotnick established that had Cabey been put on a respirator before he'd suffered his cardiopulmonary arrest on January 9, 1985, he would not have gone into the coma. Macaluso said in redirect, though, that he didn't believe anyone had been negligent in not putting Cabey on a respirator beforehand; that the arrest had been an unanticipated event.

Slotnick also tried to suggest that Cabey's memory had been substantially restored. In a sidebar he argued to Justice Crane that he be allowed to elicit statements Cabey made to Macaluso about the shootings after his coma in June and December, 1985, and to *Daily News* columnist Jimmy Breslin, who visited Cabey in November 1985, to demonstrate how much Cabey was able to recall. "I'd like to show that the injury was not so irreparable, and I would like to show, yes, Darrell Cabey is not the sponge that Mr. Waples would like him to be or brought him out to be before this jury," Slotnick said.

Macaluso explained, however, that the two versions of the shootings Cabey gave to him in March and November were substantially different from one another, and furthermore he felt that the memories Cabey recalled in June 1985 seemed more genuine and sincere than those he recalled six months later. Cabey's memory was fragmented, Macaluso said.

Crane denied Slotnick's request and later ruled that the prosecution had proven its point that Cabey was unfit to testify in this trial.

May 28

The reason I avoided referring to this medical testimony of the prosecution earlier was so that I could now present it alongside all of the subsequent testimony of experts who were to use this information to try to prove certain facts about where the youths were and precisely how they were positioned in relation to Goetz when they were shot.

The defense first called Joseph Quirk, a retired New York City police officer whose expertise was in ballistics and the re-creation of crime scenes. He said in his nineteen years on the force he had re-created crime scenes in trials "anywhere from three to five hundred times."

In order to do this, tape had been placed on the floor in the well of the courtroom to delineate the dimensions of the back third of the subway car. And, in a brilliant ploy, Slotnick had convinced the judge to allow Quirk to use four black youths, all members of the Guardian Angels, instead of court officers in his re-creation. Slotnick's contention was that the four youths had been specifically selected because they were identical in height to the four youths shot, but the underlying intention was to give the jury the chance to get the feeling of what four tough guys would look like—even if they weren't huge guys—together in one end of a subway car. They were also dressed in a rough, streetwise fashion, and they definitely produced something of a shock effect.

Quirk's re-creation, which we were reminded was strictly hypothetical but supposedly consistent with extant ballistics evidence, was a scenario in which all four of the youths were surrounding Goetz before he fired. Quirk also aligned their bodies so that all four were facing Goetz when he started to fire and merely recoiled by reflex just before they were hit. In this scenario the shots were fired extremely rapidly, from left to right, leaving no time for Goetz to think between shots.

The major challenges of Quirk's re-creation to the prosecution's contention of how the shootings occurred involved Barry Allen and Darrell Cabey. The two sides generally agreed that Canty was shot first and at close range and differed on Ramseur only in that the prosecution would have Ramseur farther away from Goetz, perhaps having leaped from his seat after the first shot was fired. With Barry Allen, however, Quirk asserted that rather than having been shot while running away, Allen was standing close to Goetz and had exposed his back by ducking down. Quirk had Cabey standing directly in front of the seat by the conductor's cab and hypothesized that Cabey was hit with Goetz's fourth bullet, that he then fell backward into the seat, and that the fifth shot was the one that struck the steel panel.

The question of whether Cabey was hit with the fourth or fifth shot was crucial in this case, because were it the fourth shot, it would negate the prosecution's contention that Goetz fired the fifth shot in a premeditated manner, after a pause in which he moved to stand directly in front of Cabey. Waples was arguing that after the fourth shot Cabey was seated, paralyzed with fear rather than by a bullet. Slotnick's counterargument was that Goetz's and Boucher's recollections were wrong.

What enraged Waples about Quirk's testimony during Slotnick's direct examination was that Quirk consistently stated not just that the theories he was espousing were *more likely* than others, but that the prosecution's theories were in fact *impossible.* He said that none of the youths could have been shot in the back while running, and that Cabey was "most definitely standing up" when shot. "From my experience, there is no way" Cabey could have been seated, Quirk testified. For that to be possible, he said, the slight downward angle of the bullet as it passed laterally through Cabey's body "would be much greater than it is."

As a result, tempers ran extremely high during Waples's cross-examination that afternoon. Waples and Slotnick became angrier at each other than at any other point in the trial, and Waples was so infuriated with Quirk's testimony that he let his temper get the better of him and unnecessarily antagonized and alienated Quirk.

Waples had to demonstrate that there was a much broader range of possibility, even within the confines of the established facts, for how the shootings might have occurred than Quirk had thus far admitted. But Waples appeared tense while he attempted this. Once again I noticed his hands occasionally trembling and thought his questions were perhaps too direct and heavy-handed; he lacked the smoothness so characteristic of Slotnick's style.

He began his attack by quizzing Quirk about his relationship with the defense team. Obviously, he had been hired by Slotnick and his function here was to demonstrate and lend credence to the defense's theories of how the shootings took place. Waples asked Quirk how much he was being paid.

"If I am directed by the Court to answer it, I will," Quirk said.

"Mr. Quirk, it's a measure of . . . interest [that] Mr. Waples is entitled to delve into," Justice Crane responded. "I would appreciate your answering the question."

"I expect to be paid about $1,500," Quirk stated.

Waples went further to imply that Quirk might need the money and so had an additional motive to kowtow to Slotnick's

theories. He pointed out that because Quirk was retired, pros-
ecutors used him less often as a witness in these matters than
when he was on the force.

"Mr. Quirk, the freelance ballistics business is not the most
lucrative in the world, is it?"

"I think it's pretty good," Quirk said, a bit defensively.

"But you're making your primary living doing other things?"

"I have a good pension," Quirk replied.

Waples then stressed that Quirk's theories were only as
good as the information he was provided and had Quirk admit
that if the information he was provided was faulty, the con-
clusions he would draw would be equally flawed.

"You've heard the phrase, 'garbage in, garbage out'?"
Waples continued.

"Yes."

"Basically, it means that if a person who's engaging in
some kind of computational process or reasoning process has
bad data to work with, the end product, the conclusion, the
result, is not going to be very reliable, right?"

"That is correct."

"That certainly applies to the field of ballistic science,
right?"

"That is correct," Quirk repeated. "That is why you use
investigators."

"Particularly to effect opinion evidence to your own, which
is based upon hypothetical questions posed to you?"

"It is not entirely hypothetical," Quirk said, becoming
testy. "That is why you investigate, to get facts. As many facts
as possible. That is where your opinion is."

"You're basing your opinion on the hypothetical—"

"You're lumping my whole life history into hypothetical
questions," Quirk cut him off. "The answer is not all my
assumptions are hypothetical. A good deal of my assumptions
are facts."

"All the hypothetical questions were given to you by
Mr.—"

"You didn't particularly point out this particular day, this
particular hour, this particular case. You rounded the whole
thing into my experience as being hypothetical," Quirk complained.

Waples antagonized Quirk to the point where Quirk began to do his best to frustrate Waples's questioning. And Waples was further flustered by a whole series of frivolous comments that Slotnick was interjecting in a sly effort to distract and disrupt his train of thought. Waples on a few prior occasions had shown a tendency to lose his train of thought when distracted, and Slotnick used this against him here. Once, while Slotnick was making an objection that Justice Crane overruled, Waples added, "I object to the interruptions." And on another occasion, Waples even complained, "Mr. Slotnick has stolen my train of thought, Judge."

"I am sorry," Slotnick said.

What Waples was paving the way for, however, was that the information Slotnick gave Quirk, particularly about Barry Allen's wound, was in fact inaccurate. He attempted to prove this by showing Quirk recently taken photographs of Barry Allen's back, which revealed that his bullet wound was in a different place from where Quirk believed it to have been. Waples also had another photograph showing the scar where a piece of the bullet had later been removed from the front of Allen's left shoulder, and photographs of Ramseur's wounds, which were less controversial.

Waples asked Quirk, "You were basing your opinion upon a hypothesis that a bullet entered the upper-left shoulder in the back and traveled downward and lodged in the lower back area near the spine, correct?"

"That's correct," Quirk answered.

The photograph of Allen's back, however, showed that the bullet had entered Allen dead center in the back, directly above the spine, and had traveled across the left side of his back, lodging near the top of his arm. Waples contended that this made Quirk's hypothesis "physically impossible," and Quirk agreed.

Waples's production of these photographs clearly surprised and infuriated the defense team. In a sidebar they claimed they had based their theories on the shooting of Allen on the testimony of the prosecution's witness, Dr. Adler, who on a chart had placed Allen's wound to the left of the spine. Slotnick and Baker contended that Waples was now impeaching the testimony of his own witness, and that such impeachment was not allowed.

"I am doing nothing improper," Waples insisted. "The defense has come on with a preposterous theory today, which has caused me to need to present refining evidence concerning exactly where these people were shot. It was unnecessary for me to even photograph these individuals, based upon my assessment of how the case would be presented. I didn't find it necessary to have these photographs beforehand. [But w]hen I realized where the defense was going, I decided to—in the last week or so, that I should photograph Barry Allen and James Ramseur, and I did. That's what I have done."

"We have gone based on facts in evidence," Slotnick countered. "I will not be sandbagged at this point. I am entitled to a mistrial, assuming what he is telling us is correct. I put experts on [the witness stand] based on his record, not mine."

"Well, he is saying there is a refinement of his record," Justice Crane offered, trying to defuse the situation. "The photographs will show—"

"He is impeaching his prior medical evidence," Slotnick insisted and added moments later, "I would like to reopen my direct, assuming his photographs come in, assuming Your Honor doesn't grant a mistrial at this point. I am assuming I will be granted a mistrial."

"This is outrageous," Waples said.

"There is no such trial by ambush in this state," Slotnick shot back. He and Waples were talking very loudly now.

"This is ridiculous. Trial by ambush—This is the ambush. The defense—The trial—"

"Please," Slotnick said.

"Gentlemen, take it easy," Justice Crane said, trying to hush them up.

This was as unruly as the trial ever became. In fact, I think if it had gone just one degree further, we would have heard the judge's gavel striking. For the first and only time, I noticed the gavel lying at the front of the judge's bench.

"It's warm in the courtroom, and I think we are all getting a little hot under the collar, except Mr. Baker," Justice Crane said during another exchange in which the two attorneys were

arguing loudly. He decided in the midst of the present sidebar
to end the arguing by adjourning for the day.

June 1

Before cross-examination of Quirk resumed, Justice Crane
formally denied the defense's application for a mistrial but
struck from the record the questions Waples had posed to
Quirk based on evidence that conflicted with Dr. Adler's original testimony. Justice Crane explained that "a question which
assumes a material fact which has no support in the evidence
is improper and must be excluded." Moving the entry wound
from where Dr. Adler had placed it "departs from the evidence," Justice Crane said, "and if the People intended to
establish a more middle location for the entry wound, it seems
they would have had to have that in the record by now."

Quirk's hypothesis of how Allen was shot when ducking
was allowed to stand unimpeached, therefore; but Waples did
get Quirk to admit it was also consistent with Allen's wound
that he might have twisted his body, turning to run, when hit.
Still, our new understanding of the parameters of possibility
concerning the shooting of Allen clearly had helped the defense's case. Allen could not have been shot directly in the
back while running away, as Waples had suggested in his
opening statement, because such a straight-on shot, given the
actual location of his wound, would have severed Allen's spine.
The bullet struck Allen at a sharp angle, suggesting that the
interval between the shots aimed at Canty and Allen had been
too brief for Allen to have had time to flee.

Quirk also admitted, concerning Darrell Cabey, that it was
also physically possible that the lateral shot across Cabey's back
could have occurred with Cabey sitting down. Waples borrowed
a chair and demonstrated in front of Quirk how Cabey might
have "jerked his right arm"—as Goetz had mentioned in both
taped statements—and, body slightly tilted, flinched to his right
just before Goetz fired. Goetz, Waples suggested, was standing
either directly in front of Cabey or slightly off to Cabey's left.
Quirk agreed that the angle of Waples's body to where Goetz

might have been standing with his gun pointed at a seated target was consistent with the wound that Cabey sustained.

The defense's next witness, Dr. Dominick DiMaio, presented Waples with the same kind of challenge as Joseph Quirk. A former New York City medical examiner who said he had performed over twenty thousand autopsies in his thirty-one-year career, DiMaio was brought in to discuss the medical evidence concerning the youths' wounds to support Quirk's physical re-creation of the shootings. Based on his examination of hospital records, DiMaio asserted that none of the youths was shot with his back facing Goetz, and that Darrell Cabey had to have been standing when he was shot. He said that Cabey must have then fallen backward into his seat after the bullet had severed his spine.

"Can you say that to a medical certainty?" Slotnick asked.

"Absolutely," DiMaio said.

DiMaio first explained his findings, using court officers as visual aids because Waples had protested against the further use of the four Guardian Angels for this purpose. Then, after a break during which DiMaio quickly looked through a package of X rays of the youths that had just been delivered to the defense team, DiMaio claimed that the X rays amounted to definitive proof.

Once more the focus of the testimony was on the wounds of Allen and Cabey. The path of the bullet that went through Allen, DiMaio stated, "entered and proceeded on a horizontal plane." He said you could see this by the trail of metal fragments that ran from the spine to the "left arm area," where the remainder of the bullet was lodged.

"[I]f you look at the X rays, it is almost a perfect straight line," DiMaio said.

"Is that indicative of a shot going from back to front?" Slotnick asked DiMaio.

"No."

"What's it indicative of?"

"It's a bullet wound that proceeded horizontally across the back and, as I tried to demonstrate, the body was not to the back of the shooter, but the side was to the shooter."

In the case of Darrell Cabey, DiMaio explained the reason he concluded Cabey had to have been standing while shot was because of the bullet's path inside his body. The bullet, he said, entered Cabey's body in the seventh intercostal space—between his seventh and eighth ribs—and traveled horizontally across his back until it struck the eighth vertebra of his spine. Then "from the midline it went up," he said, striking and damaging the sixth rib on Cabey's right side and lodging "in the soft tissue" somewhere nearby. This lateral path and subsequent upward turn of the bullet could not have happened if Goetz's gun had been aimed in a downward direction, DiMaio declared.

"[I]f he's standing, the bullet can go horizontally across, strike the spine, and the spine could deviate [the bullet] upwards slightly. That is possible," DiMaio said. But, he asserted—taking into consideration the downward angle created by a standing Goetz and a seated Cabey, and because the bullet entered through the seventh intercostal space, unimpeded by bone—the bullet "would have to continue in a downward path" if Cabey had been seated and could "no way" have struck the eighth vertebra. "It may strike the tenth or something else," DiMaio said, but "in no way could it [then] come up to the sixth rib. You follow me?"

"If Darrell Cabey is seated in that chair," Slotnick said, "and I'm Bernhard Goetz, and I approached him in any manner whatsoever, and fired directly into him, after saying something like, 'You don't look bad; here's another,' is there any position that I could be standing in, firing into him, that would duplicate the bullet wound and the path of the bullet in Darrell Cabey?"

"As long as he's seated, there's only one position," DiMaio answered. "You'll have to get almost to your knees to inflict the wound."

June 2

In cross-examination Waples had an X-ray-viewing machine set up in front of the jury box and asked DiMaio to point out the location of the lodged bullet in an X ray of Allen and to decipher whether it was in back or in front of his shoulder bone. "I would have to say it is behind the head of the humerus, because of its brightness," DiMaio said. This issue was somewhat important because it affected the angle of the bullet's path: whether it had been an almost straight side shot, as DiMaio insisted, or if it had traveled more from back to front. Later DiMaio conceded, "I'm not a radiologist" and could not readily explain how the bullet could have been lodged in the back of the shoulder and later extracted from the front, as the recent photographs of Allen showed. "I wonder if that bullet didn't migrate," he mused.

DiMaio was an obstinate witness, and throughout Waples's cross-examination he stubbornly insisted that his findings were irrefutable, no matter how logical Waples's counterarguments were. Again concerning Allen, Waples asked DiMaio why it was impossible for Allen to have been running away when shot. DiMaio said it was because of the sideways angle of the bullet. "When a man is running, he is usually presenting his back to you. . . . [T]he bullet would not have gone from right to left."

"Okay," Waples said. "Doctor, you are making certain assumptions about the way people run, right?"

"It's not an assumption, it's a practicality," DiMaio answered. "It's an obvious fact. Nobody runs sideways," he added.

Waples then demonstrated a way that Allen could have been running—southward, about ten feet from the shooter—with his torso twisted so that his back was exposed at the approximately proper angle. He added that the forward motion of the subway car, combined with some possible "lurching and swaying," could throw a person into some "peculiar positions," especially someone who was "frantically trying to get away from a person with a gun." DiMaio conceded Waples's point somewhat but insisted that for Allen to have been hit in the manner he had while running was, ultimately, "impractical."

Concerning Darrell Cabey, Waples argued that the way Cabey's spinal cord was transected, if Cabey had been standing when shot, he would have immediately "dropped like a rock." Waples suggested it was unlikely, even if Cabey were standing right next to the seat, that he would have fallen into it and not onto the floor. DiMaio didn't give in to this argument, however. While admitting that Cabey had to have been very close to the seat to have landed there, "The tendency is to fall backwards," DiMaio declared.

In redirect, Slotnick offered that the same "lurching and swaying" of the subway car that Waples argued could have jerked Allen into a "peculiar position" when hit might also have pushed Cabey backward into the seat, so those types of hypothetical arguments worked both ways for the two attorneys. Waples asked DiMaio, though, if "all other things being equal," DiMaio didn't consider it "a much more probable conclusion" that Cabey would have been seated when shot than to have fallen there.

"No, I never assume that. Without having facts, I would never assume it," DiMaio replied.

Finally, Waples tried to again demonstrate how Cabey could have been shot while seated had he bent over slightly and twisted his body, creating the proper perpendicular angle between the side of Cabey's back and a downward-tilted gun.

"Doctor, when a person is leaning to the right-hand side, he can place his body in a position where he would receive a shot at the seventh intercostal space, correct?" Waples asked.

"Yes."

"That would proceed directly across his body and transect the spinal column at [the eighth vertebra]?"

"No way."

"You say that's impossible, sir?"

"No, it's impossible," DiMaio declared.

"Doctor, do you believe other medical experts would share your opinion concerning the feasibility of Darrell Cabey being shot in this situation?" Waples asked a few minutes later.

"Everybody has his own right and own opinion," DiMaio answered.

"Dr. DiMaio has his opinion. Is that correct?"

"Which I think is correct," DiMaio said.

Waples then began an attack on DiMaio's record during the two years he was chief medical examiner for New York City.

"Is it not a fact, sir, that you were forced into retirement because—"

"Go ahead," DiMaio interjected. "Say what you want to say."

"Because a mayoral committee . . . , appointed to oversee the office that you were running, determined that your administration was not satisfactory?"

"You are wrong," DiMaio shot back. "What the committee insisted was that at sixty-five I retire and I did. . . . I ran that office without complications."

Waples detailed, however, that in 1976 six women were found dead in one Manhattan hotel over a "relatively short period of time, and autopsies performed by your office in each instance determined the cause of death was a natural cause or nonhomocidal cause." Waples then asked, [W]asn't it a number of months later that a person by the name of Calvin Jackson actually confessed to . . . raping and strangling each of those women? Isn't that right?"

"Don't say strangle," DiMaio answered. "It was not strangling. It was smothering." DiMaio defended himself by saying, "I never did any of those autopsies, but as chief I tried to explain why there would have been certain failures." He added, "Only God can tell you when a person is smothered."

"Didn't that cause an uproar, Dr. DiMaio?"

"Sure it does. Why not?" DiMaio said. He also derided the committee's actions against him as "purely political."

In redirect, Slotnick tried to indicate that the police department had been faulted more on this matter than the coroner's office. "It's unfortunate they bring a thing like this up when everybody knows the truth," DiMaio commented, though that was stricken from the record as "editorializing."

DiMaio's tainted record aside, he had been a fairly successful defense witness in my opinion. DiMaio's stubbornness frustrated Waples to the point where I think he basically conceded he was not going to get the answers he was looking for from him, and so he settled for merely undermining his authority as an expert.

The problem was that Waples seemed to be running out of time to prove the points he had to prove if we were to convict Goetz on the shooting of Cabey. All he had done in his cross-examinations of DiMaio and Quirk was leave open the possibility that Cabey *could* have been shot in the way he theorized (that is, while Cabey was seated) which was the way I also most tended to believe. If we were to convict Goetz, however, Waples would have to convince us beyond a reason-able doubt that his was the way it *must* have happened. To accomplish this Waples had a long way to go.

June 5

After the defense rested its case, Waples was allowed to bring in rebuttal witnesses, and so he called two medical experts of his own. We first heard from Dr. Melvin Becker, an expert in radiology, the medical field in which Dr. DiMaio admitted to not having expertise. Becker was the director of radiology at Gouverneur Diagnostic and Treatment Center in Manhattan, as well as an attending radiologist at Bellevue and New York University hospitals. And since 1979 he had been an official consultant in radiology to the New York City medical examiner's office.

Again the X-ray-viewing machine was set up in front of the jury box, and Becker discussed the location of the bullet fragment that was eventually removed from Barry Allen. Look-ing at the same X ray that DiMaio had used, Becker said there was no way to tell exactly where the fragment was in relation to the head of the upper arm bone.

Waples then asked, "If Dr. DiMaio, on Tuesday . . . of this week, testified or said that he could tell that this particular bullet was behind the head of the humerus because of its brightness, what would your reaction to that statement be?"

"He is using far different criteria than any other radiologist has used in making these definitions . . . ," Becker answered, explaining that the density of the lead would look the same on an X ray were it on either side of the bone.

"Is it a statement, Doctor, that any knowledgeable and competent radiologist would make?"

"I don't know any radiologist that would make that state-ment," Becker replied.

The X ray in question had been a front-to-back picture of Allen, however, and Becker was then able to show us a lateral-view X ray that he said conclusively showed the fragment lodged in front of the bone. Waples then showed Becker the photo-graph of Allen's scar where the slug had been removed, and

Becker said the location of the incision—the front of Allen's left upper shoulder—corresponded to the X ray.

"Based on this photograph and the X-ray findings, the track of the bullet would have had to be from the back across toward the front, moving to the patient's left, toward the front of the shoulder, to the front of the humerus," Becker concluded.

Slotnick's turn to cross-examine then came, and it was kind of refreshing to see him back in his natural element. Cross-examination was clearly his forte. In fact, in a sidebar during his redirect examination of Officer Smith, Slotnick stated to Justice Crane, "I'm not very good on direct."

"You're switching roles," Justice Crane noted.

"It is very difficult for me. I usually don't have to do that," Slotnick added. "[Waples] was very effective on cross-examination."

"Absolutely," said Justice Crane.

Now back on familiar turf, Slotnick seemed much more comfortable despite a case of laryngitis, which he had developed over the last few days. His laryngitis concerned him, I am sure, because he was less than a week away from having to deliver his closing argument, but he still was able to keep his sense of humor and even use his malady to some advantage. He sought everyone's sympathy, including the witness's. "Good morning, Dr. Becker," he began.

"Good morning."

"You are—You don't treat laryngitis, do you, Doctor?"

"I understand," Becker smiled.

A little later, to emphasize the point, he asked Becker to repeat that he had not read all of Allen's medical records before coming here to testify. "I'm sorry, Doctor," Slotnick said. "I have laryngitis, so I may not be hearing you properly. Did you read the Bellevue Hospital medical report in its entirety. Yes or no?"

The only substantive point Slotnick made with Becker, however, was that Allen could have been ducking in front of Goetz and received the wound he had sustained. Becker stated that was within the realm of possiblity.

Waples then asked on redirect, "Are there a whole range of possibilities of [Allen's] possible position, in relation to the gun, which could inflict that wound?"

"Yes," Becker answered. He also stated, "I wasn't there. I don't pretend to know."

June 8

Waples later called Dr. Charles Hirsch, the chief medical examiner of Suffolk County, as his final rebuttal witness. Hirsch also disagreed with DiMaio's testimony about the angle of the bullet that hit Barry Allen and then went on to contradict DiMaio concerning Darrell Cabey.

"In your opinion, Doctor, is it possible, in light of the wound you have diagnosed Darrell Cabey suffered in his back, . . . for that wound to have been inflicted upon Darrell Cabey while he was sitting in a subway seat . . . ?"

"Under certain circumstances, yes, sir," Hirsch answered. "The most essential circumstance is that his body would have been rotated slightly towards his right side, or at least the upper part of his body . . . That would make available to the shooter the target of the outer left side of his back. Beyond that, the relationship of the shooter to Mr. Cabey is governed by the range of fire and the height from which the gun was fired—whether it was fired at hip height or shoulder height, or something else—in order for the bullet to take a perfectly flat course or nearly flat course across the left side of his back before striking his spine. There are countless possible relationships that one could construct between the seated target and the standing assailant."

Hirsch then demonstrated the necessary twisting motion Cabey's upper body would have to have made, using the torso of a female mannequin as a visual aid. He reiterated, "I can't think of a single position that would make [it] impossible" for Cabey to have been shot while seated if Goetz had been standing anywhere within a quarter-circle arc to Cabey's left. "That is all there is to it," Hirsch proclaimed.

He also stated that he had read DiMaio's testimony, and when Waples asked him about the part where DiMaio had said it was "impossible" that Cabey could have been seated when shot, Hirsch said, "I disagree."

"And how strong is your disagreement, sir?"

"Objection," Slotnick offered, laryngitically.

"Overruled," said Justice Crane.

"As strong as I can [make it]," Hirsch then answered, "because it is, in my opinion, completely false."

Beyond this, however, Hirsch could do no more to lend credence to the prosecution's contention about how Cabey was shot, and this was the big weakness in Waples's case.

"Are you saying, sir, that in your opinion Darrell Cabey *was* sitting down when he was shot, then?" Waples asked.

"No, sir. That is not my opinion," Hirsch answered.

"Okay," Waples conceded. "Are you saying that that is consistent with Darrell Cabey sitting down?"

"That is correct," Hirsch said.

Hirsch asserted that Cabey "could have been standing up when shot," and stated, "I know of no way to distinguish between those two possibilities. There is—Simply on the basis of physical evidence, there is no way to do it."

"Other evidence would have to establish that, if it could?" Waples asked.

"That is correct," Hirsch said.

There was quite a bit of animosity between Hirsch and Slotnick during cross-examination. Slotnick did his best to phrase his questions in specific ways designed to make Hirsch appear to contradict himself, usually demanding yes or no answers, but Hirsch proved also to be quite clever, and would not fall into Slotnick's traps.

During one exchange, for instance, Hirsch said to Slotnick, while looking toward us, "I'm not trying to be difficult in answering your question. I don't want to give you carte blanche."

"Could you speak to me, if you could?" Slotnick responded.

"I prefer to speak to the jury, sir," Hirsch replied.

On one occasion when Slotnick demanded a yes or no answer, Hirsch responded, "Yes *and* no." Another time Hirsch said, "The answer cannot be given in a yes or no."

"Then I withdraw the question, Doctor," Slotnick said.

The only mildly successful attack Slotnick made was his questioning of why Hirsch had been called to testify from Suffolk County. He inferred that Waples had spoken to other New York City medical examiners who had disagreed with the opinion Hirsch was now espousing, but this could not be substantiated; and, after all, Slotnick had brought in Dr. Yudwitz, the neuropsychiatrist, from Massachusetts, so Slotnick should hardly have been one to talk.

In all, then, despite Slotnick's great singing and dancing abilities, he did nothing in his cross-examination to lessen the impact of Dr. Hirsch's testimony, which in my mind very much undermined the testimonies of Dr. DiMaio and Joseph Quirk. While they were obviously experts in their fields, I felt that both had slanted their testimonies toward the defense beyond what could be supported on factual grounds. In hindsight, however, the two men proved to have been extremely effective defense witnesses, having raised enough ballistic and medical questions to augment our sense of reasonable doubt.

Chapter 14

Late Evidence and Nonevidence

The testimonies of Quirk, DiMaio, Becker, and Hirsch dominated the last ten days of the trial, before both sides rested their cases and final arguments began. During that span, however, we did hear from two other witnesses, and we went on a field trip to explore a subway car that was virtually identical to the one in which the shootings occurred.

The visit to the subway car had been requested by the defense as a way to make our understanding of the crime scene more vivid. In open-court proceedings out of our presence, Slotnick argued that the car was "the most important piece of evidence in this case," explaining that the justification for Goetz's actions ultimately lay in the "positioning and confinements, surroundings and circumstances" that took place within that car. "The district attorney's office has attempted to draw a sketch," Slotnick said to Justice Crane, referring to the scale-model drawing of the subway car that was People's exhibit one in this case. "It's a terrific sketch, Judge, but it doesn't replace the real thing. . . . I know there is a counterargument . . . that these jurors are average New Yorkers and they are aware of what subway cars look like. Fortunately, in 1987, some of the lines have different subway cars than they did in 1984."

Slotnick contended that the more cramped quarters of the older-style car in which the shootings had occurred had to be seen firsthand to be fully appreciated. "You cannot get the same feeling" otherwise, he stated, adding that the photographs of the car submitted as evidence by the prosecution also "do not do the subway car justice."

215

Waples opposed the visit as procedurally "awkward," "time-consuming," and "unnecessary."

"It's basically a question of real necessity, of real value," Waples said. "Is it really necessary to go to these subway cars to allow the jury to visualize the spacial relationships that are involved in this case, the sight lines and so forth? I don't think so. We have sketches that everybody seems to have agreed are adequate for their purposes. We have photographs, plenty of photographs, of all angles of the subway car which were taken that day, not two and a half years later. And we also have a jury that is endowed with common sense and experience in riding subways. Quite a bit more experience than Mr. Slotnick has.

"It's not necessary, in my view, to transport all of these people to a subway . . . car, to allow them to feel what it is like to sit in a subway car and have other persons around you. That is something we all know about."

That morning, however, the judge and the attorneys had gone through the subway train it was proposed that we visit, and Justice Crane had apparently been surprised by several of the spacial relationships inside the car. He mentioned specifically that he had previously believed that the dent made by the bullet in the steel panel on the side of the conductor's cab had been "much higher" from the floor than it actually was. This perhaps suggested to him that the shot might have been aimed at a seated target. Justice Crane, though, said only, "[I]t went through my mind that part of the demonstration that was going on on the train this morning undercut portions of the defense's case. I won't elaborate on that."

Since Waples was not contending that the visit would prejudice his case, and since the defense was so adamant that it was a necessary part of theirs, Justice Crane capitulated to a "silent visit."

"No one will address the jurors while they are aboard," Justice Crane said. Meanwhile we would be free to move about the car—"sit, stand and look about"—as long as we wished, exploring for ourselves the various seat positions and sight angles in the car. Justice Crane explained to us later that the purpose of the visit was to "make more meaningful . . . the testimony you have heard" and "to assist you in understanding the dimensions and configurations" of the car. "It is intended to be an aid to your understanding and nothing more," he said.

⚖

May 29

The visit took place on a Friday, after the first day of Joseph Quirk's testimony, and concluded the trial proceedings for that week. We drove a few blocks in the same minibuses that took us home after we delivered our verdict, then entered the Chambers Street station of the BMT J line, going down a few flights of stairs to a platform that had long been closed to the public and boarding an eight-car train, six of the eight cars being the same R-22 model as the one in which the shootings occurred.

We first sat for a while in one car, listening as Justice Crane gave us some preliminary instructions, and at the same time watching all the commotion outside. On the platform several dozen reporters and photographers pressed against the car's windows, watching us and taking pictures. It was an extremely distracting scene and interesting in that none of us had ever been the target of so much media attention, but we also felt like fish in an aquarium with so many people looking in at us through the glass.

After about five minutes of this, the train pulled out from the station so we could concentrate on what we were there for and move around the car without an audience. The judge; the court reporter; and the attorneys, court officers, and members of the transit police who were all present with us exited then to another car, leaving us to do our investigating alone. Goetz himself, I should mention, had been excused from this proceeding and was not present. Justice Crane told us that we were not to infer anything from that fact.

Even though no talking was allowed, there still was a certain amount of communication going on through eye contact and even hand signals at times. We took turns playing the roles of the people who had been on the train; and I remember, for instance, sitting in the "Cabey" seat when another juror—Bob Leach, I think—came up and pointed his finger at me, portraying Goetz. I then demonstrated to him how I thought Cabey might have twisted in the seat to receive the bullet at the proper angle.

I and most of the other jurors made a point of sitting and standing in every position that we remembered somebody testifying to having been in or to having seen someone in, and that included going into the adjacent car and sitting where Sally Smithern said she had been, to try to determine what she might have been able to see.

Much of this, I thought, proved pretty inconclusive. I didn't think Smithern could have seen much of anything except perhaps Goetz's upper body if he had stood directly in front of the "Cabey" seat as Christopher Boucher had testified. But as for all the other eyewitnesses, everything they said they saw seemed within the realm of possibility, although views could have easily been obscured by people standing or moving around in the car.

I was impressed, however, by the narrowness of the subway car and how little space there was between the rows of seats on either side of the aisle. Although I had for many years been a frequent subway rider, being in this old-style car while contemplating the testimony I'd heard and imagining the situation that Goetz had faced did have a definite effect on me. I realized that even if only one or two of the youths had been standing in front of him with the intention of attacking him, Goetz had no real room to escape. And I also saw that while Goetz was firing at Canty, he was extremely vulnerable to an attack if Cabey or Ramseur had tried to jump him: his back was turned to them and they couldn't have been more than a few feet away.

In our deliberations both of these factors proved to be extremely important considerations; and so, although it was awkward and the situation circuslike, being very much a media event, the subway car visit was in fact very valuable, winning some crucial points for the defense.

June 2

Slotnick's last witness was Charles Penelton, a former transit police detective who was assigned to the department's major case unit at the time of the shootings. Penelton testified that two days afterward, on December 24, he went with Detective Clark to interview Troy Canty in his room at St. Vincent's Hospital, specifically because Penelton was black and Canty had been refusing to speak to white officers and detectives.

"We got to the hospital, Detective Clark left the room, and Mr. Canty said, 'I know why you're here. . . . You're a brother,' " Penelton stated. "I said, 'Yes, I'm a brother. You want to tell me what happened?' at which time he hesitated. I got up; I was going to leave the room. He said, 'No, I'll talk.'

"I asked him, 'What happened?' So he said that, 'We got on the train at 149th Street and Third Avenue, going downtown,' and the conversation started to lag at that time. So, I asked him—you know, told him to go ahead. So he says—I said, 'Where the white guy [get] on the train at?' 'The white guy got on the train at Fourteenth Street.'

"I says, 'Then what happened?' He said, 'He went to the middle of the train. He sat down.' He said, 'The doors closed. We got up and we went over and stood around the white guy.' I said, 'All of you?' He said, 'All of us.'

"Then what happened, I asked him, 'Why you pick on that guy?' 'The guy looked soft.' 'What do you mean, gay?' He said, 'No, soft.' Nothing else was said then."

"Your witness," Slotnick said to Waples.

Waples's cross-examination was brief. Penelton had taken notes when he'd interviewed Canty, so Waples did not challenge the veracity of his testimony. Rather, he used this fact to further criticize Officer Smith. "[T]he reason you made notes was because your memory is not perfect, and without notes you couldn't be certain of exact words . . . , is that right?" Waples asked.

"That is correct, yes," Penelton replied.

"That is why you made notes? That is why most officers make notes, right?"

"That is correct."

The gist of Waples's cross-examination was that Canty was heavily sedated at the time this five-to-ten-minute interview took place. According to hospital records, Canty had been given doses of Demerol and Vistaril approximately fifteen minutes before he spoke with Penelton, and Waples had previously questioned Dr. Adams about these drugs and their effects. Adams had explained that Demerol is "a painkiller" and that Vistaril "is a drug used for psychotic, neurotic disorders and also used to potentiate the effect of narcotic medication . . . Essentially it increases its strength and action."

"As a matter of medical practice, Dr. Adams, would you ever base any medical treatment upon information that you obtained from a patient who was under the influence of Demerol and Vistaril in combination?" Waples had asked.

"No, I would not," Adams had said, explaining that a patient in that condition is not considered "reliable" and "may make inaccurate statements."

"What about historical facts, memory?"

"Memory may be disturbed," Adams had answered.

Waples asked Penelton, "When you spoke to Troy Canty, he told you that he wanted the five dollars to put in the video machines, didn't he?"

"He didn't tell me what he wanted the five dollars for. He merely said he asked the guy to borrow five dollars," Penelton said.

"And he didn't say anything at all about robbing, did he?"

"Not to me, no."

"When you first went in to speak with him, he was extremely drowsy, right?"

"He was drowsy, yes."

"And during your brief interview, he kept closing his eyes?"

"That is correct."

"And, in fact, when you were talking with him he was talking in such a low voice, such a low audible tone at times, you had to bend down and almost put your ear next to his mouth to even hear, is that correct?"

"Had to bend over sometimes when he was talking, yes," Penelton answered.

"And at that time he was in bed, yes?"

"That is correct, yes."

"And he certainly appeared to you to be drugged, didn't he?"

"Yes."

"In fact, during portions of your interview, he was nodding off to sleep?"

"He closed his eyes, yes."

"And, in fact, your interview ended when he nodded off to sleep and you left, right?"

"That is correct," Penelton said.

When he was excused from the stand, Justice Crane informed us that Penelton's testimony, like that of the grand jury stenographer, Vincent Palumbo, "has been admitted at this point solely for the purpose of proving a prior inconsistent statement of the previous witness, Troy Canty. . . . [T]he statement itself is not evidence-in-chief or proof of the facts contained in the out-of-court statements. It may be considered by you only for the purpose of determining the believability of Troy Canty."

This, of course, lessened the importance of Penelton's testimony. Canty's credibility had been undermined long ago.

June 5

Waples's other rebuttal witness was Officer Dennis Driscoll, who had been Officer Smith's partner at the time of the shootings and had accompanied Smith onto the train. Driscoll testified that he was directly behind Smith as they entered the car where they found the youths, and that he—not Smith—had first approached and spoken to the person we knew to be Troy Canty. Driscoll said that while he was with Canty, Smith "was speaking to the person directly to the left on the bench." That person, we knew, was Barry Allen.

Driscoll then approached Darrell Cabey, who, he said, was in "very unstable" condition, "seated upright with his head slumped down. He didn't talk. He didn't move or make any comment."

Waples asked Driscoll what Smith was doing while he attended to Cabey.

"He was still behind me, talking, I guess, with the guy lying on the bench."

"At any point, did you see Police Officer Smith address or administer to another individual in the car?"

"I didn't see him," Driscoll said.

"What about with respect to the second person on that floor [i.e., James Ramseur]?"

"He had approached the second person on the floor just as I was finishing talking to the other guy slumped in the seat."

Waples later concluded by asking, "Officer Driscoll, did you ever, at any time, see Police Officer Smith talking in any way to Troy Canty?"

"No. Not that I remember," Driscoll replied.

Slotnick began cross-examination on the same tack Waples had used against Smith, asking Driscoll, "You were excited; your adrenaline was flowing; there may have been a person with a gun you might encounter?"

The major point Slotnick made was that for the two minutes or so that Driscoll was attending to Cabey, his back was turned and he could not see what Smith was doing, leaving open the possibility that Smith had approached Canty. Furthermore, Driscoll said that as he stood up and left Canty, "I told Officer Smith that he was having a hard time breathing . . . ," thus giving Smith a possible motive for speaking to Canty.

In redirect, Waples made the point that Driscoll had not entered in his memo book "anything concerning any admission by any of the four people who were shot to the effect that they were trying to rob the guy." But in recross Slotnick asked, "[D]id you make any notations in your memo book surrounding any conversation you had with Police Officer Smith?"

"No, sir," Driscoll answered.

"Assuming Police Officer Smith had gotten a statement from one of the people on the floor . . . and you hadn't heard it, would you have written it down in your memo book?" Slotnick followed.

"No, sir," Driscoll said.

Waples objected to that question and answer. Justice Crane, however, overruled.

The prosecution's rebuttal case constituted the last of the testimony we heard. What remained before we could deliberate was each side's closing argument and then Justice Crane's charge to us, explaining the factors and parameters of the law.

Before I detail the closing arguments, though, I'll quickly mention some of the legal arguments made out of the jury's presence, both in open court and at the sidebar, that I have learned of since the trial. I have already mentioned, for instance, that the defense offered a motion to dismiss the case against Goetz on the basis of the prosecution's failure to call Garth Reid to testify before either grand jury, and that that motion was subsequently denied.

The defense made several other motions and applications during the course of the trial. Concerning Barry Allen, they first requested that the judge compel Waples to confer immunity upon Allen after he had appeared in court and had invoked his Fifth Amendment privileges. If Allen had been granted immunity, then he, like Ramseur, would have been forced to testify in our presence. "[W]hat is being violated is the defendant's Sixth Amendment right to confront . . . those who accuse him of egregious acts and criminality," Mark Baker argued. Slotnick contended that Waples "has an obligation to be fair" in his prosecution of Goetz, but that Waples was behaving as if he were a defense lawyer for the youths.

In fact, Slotnick said, "Mr. Waples is acting as a terrific defense lawyer, and I think that eventually, when the call of financial need, and his understanding that he has done his public service [arrives], he will do very well . . . because he has proven himself quite adequate and an excellent defense lawyer in this case.

"I am, however, being deprived of the ability to cross-examine, obviously, Barry Allen. Mr. Waples is—most respectfully, and I think—I'm trying to temper the term, I don't want to say playing games—but I really think he's manipulating the ends of justice by not doing what he has a right to do, and which I think Your Honor has an absolute right to direct, which is to immunize Mr. Allen . . . I think—candidly, Judge—that this makes a mockery out of the due process rights my client should be afforded."

Waples, however, argued, "The issue here is whether the defense has a right to compel a prosecutor to give a witness the defense wants to cross-examine immunity, so that the prosecutor will be required to call him as part of the People's case. . . . There is no authority for that. The prosecutor has absolute discretion, I believe, as long as he's acting in good faith, not to give him immunity."

Slotnick was really trying to play on both sides of the fence here. On the one hand, in the cases of Canty and Ramseur, he implied to us that the district attorney's office had purchased their testimony at the cost of immunity. Out of our presence, though, he was insisting that immunity to Allen be given.

"The defense is trying to rewrite the Sixth Amendment . . . ," Waples contended. "As far as I recall, the Sixth Amendment merely guarantees the defense a right to cross-examine witnesses who are called by the prosecution. [I]t does not contemplate a right to force the prosecutor to call any particular witness."

Justice Crane called the defense's claim of a Sixth Amendment violation "a very novel argument" and asked Waples if there was a substantial distinction between Canty and Ramseur, on the one hand, who had been granted immunity, and Allen, on the other. Waples said there was, although Slotnick contended, "The only difference between Barry Allen and Messrs. Canty and Ramseur is that those two individuals were willing to perjure themselves [before] a grand jury and this witness was not."

Justice Crane ruled that "it's up to the prosecutor" what witnesses he calls, "at the risk, of course, of a trial order of dismissal, or any other parade of horribles that takes place when a prosecutor falls short of the mark. . . . The real violation here, again, would be a due process violation if there is an indication Mr. Allen has substantial . . . material exculpatory evidence to give, and the prosecutor decides then to continue in the posture of withholding a request for immunity. . . .

"I don't see any authority for me to directly demand that the prosecutor grant immunity . . . I don't control his strategy, and he has full and complete experience to know what ramifications occur if his case falls short."

Later, the defense applied for a dismissal of the charges against Goetz concerning Barry Allen and James Ramseur, because of Allen's invocation of the Fifth Amendment and Ramseur's failure to complete his testimony, thereby depriving Goetz of his Sixth Amendment rights. This application was also denied.

In addition, the defense asked for all thirteen counts of the indictment to be dismissed and for the trial to be halted in filing a "Motion To Dismiss for the People's Failure To Prove a *Prima Facie* Case," claiming that "the evidence is legally insufficient to support the offenses charged, or any lesser included offenses." This motion was made on May 21, after the prosecution had rested its case, and was argued by both sides in open court.

Concerning the "Myra" gun counts, the defense claimed that Goetz did not possess the two guns once they were in Myra Friedman's apartment. Mark Baker argued that Goetz "had given them to Myra Friedman to dispose of them" and that Goetz had "forfeited all dominion and control when he had asked Miss Friedman to get rid of those guns." Therefore, Baker said, "As a matter of law, possession is not established . . .

"Now, let's get to the main course, and why we've been here: attempted murder, assault, and reckless endangerment in the first degree," Baker continued. "I submit to the Court, to these offenses, as a matter of law, justification has not been disproved. . . .

"The key to this case and the prosecution's utter failure of proof is summed up in two words: rapid succession. Mr. Slotnick and I agree that if there is ever anything written about this trial . . . , the only title is *Rapid Succession*."

Baker then went ahead and made most of the points Slotnick would later make to us in his closing argument, the essential point being that the eyewitnesses had testified that the shots had been fired too quickly for Goetz to have had time to reassess the danger to himself that had led him to draw his weapon and to commence firing; all of the eyewitnesses, that is, except Christopher Boucher. And, Baker said, "If the People have produced no witnesses to undermine the defendant's version that he was surrounded by these four—and his statement is clear, two on his left, two on his right—then his beliefs as a matter of law cannot be demonstrated to have been unreasonable. . . . No witness puts the four victims in any place different immediately prior to these shootings than where the defendant had put them."

Baker concluded by announcing, "This case should be sent back to the junk heap where the first grand jury consigned it and from where the district attorney retained the likes of its champagne witness, Canty. I submit to the Court, Your Honor should dismiss it and bring this travesty of justice to a grinding halt."

Waples's counterargument concerning "the legal sufficiency" of the attempted murder and assault counts against Goetz was simply that, "[b]y the defendant's own admission, he shot them with the intent to kill and to maim. . . . Concerning the question of justification, that is a classic jury question," Waples went on. "There are significant and substantial questions presented by the evidence concerning whether the defendant reasonably believed that he was about to be mercilessly attacked by these four individuals, and even more substantial and grave questions concerning the reasonableness of his belief that it was necessary to fire one shot to deter this threat, much less five shots, as he did. The defendant's statements alone prove the People's case that these shootings were without justification. . . .

"In addition, . . . none of the eyewitness testimony corroborates the defendant's claim that he was closely surrounded by four persons," Waples added, refuting the defense's contentions. "None of them corroborate in any degree his claim that he was about to be beaten within an inch of his life. . . .

"With respect to the two counts of criminal possession of a weapon in the fourth degree, Myra Friedman's guns, I don't think there's any evidence that the defendant abandoned the guns when he gave them to Myra Friedman. In any event, he certainly possessed them when he brought them to her apartment.

"I need say nothing more, Your Honor. . . . The People have made a legally sufficient—far in excess of the legally sufficient case, and it's up to the jury to decide what to do with this."

Obviously, since the trial continued and we did indeed deliberate, all of the defense's motions to dismiss the case were denied.

Justice Crane also ruled against allowing into evidence any statements Darrell Cabey had made after the incident: first, to the paramedic John Filangeri; second, to a detective several hours later in the hospital, in which he had stated, "I don't know why I hung out with the others. They always get into trouble"; third, the next day to Detective Clark, "to the effect that Mr. Cabey was going to lower Manhattan, Mr. Ramseur was taking him for a job," and that "Barry Allen went over with Troy Canty and Troy asked for the money," according to Justice Crane; and fourth, in November 1985, while still in the hospital, to *Daily News* columnist Jimmy Breslin, in which, Justice Crane summarized, "Cabey said he sat down a couple of seats away and wasn't with [the other three], and that they thought he looked like easy bait, he looked like he had money. They asked him for five dollars. They didn't use any screwdrivers and . . . they were going to rob the defendant by just scaring him."

In all of these cases Justice Crane explained that the statements were made against Darrell Cabey's penal interest, that they were falsely exculpatory and "admissions of participation demonstrated by extrinsic facts." As such, Justice Crane said, "Since Mr. Cabey is not a party to this action [i.e., a defendant], the evidentiary basis for the proffer of these statements is lacking . . ."

The statements did not qualify, therefore, as exceptions to the rules against hearsay; and so the only way the defense could have offered them before the jury would have been if they could have called Cabey as a witness. Slotnick, remember, stated in his opening that he would call as witnesses any of the youths that Waples failed to make take the stand. He reneged on that promise, however. Cabey was adjudged to be unfit to testify; and Slotnick ultimately decided not to call Allen. Without the district attorney's grant of immunity, Allen could still have taken the Fifth and have been shielded from having to field Slotnick's questions. The defense settled instead, therefore, on the judge's decision to declare Allen a missing witness in his instructions to us before we deliberated.

"There is no duty on any party to call any particular person as a witness," Justice Crane told us then. "However, if you find that a witness was in a position to give relevant evidence on the side of the People, and that the People offered no reasonable explanation for failing to call such witness, you may infer, if you deem it proper to do so, that the testimony of the uncalled person would not contradict the opposing evidence or would not support that part of the People's version of the case on which the uncalled witness was in a position to testify. In this light, you may consider the failure of the People to call Barry Allen, whose absense or unavailability they have failed to adequately explain. If you wish, you may draw an inference that Allen's testimony would not have been favorable to the People."

Justice Crane also discussed in his predeliberation instructions to us the fact that Goetz never took the stand. "The defendant did not testify in this case," Justice Crane said. "I charge you that the fact that he did not testify is not a factor from which any inference unfavorable to the defendant may be drawn."

Concerning why Goetz did not testify, Slotnick told the media after the trial that the jury had seen and heard enough from Goetz through the playing of his taped statements and that there was little more that Goetz could have added beyond what he'd said on the tapes. Later, Mark Baker told me of the defense's belief that Goetz could not have withstood the intense cross-examination Waples would have mounted against him.

Goetz's role in the courtroom, then, was reduced to that of an observer. He watched silently while the drama of the trial unfolded before him, as the attorneys grappled with the witnesses and with each other over legal points. I thought about this as the trial wound down and made the following addendum to my May 28 diary entry, the first day of the testimony of Joseph Quirk:

> It's funny, but Goetz has almost been invisible in court. I mean, he's here every day, sitting at the defense table, but he doesn't react much. I did see him squirm a bit and look uncomfortable today, though, as Quirk's "scientific" analysis of how he shot four people was being played out in the courtroom before him. Sometimes, though, I almost forget about him even being a part of these proceedings, and he seems to fade behind the witnesses and the lawyers in importance.

Today—as I watched the lawyers and the judge arguing over things and with us sitting there and all the people in the courtroom—for the first time I started wondering how Goetz is feeling about this whole thing. And I found myself thinking back to those comments he made in his audiotaped statement where he said he didn't want the lawyers going through this with a microscope, et cetera, and, boy, they sure are doing that now. He'd also talked about not wanting a circus, and how he wished what was happening was just a dream. "But it's not," he'd said, and he got that right. I guess in a lot of ways this whole thing is like Goetz's worst nightmare come to life.

Chapter 15

The Defense's Summation

June 10

The closing arguments marked the beginning of the jury's sequestration, so we came to court with our bags packed, bringing clothing to last at least four days, according to the judge's instructions. By the end I had wished I had more clothing, though; the four-day estimate proved to be entirely wishful thinking. Perhaps the judge was not aware that each side's argument would run over four hours and take up a full day of our attention. Justice Crane's charge to us on the law didn't come until the morning of the third day, therefore, and the charge itself lasted over three hours, taking us well into the afternoon.

Nobody could be accused of unduly elongating the proceedings, however. Both attorneys' presentations contained some pretty high-charged rhetoric, but they also had a lot of ground to cover, with over six weeks of testimony and an indictment of thirteen separate counts.

The closing arguments also were extremely important in our understanding of the evidence. Spaced out over so long a period, there was no way that we could assimilate all of the testimony that we had heard. Thus there was a lot at stake; and each side's argument proved very effective, condensing all the evidence into a single day's speech.

Slotnick went first, laryngitis and all. He told me after the trial that he had been coached by a voice teacher over the weekend on how to get through this without losing his voice entirely. There was a microphone for him on a stand near the jury box that he used throughout his summation, although he often took it off the stand so that he could pace around the well of the courtroom. His voice was raspy, and especially toward the lunch break he clearly struggled to talk loud enough to be heard. It was also clear, though, that he was aware his condition added pathos to his speech, and he milked that for all it was worth.

"Your Honor, Mark Baker, Investigator King, members of the jury," he began, "we started this case in the courtroom listening to openings. We ended up in the subway car and we came back to the courtroom. We have watched, listened to over forty witnesses. We have seen many exhibits. And now, I come back full circle to where I was some two months ago.

"When I first opened to you two months ago—that was after listening to Mr. Waples's opening—there were several promises that I made to you. . . . I promised you that I would come back and look you directly in your eyes and ask you to acquit Bernhard Goetz, and I would do it with an honesty and integrity that you have seen in the courtroom. I promised that I would come back and tell you that the prosecution had no case against him to begin with, and . . . , as a result of that, you must find the defendant not guilty.

"I also made another promise to you. I promised you that when I came back I would reread the basic openings that Mr. Waples made to you to show you that even the district attorney, two-and-a-half years after the event, had no idea what this case is about; and I'm going to do that.

"I warn you now: it will be long; it will be tedious; hopefully it will be not that educational because you will have seen it. But I must do it. So I will start now, as I promised you, with Mr. Waples's opening. And the reason that I go about it this way is again to show you clearly that the prosecution's . . . burden that they have indicated to you, one, has not been sustained, and two, that their theory of the case was totally wrong and they looked at it from an improper prospective.

"Mr. Waples opened by asserting to you . . . that there were two things that he was going to prove—two things which would cause you to convict Bernhard Goetz. One, . . . he talked to you about a fifth shot that was fired [at] point-blank range into Darrell Cabey. . . . But the most important thing he told you—and I read from his opening—because it's all wrong and the theory of the case was all wrong, and we were caused to bring people here to show you that it was all wrong— he said to you, 'In fact, you'll hear from medical evidence that two of the four young men who the defendant shot were shot in their backs, one squarely in the center of his back as he tried to flee.' He's referring to Barry Allen. And I tell you now, succinctly—and I'll go into a bit more later on—that Barry Allen was not shot squarely in the back while trying to flee."

Slotnick then discussed the testimony of Joseph Quirk and the location of Allen's wound, declaring that if Allen had been shot as Waples had stated, "he would have had his spinal cord severed and he wouldn't have been able to come here and cooperate with the district attorney and take pictures. By the way," he added, "this is the same Barry Allen who they had the cooperation of [and] the power and authority [over] to put on the witness stand but did not. And this is the same Barry Allen that, the judge will tell you, you must assume that he wasn't called because he would testify adversely to the district attorney's case."

"Objection, Your Honor," Waples said.

"That is sustained, and the jurors are admonished to disregard the remarks and listen to my charge on the subject when it comes down," said Justice Crane.

"I'll tell you, listen to the judge's charge, and I argue to you now that Barry Allen was in this building cooperating with the district attorney's office, was available to him," Slotnick continued. "They did not call him, and you can infer that had they called him, his testimony would have hurt their case."

Slotnick continued to emphasize the evidence concerning Allen's wound, insisting that he had to have been shot "over the back" when ducking. Though the physical evidence, I felt, proved only that the shot did not hit Allen "squarely," Slotnick persisted that this was a crucial point.

"So please understand the significance of it because Mr. Waples knows what his burden must prove to you: that Barry Allen was shot squarely in the center of the back as he tried to flee. Not only does he have to prove that to you, but he's got to prove that to you beyond a reasonable doubt."

"Justice, that is incorrect," Waples objected.

Justice Crane called the attorneys up for a sidebar and then announced to us, "The instructions on the law, of course, you'll take from the Court. But what has to be proven will be in terms of elements of crimes. If there is a deviation from what was told to you on the opening, and you attach significance to the location of the shot, that is up to you. Mr. Slotnick is urging you to do so, but as to the elements that have to be proven and the standard of proof beyond a reasonable doubt, you'll take that information from me, and to that extent I would sustain the objection. Please proceed, Mr. Slotnick."

Slotnick moved on then to Darrell Cabey, and here the point he wanted to make was simpler. He quoted Waples's opening, where Waples had said, "The evidence will show . . . , beyond the slightest shadow of a doubt, that when the defendant fired the second of these shots at Cabey, Darrell Cabey was sitting down in the subway seat . . ."

"Now, those are his words, his commitment to you in his opening; what he has to prove, his theory of the case . . . ," Slotnick said, somewhat smugly. "I suggest that not only does he have a problem with 'the slightest shadow of a doubt,' as he said to you in his opening, but he hasn't proved to you in any manner, form, or shape whatsoever that Darrell Cabey was shot while sitting down."

To support this he briefly mentioned the testimony of Dr. DiMaio and contended that Waples had purposefully avoided asking Dr. Becker, the prosecution's radiology expert, whether Cabey could have been shot while seated, because Becker would have also agreed it was impossible. Slotnick also criticized Waples's use of Dr. Hirsch, a medical examiner from Suffolk County, reiterating his inference that Waples had first consulted New York City medical examiners who could not support Waples's theories. "I wonder if Dr. Hirsch in Suffolk County weren't available, where he would have gone for another person like him," Slotnick mused.

After this early emphasis on the expert testimony concerning how Allen and Cabey were shot, Slotnick centered his argument around the contention that all the shots had been fired in rapid succession, with Goetz standing in one location and merely pivoting as he aimed. Slotnick focused on the fact that every eyewitness except Christopher Boucher had testified that the shots occurred in one quick cluster, that they did not hear a pause before the final shot, and they did not see Goetz standing in front of Cabey. He referred specifically to Garth Reid's statement that the shootings occurred in "a snap of time" and Armando Soler's estimate that the shots were fired in "about a second." He mentioned also Joseph Quirk's having testified that "one-and-a-half seconds" was the amount of time it would have taken for Goetz to have fired without hesitation and emptied his gun.

"The fact of the matter is that Armando Soler tells us that it was in rapid succession, which is a major key in this case in terms of how and why Bernhard Goetz did what he did," Slotnick said.

Goetz, he asserted, was in danger and was surrounded and merely unloaded his weapon as quickly as he could. Slotnick referred to Dr. Yudwitz's testimony about the autonomic nervous system to explain Goetz's firing in rapid succession: Goetz had a rush of adrenaline, his mind switched on to "automatic pilot," his body was in control and remained in control until all of his bullets were gone. Slotnick contended, therefore, that Goetz had no chance to reassess his situation, much less the time to move toward Cabey, and also that the youths had no time to flee.

The two crucial presuppositions to the defense's "rapid succession" hypothesis that Slotnick sought to support were, first, that Goetz was justified in feeling threatened, that his assessment of the situation was correct and the danger real; and, second, that Goetz had been surrounded by the youths, who had acted in concert, all as a group. He did this with gusto.

"There is no question that Bernhard Goetz was surrounded by four people [who] meant him ill," Slotnick asserted. "But the issue at hand . . . for you to consider [is] did Bernhard Goetz believe that he was about to be robbed, that he was about to be mugged, that he was about to be injured? I trust, if you respond 'yes' to that question, you can all rapidly go home."

Concerning the danger Goetz said he sensed, Slotnick again quoted from Waples's opening: "Undoubtedly some passengers may have been annoyed by the rowdy behavior of these teenagers, but that's all it was, an annoyance to more gentle sensibilities."

Slotnick contrasted this with the testimonies of the eyewitnesses, which he exaggerated, particularly in the case of Josephine Holt. Referring to Waples, Slotnick said, "Did he not know that Josephine Holt would come and say that she was scared to death? That the Reids were going to tell you about the fear that they had? That Andrea Reid was telling you that she was afraid they were going to come over to her and her child? That Mary Gant was cowering in fear? What about Bernie Goetz, [who] was surrounded? Is that what you tell a jury asking to convict somebody, that all it was was 'an annoyance to more gentle sensibilities'? Was I in a different courtroom? Were we all in different courtrooms? Didn't we hear the fear that these witnesses on the subway had? . . . Let us not be shanghaied by the rhetoric of an assistant district attorney who tells you not to be swayed by 'rowdy behavior' that was 'an annoyance to more gentle sensibilities.' "

Slotnick keyed on Andrea Reid to substantiate the notion that the eyewitnesses were afraid. He referred to her as "a very sad witness . . . , a woman who is waiting to become a police officer. She sat on that witness stand, scared to death, . . . [a]nd she was willing to throw it all out the window because she was so afraid of the Cabey boy.

"She came here, and for Bernhard Goetz I say thank God I sent John Barna to tape her, because she came here and lied. She came here and lied, and we will forgive her for that and so will everybody because we understand why she did it. She did it out of fear, and I guess she did it out of necessity. She took the witness stand and she told you all sorts of things that she later recanted and realized she was wrong. And she ultimately told you why she did it, and I would like you to please try to relate her to Bernhard Goetz."

Slotnick several times repeated Reid's comment to her husband on the day of the shootings that the youths "got what they deserved," calling this "the most important part of her testimony. She told us that from what she saw on the subway car they all—'They got what they deserved,' and it is our position that, for Bernhard Goetz, they received what the law allowed.

* * *

"Andrea Reid, who was a witness to the event. Andrea Reid, who saw what happened, who sat here on the witness stand, fearful, in total trauma, told you that her first reaction was, 'They got what they deserved.' It's pretty strong words from a witness who saw exactly what happened."

Reid lied, Slotnick said, when she testified that she wasn't sure the "white man" she told her husband the "four punks" were "hassling" was Goetz. She also lied about what she saw the youths doing before Goetz fired, Slotnick argued, and about how many of the youths she saw standing around Goetz.

"She is deathly afraid," Slotnick stated. "She doesn't want to be labeled as telling somebody something that helps Bernhard Goetz because she is worried about Darrell Cabey's family, but that's no excuse. I am worried about and the system worries about Bernhard Goetz."

Slotnick's other tack in arguing that Goetz was in a fearful situation was to discuss the natures of Canty and Ramseur. "Troy Canty," he said, "came here all spiffed up in a nice suit telling us things that were absolutely and totally untrue." He ridiculed Canty's testimony, asking us to see through it, which, of course, we already had. "I think he said 'I don't remember' to me about two hundred times," Slotnick said, and also criticized Canty's frequent answer, "That's what I remembered then," calling it "a statement tailored by lawyers so you don't have your client committing perjury." He also mocked the district attorney's grant of immunity to Canty, asking, "Immunity from what? Immunity from panhandling?"

Slotnick went all through Canty's criminal history, calling him "someone who was freebasing drugs, who was a thief, who was a criminal, and who was the leader of a group." He spent less time on Ramseur, referring to him merely as Canty's friend "whose testimony was stricken, but who you had a good look at. You saw the fear and hate and anger that radiated out of him when surrounded by court officers. Can you imagine what he looked like when he surrounded Bernhard Goetz with three of his other friends?"

Referring to Goetz's prior mugging, Slotnick argued that the youths were engaged in the same kind of group conduct as those who had beaten up Goetz in 1981. He referred to them as a "gang of four," the same phrase he had used for them in his opening, and said that Goetz "had no obligation to allow that to happen again."

"It was not Bernhard Goetz's . . . fault that he was surrounded by these four men who he reasonably believed meant to do him harm, and that's the crux of this case," Slotnick declared. "There [is] no obligation to allow yourself to be robbed, beaten, or brutalized and if . . . Bernhard Goetz reasonably believed that was going to happen to him he had a right to take the action that he did take."

According to the law, Slotnick said, "You will find that no matter what role anybody had in that action, the fact that they were working together made them all criminally liable and culpable. No one has been excluded.

"It was four of them that surrounded Bernhard Goetz in the same way that in 1981 Fred Clark and his two friends beat and injured Bernhard Goetz. By the way, the Troy Cantys and Barry Allens and James Ramseurs and Darrell Cabeys, who prey on others, who prey on people for their property, who prey on the good people in this community, like the Fred Clarks who also prey on people, . . . the young, the old, the soft looking, the easy bait, those people take a chance when they go out to prey that it may backfire on them."

Slotnick dealt with the eyewitness testimony concerning how many of the youths were seen standing in front of Goetz. Andrea Reid, he argued, told his investigator she saw two or three. Victor Flores testified he saw two, but Slotnick contended that Flores's view was blocked from seeing a third youth because of the narrowness of the subway car.

Principally, though, Slotnick relied on Goetz's own statement that he had been surrounded and sought to support this with a verbal barrage beginning with a quote from Canty's testimony: " 'When you were standing in front of him, where were Barry Allen, James Ramseur, and Darrell Cabey?' And he responds, 'They could have been with me, I can't be sure.' . . . Remember the witnesses talking about [Canty's] inconsistent statements? Remember Detective Penelton saying, 'He told me, "All of us surrounded him' "? Remember Smith saying, " 'We tried to rob him' "? Remember Bernhard Goetz saying, 'I was surrounded, two to the left and two to the right'? Remember Canty now . . . , 'They could have been standing with me'? Remember Andrea Reid, 'They had got what they deserved'? Remember Mary Gant, Josephine Holt, and Garth Reid, all who were afraid of these people? And remember where they got shot and . . . where they ended up? James Ramseur was on the floor . . . , and Troy Canty told you . . . he, in fact, fell on top of James Ramseur. It was so fast."

This was actually a very significant point. Slotnick also tried to attach significance to where Barry Allen was found in the subway car, but that didn't hold up because we had heard John Filangeri's testimony that he had found Allen crawling around on the floor. Ramseur, however, was said to have suffered a severe enough injury that he was unable to move once he had fallen, and Ramseur's position on the floor next to Canty suggested strongly that he had been near Canty when shot.

"James Ramseur said to Troy Canty, 'Get your feet out of my face,' " Slotnick continued. "Right here. Right in this little area. They were surrounding him. There is no doubt."

Another of Slotnick's major tasks was to discredit Goetz's statements and Christopher Boucher's testimony regarding their description of the fifth shot fired at Cabey. He insisted that the other eyewitnesses' recollection of the rapid succession of shots made such an occurrence completely impossible. "Did anybody other than Christopher Boucher . . . indicate that that was a possibility?" Slotnick asked. "Anything is a possibility in life. People don't get convicted on possibilities. . . . Was there a separate fifth shot? All the witnesses said no. . . .

"[T]he witnesses said the bullets were in rapid succession, and the witnesses did not indicate that thereafter was a pause or a hiatus, a walking over and a fifth shot. Most of the witnesses that saw Bernhard Goetz after the shooting, after he unloaded his gun, they saw him put it in his waistband, hold it to the side, and that was the end of the shooting."

As for Christopher Boucher, Slotnick conceded, "he is an enigma. What he tells you is absolutely and totally impossible under the physical evidence. He goes through a sequence of time that is much too much time as compared to the other witnesses.

"He is completely inconsistent with every other witness. What he says is that he sees Bernhard Goetz standing before [Cabey's] seat . . . going bang. Now, again, we know that that couldn't have happened. The angle is wrong. We know Darrell Cabey was shot on the left side, straight across . . . He said he saw no jerk, nothing whatsoever in terms of the hypothetical that the district attorney tried to garner up to make this become real for you, because it's just not. . . .

"What he tells you is that . . . [h]e is looking ahead. He hears pops. This woman falls over his friend. His friend struggles with the woman and child to get them up. He finally takes a look over and sees what he sees. By that time all the shots are gone. By that time the gun is emptied, and it's over. And he goes over it again and again and again. He said, 'Yes, I heard popping sounds, then a woman fell over my friend . . . and my friend and I tried to lift her up.

"It's over. The rapid succession, 'a snap of time,' is over. Why did he fantasize? Why did he say that? I don't know. All I can tell you, understand the stress and trauma that happens.

"Did he see Bernhard Goetz? 'I saw him in profile.' It just doesn't work out. It's not part of the evidence. I asked him, 'Are you traumatized?' He actually said no. Of course his friend [Loren Michals] said he was."

Slotnick referred also to the police report made on the day of the shootings in which Boucher said there were two people seated where Cabey was when he saw Goetz fire at Cabey. Boucher had denied he'd ever said this in his cross-examination, but Slotnick now insisted "the police report is in evidence" and urged us when we deliberated to "call for it" and look it up.

"His testimony has to basically be disregarded," Slotnick concluded. "And he is the only person [who] comes close to saying something like that."

* * *

"Mr. Waples wants you to believe that Bernhard Goetz walked over to Darrell Cabey and said, 'You don't look bad; here's another,' bang. Well, that is belied by lots of facts. . . .

"Where does the DA get this? Where does he get his theories from? He gets his theories from the most unreliable source in the world, the statement of Bernhard Goetz. Why is it unreliable? Am I undermining my client? The answer is no, and I'll tell you why.

"Nine days after the event, nine days of pain and suffering and running, nine days later a traumatized, sick, psychologically upset individual walked into a Concord, New Hampshire police station and made a statement on audiotape, and you heard it. . . . He fantasized—exactly what Dr. Yudwitz said happened. The mind went off and the body went into automatic pilot. . . . Bernhard Goetz's statement . . . is not trustworthy. Up to the moment of fear, it is trustworthy. Up to the point where the body takes over and goes into automatic pilot, the mind shuts off, it is trustworthy. After that, it is like every other witness in this case; it is not trustworthy. Because everybody who saw this case, everybody who testified, past the moment of fear, [is] essentially not very trustworthy."

Slotnick referred to Goetz's audiotaped statement where he described what he was feeling when he passed the point of fear. "He told Officer Foote . . . , 'The upper level of your mind, you just turn off. . . . The important thing is to react. You go in a different state of mind and a lot of things happen. As I explained, it is—it's your sense of perception that changes. Your abilities change.' . . . And Officer Foote asks him a question. He said, 'The exact truth is I don't know; it doesn't matter. I could have been right on them. I could have been fifteen feet away from them. A different level of your mind is controlled, and that level of your mind just does it.'

"You can't trust anything from the mind that doesn't know if he is fifteen feet away," Slotnick concluded. At another point he quoted Goetz's description of how he shot Ramseur: "Ramseur 'tried to run through the wall of the train, but he had nowhere to go. Nowhere to go.' Where did he get that from?" Slotnick asked. "One more time, the tape in New Hampshire, the automatic pilot of Bernhard Goetz's mind. He knew about as much about Ramseur and his bullet wound as you all before you came in here."

Waples, Slotnick stated, "framed his case around posttraumatic statements. He framed his case around unreliable statements. He framed his case around a man who at the moment of fear, after he realized he was surrounded, did what was to him a terrible thing. A man who nine days later spoke in Concord, New Hampshire, anguished with pain, anxiety, and all the other horrors that are tended to someone who's truly a victim.

"He told you in his opening, Bernhard Goetz was not acting defensively, not to protect himself from a robbery and an assault, but offensively and aggressively, with a deliberate, cold-blooded intention to kill or cripple the men he was shooting at. What he essentially is telling you, Bernhard Goetz walked on that train that day as a hunter rather than someone who's going down to Chambers Street have some pre-Christmas drinks with his friends.

* * *

"When he entered the train on December 22, 1984, Bernhard Goetz was all smiles and happy," Slotnick rebutted. "He was going to have a drink. It was these four that have distorted and destroyed his life for the past two-and-a-half years. And now I ask you to put an end to that pain and suffering and I ask you to understand some of the statements that he makes because he's angry and he's in pain. . . . He didn't walk on the train hunting. He walked on a train to enjoy some Christmas cheer. . . . Three days before Christmas. 'It was a day like any other day.' A day that these predators were going to go out and plunder decent, decent people in our community."

Slotnick quoted from Waples's opening: "You'll come to realize that Troy Canty, Barry Allen, James Ramseur, and Darrell Cabey were shot not so much for what they did in the subway, for even by the defendant's version—his potentially self-serving version—they did very little."

"Now that is an insult," Slotnick said. "If you want to believe as he does that Bernhard Goetz went to Concord, New Hampshire to make up a story to get him off, then you've got to listen to the tape and say to yourself, 'Why does he tell Officer Foote that . . . when the other one had his hand in his pocket . . . "I knew the bulge in that pocket wasn't a gun"? . . . Why does he tell that to Officer Foote if this is a phony, self-serving statement?' You see? It is not, because

Bernhard Goetz, when walking in nine days later in Concord, New Hampshire, could have concocted a hell of a story."

Slotnick concluded that in spite of his fantasies about things that hadn't happened, Goetz in his statements had been open and honest, and, to the best of his ability, had "told the truth."

Before he was done, Slotnick also discussed the other counts in the indictment against Goetz besides those involving attempted murder and assault. The strongest argument he made concerned the reckless endangerment charge, referring once more to Waples's opening.

"Greg Waples said to you the bullets were ricocheting all over the car," Slotnick said, and he asserted, "not only didn't it ever happen, but he knew it didn't happen." Detective Haase had testified that when the stray bullet hit the metal panel on the side of the conductor's cab, the impact mark showed clearly that the bullet wouldn't have ricocheted but merely fallen down. The only evidence that indicated a bullet did ricochet was a piece of bullet, part of the lead core, that Haase found well away from the impact mark, on the subway car floor, and Victor Flores's recollection that he heard a ricochet hit a ceiling fan.

Detective Torres, however, who arrived on the scene an hour and a half before Haase, had testified that he had seen the fragment on the "Cabey" seat with the other pieces: more of the core and the copper jacket. Haase had testified that the crime scene had not been properly secured before he arrived, so in all probability the fragment had somehow been knocked to the floor and then kicked around. And in a later inspection of the car, including a thorough check of the ceiling fan, according to Slotnick, no other dents made by bullets were found.

Slotnick ended his argument by briefly discussing the four weapons possession charges Goetz faced. Concerning the "Myra" guns, Slotnick said, "the judge will charge you about Myra Friedman. . . . If you find that she's an accomplice in the possession of those guns, I indicate to you you must corroborate her testimony. Obviously, no such corroboration exist[s], and I ask you to acquit Bernhard Goetz on those counts."

The other two weapons possessions charges Goetz faced dealt with the gun he used in the subway incident. Slotnick urged us again to listen to the judge's charge and consider that Goetz was not carrying his gun with unlawful intent.

"He didn't have an unlawful intent for its use when he walked out of [his] building, when he walked to the sidewalk, when he walked into the subway station, even when he sat down in the subway seat," Slotnick said. "It was only after he was surrounded and he knew what was going to happen and he had his belief that any intent to use the weapon first materialized. If you find that he developed the intent to use that gun when he was surrounded, when he reasonably believed he had to use it, that he never harbored any initial intent to use it, lawfully or unlawfully, you can acquit him of that very, very severe charge.

"Criminal possession of a weapon in the second degree is a very, very severe charge. We indicate to you, again, that the shootings were justified and not unlawful. . . . We tell you now Bernhard Goetz had no intention to use those weapons unlawfully. We tell you now that from what you have seen in the past two months, you know he had no intention to use those weapons unlawfully. He took pains to get—to attempt to get a pistol permit. Anybody who takes such time to get—to get a weapon has no intention of using it unlawfully. Clearly it is not unlawful in terms of its use.

"Now, I can't come back. It is over," Slotnick said in a melancholy tone. "I have made my final statement. I tried to marshal the evidence as best as I could. I have been long; I have been tedious, hopefully not too boring. This is it. The life of Bernhard Goetz is spread across the table. . . . You know I have no burden. Mr. Waples has it all.

"They came in here without a case. Please let them walk out without a conviction. . . . As to Bernhard Goetz, understand what I have done, what I did not have to do. I did not have to show any scientific proof, but I have just had to show you that [Waples's] theory was made out of a tape. . . .

"And since I will not be able to address you again during the course of this trial, I ask you to please do one thing. Because it's Mr. Waples who has the burden. It's Mr. Waples who must prove his case beyond a reasonable doubt as to each and every element. It is he who has the right to speak to you last, not me. I ask you to do one thing when he raises a point, strikes a chord; please say, 'What would Slotnick say about that?' Please try and remember what I have said to you in terms of what is in this trial, and if I am presumptuous, I am presumptuous; I apologize. But I ask you to consider our point of view when you hear the very clever argument of Mr. Waples.

"Providence has sent me a message: my voice is about gone. I thank you for your time, patience, and attention. I just hope you remember. Thank you."

"Thank you, Mr. Slotnick," said Justice Crane.

Chapter 16

Waples's Bombshell

June 11

Slotnick's closing argument had begun at about 10:30 a.m. and had been delivered in four parts, with short breaks taken before and after the lunch recess to give Slotnick's voice a rest and to help us remain alert. Waples's speech, though, began earlier—almost as soon as we arrived the next day, at 8:30 a.m.—and was presented in three parts with only a half-hour segment left for after lunch. It was a riveting argument, so maintaining concentration was not a problem. And it also included a real attention grabber: a demonstration of why, according to Waples, Darrell Cabey "could not have possibly been shot while standing up"; why he had to have been struck by Goetz's fifth shot "when he was sitting down, just as Christopher Boucher testified."

"Good morning, folks," Waples began. "Try to bear with me for about the next four hours, and then I will walk out of your lives forever.

"Almost a century ago, the highest court in New York wrote, 'The worst man has the same right to live as the best and no one may attack another because his general reputation is bad. The law protects everyone from unlawful violence, regardless of his character.' This case, I submit, presents a monumental challenge to this most precious tenet of a free and democratic society.

"Mr. Slotnick, in his pitch to you throughout this trial and in his summation yesterday, has in essence asked you to return a verdict that will legitimize the idea that the law does not apply equally to all persons, that some persons are above the law's sanctions, and, worse, that some people are below the law's protection.

"Bernhard Goetz, by his own admission, did everything within his power to murder four young men in the subway system shortly before Christmas in 1984. By some stroke of fortune he succeeded in killing none of these young men and he succeeded in maiming only one, but . . . the question before this court is whether the law . . . will hold the defendant accountable for the terrible and irredeemable crimes he committed on December 22.

"I do not minimize the great personal challenge that each of you who will be retiring to the jury room to deliberate in this case faces. . . . This is a sad and, at times, confusing case. The defendant is alternately a pathetic and pitiable man and, then, contemptuous and contemptible. . . .

"Pity the defendant all you want. Feel sorry for the defendant all you want. But you must not acquit the defendant because, in this case, you can do so only by abandoning your duty and your oath to judge this case solely on the law and solely on the evidence; and therein lies the great personal challenge that you, folks, will face in this case.

"Are you going to judge this case with your hearts or with your heads? Are you going to decide this with emotion or with logic? Is justice going to prevail in this courtroom or are you going to capitulate to the fear of crime Mr. Slotnick has sought to exploit and to manipulate? . . .

"Mr. Slotnick put a question on the table maybe of whether the lives of the four young men that Bernhard Goetz shot are worthy of anyone's consideration. But Troy Canty, Barry Allen, James Ramseur, and Darrell Cabey are not on trial in this case. What is on trial in this courtroom is a question of law, a question of civilization here. It's a question of whether the defendant was acting within or without the bounds, the proper bounds of self-defense when he rose up off his seat and emptied his pistol into the bodies of four persons, four human beings, on December 22. The question is whether the defendant was legally right or legally wrong when he shot two persons as they were trying to flee from him. The question is whether the law will place a stamp of approval on what the defendant did that Saturday afternoon when he advanced on a seated and totally helpless Darrell Cabey and said, 'You look all right; here's another' before blasting away with another shot, at virtually point-blank range. . . .

"This case cries out for justice. Darrell Cabey cries out for justice," Waples continued, shifting the focus of his argument to concentrate on the shooting of Cabey.

"Forget about the shootings of Troy Canty, Barry Allen, and James Ramseur for the moment. In fact, assume for the sake of argument that the defendant was legally justified in shooting each of those three individuals, was legally justified in firing the first three shots at them. The question remains, how can that possibly condone, how can that possibly excuse the totally needless injury that the defendant inflicted on Darrell Cabey?

"Regardless of all that went before, the last two bullets that the defendant fired at Darrell Cabey stand in a class of horror by themselves, stand separate and apart from all the shots that were fired before," Waples said. "[T]he circumstances surrounding the firing of the last two shots were so different, the shots were so sadistic and unnecessary, as to make any possible claim of justification as to that injury, that attempted murder, almost a cruel joke. . . .

"Deep down inside, each of you must know, if you are honest with yourselves, that no matter how much you may sympathize with this defendant, you cannot wink at this, 'You look all right; here's another,' fifth shot, because no reasonable person would have fired that shot or even contemplated firing that shot.

"Now, . . . in his presentation of evidence and in his summation, Mr. Slotnick devoted a substantial amount of effort in trying to drag an act of the defendant—who himself admits was cold-blooded and murderous—under the skirt of the laws of protection . . . Mr. Slotnick is many things, including a genius and resourceful lawyer, but he isn't an alchemist. He can't spin gold from straw, nor can he transmute a totally sadistic, hateful attempt to murder into a perfectly legitimate and blameless act of self-defense.

"Subject the defense evidence and subject these defense arguments to the acid test of logic," Waples told us and added later, "[W]hen you try and fit the defendant's conduct within the law of justification, you may discover that it is more than a little like trying to pound the square peg into a round hole. It just doesn't fit, folks."

Waples, of course, quoted extensively and often from Goetz's taped statements as he argued about what happened in the subway car and about the motives behind Goetz's actions. He mentioned Slotnick's criticism that the prosecution was relying too heavily on Goetz's statements but said "no apology is going to be offered in that regard."

"In the first place, ask yourselves, why should you disbelieve the defendant's tape-recorded statements? Why should you disbelieve the statements of the one witness above all others who have marched into this courtroom who should know exactly why and what happened on December 22?" Waples stated that there was not "the slightest basis for dismissing these admissions as the product of a fertile imagination." He argued that "the rush of adrenaline only sharpened [Goetz's] cognitive powers," quoting the audiotapes where Goetz spoke of how "being afraid . . . makes you think and analyze and it speeds up your mind. . . . You react, not from second to second; you react from maybe a tenth of a second or a twentieth of a second."

Waples went on to declare, "The richness of the detail he recalled—especially in the audiotaped statement—is simply staggering," and that "[t]he only way he could recall those minute details is because he was there: because he lived it; because he perceived it; because it went into his mind. He reacted to it; he processed it; he assimilated it. He lived each split second. It was each frame of a filmstrip being frozen in his mind."

Slotnick's contention that Goetz's statements were not reliable "has no basis in fact," Waples said, arguing that "almost every major detail . . . is corroborated" by eyewitness testimony and the physical evidence. Waples then went over Goetz's description of what happened in his statements and discussed the corroborating testimony point by point.

During his audiotaped statement, Goetz described through
which doors of the subway car he had entered, where he'd
sat, and the locations of the four youths. He also drew a diagram
indicating the same for Officer Foote. All of this was exactly
corroborated by Troy Canty's testimony, Waples said.

"The defendant said that Troy Canty and Barry Allen both
came over to him," Waples continued. "Troy Canty said that,
as far as he knows, he alone approached the defendant, but
now the defendant's version is accurate because at least three
independant witnesses have said they saw two persons standing
over the defendant before the shots were fired: Josephine Holt
saw that; Garth Reid saw that; Mary Gant saw that."

Canty also admitted two other details in Goetz's statements:
that he had asked Goetz for five dollars, and that he was the
first one shot. (Another detail that Canty didn't mention and
Waples did not bring up was Canty's having said, 'How's your
day?' to Goetz when he first sat down across from Canty, and
Goetz's having muttered, 'Fine' in return. Andrea Reid recalled
this exchange, but she testified that she thought the man talking
with Canty might not have been Goetz and might have exited
the train.)

"The defendant on the tapes said that after he shot Troy
Canty, he then turned his attention on number two, who is
Barry Allen; and the defendant said that Barry Allen was trying
to run through this crowd of the subway car [i.e., southward
at an angle toward the long bench on the west side] when he
got shot. Mr. Slotnick says that did not happen, but you know
it did because at least two independent eyewitnesses told you
that.

"Victor Flores saw that. Victor Flores was sitting right here
[on the southwest long bench]. When he heard the shots, he
looked up and he was looking right down the gun barrel of
the defendant as he was looking straight in the faces of the
two persons who were running towards him. But they never
got there because they got shot in their backs, or as their backs
were turned towards the defendant.

"You also know Andrea Reid told you that when she heard
the shots, she looked over and she saw two persons moving
away from the defendant.

"You also know Barry Allen was shot squarely in the center of the back. If that isn't squarely in the center of the back, I don't know what is. I never said that the shots that went into Barry Allen's back went perpendicular to it; I said he was shot squarely in the center of the back. That is what the evidence shows."

Next Goetz pivoted to his right and fired his remaining three shots. "Garth Reid saw that happen," Waples stated. "Garth Reid saw the defendant firing two shots in this direction and then saw the defendant turn and fire additional shots towards the other end of the car."

The third shot was fired at James Ramsuer, who looked like he was "trying to climb through the wall of the subway car," according to Goetz. Then both the fourth and fifth shots were fired at Darrell Cabey. "You know the defendant was accurately recalling that fact because we have Darrell Cabey's jacket and it has two bullet holes in it. Not one, two. Detective Haase pointed them out . . . ," Waples said.

"The defendant said he fired the first of two shots at Darrell Cabey when Darrell Cabey was standing up. That is what the defense's own expert said had to have happened. You know the defendant was accurately recalling that detail. The defendant's own tape said that he fired the second of two shots at Darrell Cabey while Darrell Cabey was sitting down. You know that happened, you know the defendant was accurately recalling that detail, because Christopher Boucher saw it happen. Dr. Hirsch testified it was certainly possible.

"The defendant's own tape insisted, *insisted,* that he fired five shots, five shots altogether, and you know from the physical evidence that five shots were fired. . . . We have one shot into each body and we have the miss. Struck the wall in the subway car.

"The defendant's own tape after the shooting was over said that he went over to the individual who had asked him for money and considered gouging his eyes out and bent over to him and said words to the effect, 'And let this be a lesson to you.' You know the defendant was accurately recalling that detail because Victor Flores said that he saw the defendant kneel down close to the face of one of the individuals. He saw that: Victor Flores."

Waples also detailed how Goetz remembered noticing two women on the floor of the car, a black woman and a white woman whom he was afraid he'd mistakenly hit, and that the train conductor, Armando Soler, testified to having helped these women off the floor. Goetz also remembered saying to Soler, "I don't know why I did it. They tried to rob me," and Soler had also corroborated this fact. Finally, Goetz described how he had moved down to the south end of the car and fled the train by jumping down onto the tracks. "Now, once again, ladies and gentlemen, you know that the defendant was accurately recalling that detail because Victor Flores and Armando Soler both saw the defendant do exactly what he said he had done on the tapes," Waples stated.

"This wealth of corroboration—nearly a dozen and a half major details—stands as the most convincing proof there can be, I submit, that the defendant was not hallucinating or fantasizing or fabricating when he recalled how he shot at human beings as they were running away from him and how he shot at Darrell Cabey when he was down in his seat," Waples asserted. He then rebutted Slotnick's attack on Boucher, arguing that Boucher was "not a raving lunatic or a crackpot," and asking, "If Christopher Boucher did not see the defendant firing into a person who was sitting in that small seat, what did he see?

"Do you think it is simply some enormous coincidence that Christopher Boucher and the defendant both saw a person being shot while in that small subway seat?" Waples asked. "Is it possible that both of these men, the defendant and Christopher Boucher, had the same vision, the exact same vision, the exact same terrible dream, on December 22? Well, that could happen in the twilight zone, but not here."

Waples called Boucher an "intelligent and reliable witness" and defended the clearly erroneous part of his testimony by stating that just because "Boucher did not actually see . . . Darrell Cabey turn or flinch an instant before he was shot is hardly proof that that did not occur. You have to remember that Christopher Boucher was about forty feet away from that event," Waples said, "and—certainly understandably—that from that distance he would not detect every slight and subtle motion that Darrell Cabey was making at the instant the gun was fired, particularly when, as Boucher said, most of his attention was riveted on the gun. His eyes were riveted on the gun."

The discussion of Boucher's testimony once again placed the focus of Waples's argument on the way that Goetz shot Cabey, and it was at this point that Waples said, "[N]ow let me take the bull by the horns and prove to you, . . . in a way that was ignored by the . . . so-called defense expert, why Darrell Cabey could not have been shot—could not have possibly been shot while we was standing up; [why he had to have been] struck by the bullet while he was sitting down, just as Christopher Boucher testified. The answer is this: Darrell Cabey's coat, Darrell Cabey's jacket."

Waples brought out the jacket and showed it to us, pointing out the two bullet holes in the left side, which Detective Haase had detailed in in his testimony [see p. 49] but Joseph Quirk had completely ignored. The hole that was higher up, in the upper back area, was the one that had blood around it, Waples said, so that was from the shot that crippled Cabey. The other hole, farther to the front and lower on the jacket, Waples claimed was made by the shot that missed.

In a dramatic gesture Waples then took off his jacket and donned Cabey's. Usually an attorney would seek the judge's permission before presuming to remove his jacket, but I interpreted this action as an indication that Waples had perhaps become fed up all of Slotnick's shenanigans; now Waples was pulling a stunt of his own.

Waples argued that it was impossible for the fourth shot to have been the one that crippled Cabey, as Dr. DiMaio had suggested, because the fifth shot could not have passed through Cabey's jacket and then struck the panel on the wall of the conductor's cab at the proper place while Cabey was sitting down. He sat in a chair and demonstrated that the dent in the panel was slightly higher than the hole in Cabey's jacket; and since Goetz would have been shooting downward at Cabey, the gun, the jacket hole and the panel dent could not therefore be aligned.

"The only way this bullet hole could have been sustained," Waples insisted, was "if Darrell Cabey was standing" and a bullet "passed loosely through his jacket, not grazing him, and then struck the wall. There's no other way it could have happened. Darrell Cabey could not have been sitting down when the fourth shot was fired at him, which missed." Waples insisted that this proved Goetz was right that he had indeed missed Cabey with his fourth shot, leaving open the possibility (Waples argued it was virtually positive proof) that Goetz was right about the fifth shot too, that Cabey had sat down before Goetz fired at him again.

Waples did not offer in his demonstration any specific position Cabey might have been in that would align the gun, the jacket hole and the panel dent, but he seemed to suggest one scenario that coincided with a theory of my own. Goetz said in his taped statements that Cabey was holding onto the strap above his seat "pretending he wasn't with" the others "like . . . he wasn't aware of what was going on." I believed it likely, therefore, that Cabey was standing facing the seat, as most straphangers do, rather than facing the aisle as the defense had argued through Quirk's demonstration. In either case, Cabey would have been standing in profile to Goetz; but according to my theory, Cabey's right side would have been exposed to Goetz rather than his left, rendering impossible the defense's argument that the fourth shot crippled Cabey because the bullet entered his left side. I believed that the left flap of Cabey's jacket could have been hanging out over the seat—especially since the pocket was weighted with a screwdriver—and the fourth bullet could have travelled through it inside out and then struck the panel. Cabey then could have turned around and sat down, and, as the fifth shot was fired, flinched to his right, exposing his left side.

The demonstration had an extremely strong effect on me, and I felt that if the evidence supported Waples's hypothesis, Goetz was certainly guilty on this. I found out later, in our deliberations, that not all of the jurors agreed with me, but I don't believe they could have ever made me back down. I would have fought to the bitter end to get Goetz convicted, and either the jury would have ended up deadlocked, or else I would have turned the others around.

Waples next combated Slotnick's "rapid succession" defense of Goetz's actions, saying that "rapid is a relative term" and arguing that while some of the eyewitnesses described the shots as sounding like firecrackers going off, others suggested the shots were "considerably more methodical."

The witnesses Waples referred to as having heard spacing between the shots had all been discredited, however, by Slotnick. Waples refuted Slotnick's contentions that neither Sally Smithern nor Solitaire MacFoy was actually on the train, while stressing MacFoy's testimony that the shots "seemed very deliberate." Andrea Reid's testimony also disputed that the shots were closely bunched together, Waples said; and he defended her testimony by arguing that John Barna, in his conversation with Reid, had tried to put words into her mouth. Christopher Boucher, of course, had also testified that there was a pause between the fourth and fifth shots; and Waples argued, "Can all these witnesses who give testimony that is unfavorable to the defense be lying or mistaken?"

Waples also called Dr. Yudwitz's testimony "totally meaningless" since "Yudwitz admitted that the individual response to stress and fear is unique." And again relying on Goetz's taped statements, Waples contended that Goetz revealed a moment-to-moment awareness of what was happening, demonstrating that he never lost control.

He referred first to Goetz's statement that because of the way Canty was smiling he made up his mind to shoot them all and preplanned his pattern of fire. "This is the antithesis of someone on automatic pilot," Waples stated. "How can someone on automatic pilot lay down a plan?"

Waples then went through Goetz's "gruesome, blow-by-blow account" of the shootings, declaring that Goetz's perceptions that Allen and Ramseur were trying to escape and that Cabey was holding onto the strap, trying to pretend he wasn't part of the group, proved that Goetz "had an opportunity to reflect" and to choose not to shoot.

Even if things were happening in split seconds, Waples argued, Goetz's "ability to perceive" what the youths were doing meant that he had "the opportunity . . . to recognize [that] the threat . . . had been neutralized" and the capacity to stop firing his gun. Once again, this was most blatant in the case of Darrell Cabey, Waples suggested, stating, "If, as the defendant admits, he had the opportunity and the ability to perceive that Darrell Cabey was sitting down in his seat, doing absolutely nothing to threaten him, he had the opportunity to make a decision not to fire that fifth shot."

Goetz, "in his own statement, indicated clearly he had the opportunity to avoid this needless bloodshed," Waples continued. "And the question persists: Why? Why? There's an answer, folks. It's been staring you in the face for the last six weeks, since April 27. The answer is Bernhard Goetz. . . .

"Anger alone—a blind, self-righteous, organic fury—can explain the sequential shooting of these four young men," Waples asserted, prefacing a scathing psychological profile of Goetz. He also now shifted back his focus from the shooting of Cabey by suggesting that that "sadistic and unnecessary" attack also "raises grave questions" about whether the preceding shots into Canty, Allen, and Ramseur "had even a gleam of legitimacy."

"If there's one fact that towers above all others, it is that the shooting of Darrell Cabey was different: different in kind; different in degree; different in the defendant's culpability from all the shots that preceded it," Waples said. "But perhaps even more importantly, the manner in which the defendant assaulted Darrell Cabey should cause alarm bells and sirens to go off in your head when you scrutinize the circumstances surrounding the firing of the first three shots."

Waples said Goetz was "anything but a typical New Yorker" and argued that beneath Goetz's "placid and unassuming exterior . . . there lurks a dark spirit." He called Goetz a "deeply suspicious, paranoid individual, intellectually rigid, who's seething inside with suppressed, self-righteous anger, and an individual who is obsessed with crime and his own solutions to problems of crime and disorder in our cities." As in his opening, Waples once again referred to Goetz as "an emotional powderkeg . . . waiting to detonate" that sooner or later had been certain to explode.

"Search the defendant's background, ladies and gentlemen, and you'll find a tantalizing hint of what happened in the subway in 1984," Waples went on. "The emotional instability; the self-righteous arrogance that more than a little resembles a superiority complex; his infatuation with guns." Waples pointed out that Goetz bought a pistol in Connecticut—one of the "Myra" guns—over ten years before he was mugged. And of the mugging incident itself, Waples said, "without belittling [its] significance, there are thousands and thousands of New Yorkers who have had experiences and encounters with violent crime . . . far more harrowing than that which the defendant experienced on Canal Street in 1981, and they did not run amuck. . . .

"What that mugging did, I submit, is this: it nurtured an obsession the defendant had with a problem of crime and punishment in a mind that was fertile to the growth of those ideas. The defendant's personal experience with crime and criminal justice system bureaucracy that stems from his 1981 assault offended [his] scientifically precise mind. It's not so much the mugging itself but the aftermath of the mugging that really tormented and tortured this defendant.

"When you listen to the tapes, you can almost taste the bitter indignation that he feels almost four years after the incident, because Fred Clark, the young person who beat him up, was detained for only two hours and thirty-five minutes while he, the victim, was detained processing the case for six hours and five minutes. He carries those numbers down to the exact minutes in his head for four years."

Waples mentioned Goetz's offer to lie in order to charge Fred Clark with attempted robbery and commented, "How presumptuous can one get? Here you have a person who is so cocksure about [the] superiority of his own system of values that he presumes that it is right and moral for him to lie, to deliberately fabricate evidence, so that some person who he in his own mind branded a criminal gets the kind of punishment the defendant feels he deserves."

After the mugging, Waples said that Goetz "set his own standard of conduct and behavior . . . , disdaining the laws that he did not feel [were] worthy of his respect and obedience. The defendant began carrying a gun in direct violation of the laws of New York. In addition, he actively encouraged his friends to do the same by selling them guns at cost." Goetz also, according to Waples, "evolved from a helpless and frustrated victim into something closely resembling an avenging angel." This was one of several statements to which Slotnick objected.

"Yes," Justice Crane said. "Please, Mr. Waples, would you desist [from applying] those kinds of labels and epithets and try to draw inferences from facts? I don't want the jury to get the idea any part of their deliberations involves emotional sympathy or bias."

Waples continued on this tack, though, arguing that "following this transformation was the moral superiority and the contempt that the defendant has for people who he regards as society's vagabonds in this defendant's supremely arrogant mind." He referred to the part of the videotape where Goetz described having drawn his gun on the drug addict who had asked him for money and then had issued some mild threat. "[T]his unfortunate soul offended the defendant's dignity," Waples argued, calling Goetz's response "totally unnecessary" and his explanation "chilling": "I just—Okay, okay, it's true; I was pissed. But I didn't shoot him. He deserved to die."

Discussing the events that led to the shootings, Waples contended that rather than being happy-go-lucky when he entered the subway system, Goetz said he was going to meet friends for a drink after having become "frustrated" with an electronics project he was working on that day. He then "sat down in the midst of this group of four rambunctious youths. Right in their midst," Waples stressed; then commented, "In light of the defendant's self-confessed paranoia about crime and . . . the obsession he has with his personal safety, one really has to wonder why the defendant deliberately seated himself in an area of the car that is not only in the middle of this group of rambunctious young teens, but . . . where he is at least psychologically isolated from all the other passengers on the train. . . .

"[D]on't you think it seems likely when the defendant got on the train and found where he was and found where he says all the other passengers were, he would have gotten up and walked over to an area where he could have felt more safe and secure? Now, of course, that seems like it would be the logical thing to do for a cautious and prudent person who sincerely felt as much in fear for his personal safety as the defendant would have you believe he did," Waples said. And he argued, "You really, really should be wondering, folks, whether . . . he wasn't secretly hoping, if only on a subconscious level, that one of these rambunctious kids would make his day, one of these persons would do something stupid, would provide him with some excuse, some pretext that would allow him to draw his gun and take a lifetime of revenge out on them."

Waples later discussed the law concerning justification for situations where a person is permitted to use "deadly physical force." First, Waples said, the law makes a distinction between defending oneself from an assault or a robbery, the difference being that when robbery is involved there is no "duty to retreat." "Time after time on the tapes the defendant said he did not fear a robbery," Waples stated; and "[i]n this case there is no evidence that the defendant tried to retreat from this encounter before he used deadly physical force." He also explained that we would be asked to apply the evidence to what "the law calls a 'reasonable man' standard . . . to decide whether the defendant had a sufficiently strong basis in reason to figure he was about to be savagely beaten . . . ; whether that belief was the product of an obsessed and paranoid and disturbed man, or perhaps even a pretext concocted by a person whose fanatical frustration with the criminal justice system had finally reached its limit, a person who, for no very good reason, suddenly decided that these four persons deserved to die.

"I have the burden of proof but I don't have to prove the defendant's either a quack or a cold-blooded murderer to prove my case," Waples said. "All I have to do is prove . . . that it was unreasonable, and I submit that that's this case. . . . The bottom line in this case is that the defendant had no reasonable ground for believing he had to shoot four human beings after two of them came up to him and one of them asked him for money."

To further argue against the defense's justification contentions, Waples explored the nature of the threat. He pointed out that from the time the youths boarded the train in the Bronx, "None of the four tried to rob anybody. None of the four tried to shake anybody down for money. None of the four physically harassed or physically threatened anybody during the train ride downtown.

"Many passengers were not alarmed in the slightest by anything that this group did," Waples added. "Even among the passengers who were attentive to this group, the atmosphere was one of attentiveness, not fear."

Waples then discussed Canty's motives in approaching Goetz. "In the first place, you have to bear in mind this group is going downtown for a very specific purpose: to rob video machines. Troy Canty had done this for years. He knew he had a gold mine in this kind of action. . . . Canty knew that breaking into video machines was neat, clean work [that] paid rich dividends with very little risk.

"How many times had he done it? Hundreds of times. How many times had he been caught? A handful. Even on those rare occasions when the authorities succeeded in nabbing him, what happened to him? He was charged with a misdemeanor. That's all. He knew that. He got what, the most, thirty days in jail? That was a small price for Troy Canty to pay for the hundreds of dollars that was available to him. But breaking into video machines is one thing. Robbing people is quite another.

"Canty may not be the most highly educated person in the world, but he is not dumb. He is shrewd and he is streetwise and Troy Canty knew in December of 1984, as he knows now, that there is a big difference between robbing people and breaking into video machines. . . . Canty knew that there was a difference between a felony and a misdemeanor, big difference between going upstate to prison with murderers and rapists and spending a few weeks on Rikers Island with the boys.

"Canty, I submit, is simply too shrewd to try to rob the defendant in front of a carload of passengers," Waples said, arguing also that a group "taking care to wear reversible jackets so they could avoid apprehension" would not have tried to rob someone "in front of a trainload of passengers that they have been riding with for thirty minutes . . . , conspicuously calling attention to themselves: playing on the bars, pounding on the seats, talking to people, approaching people for matches. That makes Mr. Slotnick's robbery hypothesis somewhat absurd."

About the testimony regarding Canty's alleged inconsistent statements, Waples said, "I do not suggest that Police Officer Peter Smith is a liar, and I don't suggest that you brand him as one. I do suggest, however, that all of the evidence, when considered as a whole, demonstrates that Police Officer Smith's testimony in court is not reliable. It's not trustworthy; it should not be considered by you. . . .

"The prosecution does not dispute for a moment that Canty said what Penelton said [he said]," Waples stated. "Penelton was a careful detective. He did what Smith should have done if Smith had heard what he said he heard. He made notes, and he transcribed the notes into a report, and he forwarded the report to the appropriate officials involved in the investigation."

Because Canty had been given doses of Demerol and Visaril fifteen to twenty minutes before his conversation with Penelton, however, Waples argued that Canty's statements should be considered unreliable. "There is no doubt Canty said it, but how can you possibly know it's true, because those drugs can cause hallucinations; they can cause confabulations; they can cause people to misrecall facts."

Waples next challenged the reasonableness of Goetz's decision to draw his gun and shoot the youths. The two factors that Goetz in his statements said led to his decision, according to Waples, were, first, that he felt surrounded and, second, that he saw "the smile in Canty's face and the shine in his eyes."

Waples argued at considerable length that Goetz's sense that he was being surrounded by all four of the youths was not supportable by the evidence. In Goetz's own account of what happened, only Canty and Allen approached and stood in front of him, Waples said, reiterating that the eyewitness testimony corroborated this fact. He contended that Ramseur and Cabey perhaps stood up, but that they never advanced toward Goetz from where they'd been sitting; and that Goetz felt surrounded only because he chose to sit in their midst. "If he was intimidated by James Ramseur and Darrell Cabey, it was only because he came into the area in which they were standing or sitting, the space they were occupying before the defendant boarded the train."

Quoting from the videotape, Waples recounted where Detective Clark asked Goetz, "Question: 'Bernard, one and two' —referring to Troy Canty and Barry Allen—'come over to your left. What [do] three and four do?' Answer: 'They were just kind of—All they had to do was stand there. Does it matter? Does it matter?' . . . The answer, of course, mattered to Detective Clark," Waples said.

Goetz did describe that one of these two—which Waples said had to be Ramseur because Cabey had his pockets zippered shut—put his hand in his coat pocket and created a bulge to suggest that he had a gun. But Goetz insisted he knew this was a ruse.

Meanwhile, Clark continued to press Goetz about what, if anything, Ramseur and Cabey had done. Waples went over the pertinent portions of the transcript with us. "When these two made [their] move, did they move in on you too?" Clark asked. Goetz's answer was ambiguous. "The important thing is you have to try to keep track of everybody but at the same time you don't want to look too much . . . because you don't want to provoke an attack. . . . These two were moving around," Goetz then said. "They were paying attention to me, I believe, but only in a—in a quite casual way." "Did you feel threatened by them?" Clark asked. "They were all together, because they were all talking and joking with each other," Goetz responded. "So you knew them to be as a group before?" "Correct," Goetz said. "And now, if that's—if that—if that is an unreasonable conclusion—Now, if you feel that is unwarranted, that—that—"

Waples also read from the videotape where Goetz said that, after seeing the look on Canty's face and the shine in his eyes, he "snapped" and decided "to waste them all."

"This defendant . . . said that he has a right—legal right, mind you—to try and kill these four young men, not on the basis of what Troy Canty said to him, not on the basis of what Troy Canty did, but on the way that Troy Canty smiled . . . ," Waples said. "That, I submit, is not a . . . sufficiently reasonable basis to have a legal right to take out a gun and shoot to kill. . . .

"Now, please understand that I am in no way condoning what Troy Canty did on December 22," Waples said. "It was stupid, it was inexcusable, [but] it wasn't criminal . . ." Rather, Waples described it as an "an annoying and intimidating encounter" that is an "unpleasant" but unavoidable element of city life. "Reasonable people, even people who have been victimized by crime in the past, realize that there's an enormous

difference between life's petty annoyances and a lethal threat
which may justify someone pulling a gun and shooting," Waples
stated, later adding, "I suggest a solution for the defendant [is]
to pack his bags and go somewhere else where his fragile
sensibility will be less easily assaulted."

Waples also argued that "[a]fter the first shot at Troy Canty,
each succeeding shot became progressively more unnecessary
and hence less justifiable than everything that preceded it."
He made an effort to distinguish Ramseur and Cabey from
Canty and Allen by arguing that rather than being a "gang of
four," as Slotnick professed, the youths were actually "more
or less like two couples traveling together." Canty and Allen,
Waples said, were long-time friends who "live in the same
building" and "go out and break into video machines together
on a regular basis," while Ramseur and Cabey were just "tag-
alongs that particular day."

"The defendant had no right to shoot James Ramseur and
Darrell Cabey just because of what Troy Canty did or what
the defendant in his own mind felt Canty was about to do,"
Waples stated. "There has to be more. There has to be a
reasonable basis to expect or believe that Darrell Cabey and
James Ramseur are involved in whatever is going on."

Like Slotnick, Waples spent a minimal amount of time
discussing the gun-possession charges. Concerning the unlicensed gun that Goetz used on the subway that day, Waples
said the defense "doesn't dispute [Goetz] possessed the gun,"
and that there was "no doubt . . . that the gun was loaded
and operable." That, Waples told us, was all that was involved
in count one of the indictment: criminal possession of a weapon
in the third degree. He added, for the purposes of proving
Goetz's guilt on the twelfth count, second-degree weapons
possession, that "there's no doubt [Goetz] was prepared to draw
that gun and use it at the slightest excuse, the slightest pretext,
because he felt that was right and legal technically."

About the "Myra" guns, Waples stated that they were "not
toys," but rather "real guns" that were part of a "small arsenal"
Goetz was keeping in his apartment at the time of the shootings.
Waples further argued that "Myra Friedman was not an ac-

complice to anything. She was a victim. The defendant gallantly foisted these guns off on her because he did not want to have them in his apartment when he surrendered. . . . Even if she were an accomplice, however, there's ample corroboration that establishes that these were the defendant's guns," Waples added, citing the testimony and documentation that proved Goetz was the original purchaser of the guns. "Those are the defendant's guns," Waples asserted. "They were test-fired; they were operable. That is all we have to prove for criminal possession of a weapon in the fourth degree."

Waples concluded his argument by insisting that rather than acting in justifiable self-defense, Goetz had aggressively lashed out at the youths, "propelled by his hateful frenzy." He offered that "[t]his strange and troubled man may actually believe that, in the bottom of his heart, what he did to Troy Canty, Barry Allen, James Ramseur, and Darrell Cabey was right and just and legal." But, Waples said, "You are the jury, folks, not Bernhard Goetz. . . .

"What the defendant has done in the name of self-defense in this case is ugly; it's cold-blooded; it's savage," Waples said. He then quoted Benjamin Franklin: " 'The citizen that will tolerate oppression and injustice in the name of security deserves neither liberty nor security.' "

"I hope that each of you is . . . as willing to uphold and defend Darrell Cabey's liberties as you are to honor and protect the defendant's, as you are sworn to do," Waples said. "If I have misjudged you or if you have misjudged yourselves, then I shall be disappointed; but the cause of justice shall suffer more.

"The evidence in this case has established that on December 22, 1984, Bernhard Goetz systematically and remorselessly shot four individuals in a subway car. Only you have the power to say whether . . . the defendant was behaving as a reasonable person, behaving in a manner that deserves the laws of protection . . . , or whether what he did simply cannot be tolerated by reasonable men because it makes a mockery of the notion of self-defense." Waples added, though, "Nothing you can say or do with your verdict will ever enable Darrell Cabey to walk another step again."

"I object," Slotnick said.

"Let's not appeal to emotion, please, Mr. Waples. Sustained," said Justice Crane.

"All I ask you, at this point, is to be faithful to your oaths as jurors," Waples continued. "Obey the law. Decide this case on the evidence. Be fair. Do what is right. The defendant is entitled to nothing more and we, the People, deserve nothing less.

"I thank you for your attention. I am sorry I have taken so long."

⚖

We were then excused from the courtroom and were brought back in shortly afterward only so Justice Crane could excuse us for the day. "All that remains is the charge before I give the case to the twelve of you for your deliberations," he said. He told the court officers we were free to watch the basketball game that night—the Lakers and Celtics were in the midst of the final series for the NBA championship—but, he warned us, "I need to start you at 9:00 a.m. tomorrow, so get a good night's sleep. Don't stay up too late in case that game goes into overtime."

Out of our presence, a controversy raged over Waples's demonstration of the shooting of Cabey. Slotnick began by requesting a mistrial, then argued instead for the right to reopen his case in order to rebut what Waples had said. He insisted that Waples's argument that two bullets traveled through the jacket was insupportable by the evidence. "There was never an inference that [the holes were] made by two bullets. Never," Slotnick insisted; and he said, "There is no place in the record for that type of assumption or inference."

The defense's contention was that the two bullet holes had been made by a single bullet, that the material of the jacket had been folded over or bunched up in some way. Slotnick asked that he be allowed to "bring in a ballistics expert to indicate and to prove to this jury that . . . all of the holes were made by one bullet consistent with the wound to Darrell Cabey," adding that "we don't try cases by ambush or deception."

"It is not a deception," Waples countered. "It has two holes in it. Two bullets did go through it."

"You know they were made by one bullet," Slotnick said to Waples.

"I cetainly do not," Waples shot back.

Justice Crane then asked to see the jacket and Frank King of the defense team demonstrated how the holes could be aligned with the path of a single bullet. Waples remarked, though, that "[a]ny two bullet holes can be lined up."

Waples's demonstration was based on the testimony of Detective Haase, who pointed out the extant bullet holes when the jacket was placed into evidence. After examining the transcript of Haase's testimony, Justice Crane ruled in favor of Waples and denied the defense's motions, saying that Waples had made a legitimate inference drawn from the record (that is, the existence of two bullet holes) that the defense had a full opportunity to confront during Quirk's testimony. Haase was never asked if the holes had been made by one bullet or two.

"[A]s far as I can tell, and as far as my memory goes, this could have been made by two separate bullets or could have been made by a single bullet. It is fair to infer either one and Mr. Waples can't be faulted for having taken the advantage," Justice Crane said.

Slotnick then pleaded to the judge for "three minutes" to explain the defense's counterargument to us, arguing that "to allow this jury to believe that the holes in this jacket were caused by two bullets is dishonest, deceitful, and untrue." Justice Crane denied him this as well.

The defense team continued to argue that Waples's theory was impossible, however; and eventually they did win some key concessions from the judge in this regard.

Slotnick insisted that Detective Haase had testified both bullet holes had been made by a bullet passing through the jacket from the outside in. He pressed Waples to re-create his demonstration before the judge. "I'd like Mr. Waples—other than walking away with his hands on his hips—to show us how he thinks it could have happened," Slotnick said.

Waples refused for the most part, saying, "This case is over as far as I'm concerned." He did relent to show how he believed the flap of Cabey's coat had been hanging outward, away from his body, but he declined to be drawn into a discussion about through which direction the bullet had passed.

"Judge, if the jury doesn't buy it, that is their business," Waples commented.

"The problem is, the jury may think it has some mystical quality," Slotnick retorted. "They are supposed to be told what this case is about in English."

"The district attorney just demonstrated the bullet went in there [i.e., inside to outside]," Frank King then stated.

"I was not demonstrating anywhere," Waples replied.

"You just did," King challenged.

"I was demonstrating how the coat was."

"But . . . your expert says the bullet went in from the outside of the coat. You're saying the . . . bullet went in through this way now."

"I wasn't saying that," Waples insisted.

"Am I wrong?" King continued. "Did you just pull your coat [out] and say the bullet went in this way?"

"I pulled the coat out," said Waples. "The bullet is going this way, that way. Doesn't matter."

The defense team contended that this mattered a great deal, though; and Justice Crane stated that, based on his rec-ollection of which way Haase was pointing, he agreed with them that Haase had said the holes on the outside part of the jacket were both entrance holes and that inside were the exit holes. This ruined the alignment of the gun barrel, the jacket, and the panel dent that I had imagined, because it meant that Cabey would have to have had his left side exposed to Goetz rather than his right side. Cabey, therefore, was standing facing the aisle, and, in that case, Justice Crane believed, for the bullet to have passed through the left side of Cabey's jacket where it did and still to have missed his body, the bullet could not possibly have struck the panel. Rather, it would have likely struck the storm door on the north end of the car.

According to Justice Crane, then, Waples's hypothesis that two bullets passed through Cabey's jacket *was* impossible, even if the inference that it had happened was fair. The only way he felt it could have happened were if Goetz had fired a sixth, unaccounted-for bullet that neither struck the panel nor Cabey's body. Justice Crane also stated that he believed Cabey would have had to have been seated to align the bullet hole and the dent in the panel properly because the dent was so low (only thirty-four inches from the floor) and Haase had testified that the bullet struck the panel flatly, not at an angle toward the ground.

Because Justice Crane did not want us to be "looking for a sixth bullet," he declared that he would add an admonition into his instructions to us that we were "not to speculate that there was yet another bullet unaccounted for, or on facts not in evidence or not reasonably inferrable from facts in evidence, or on facts that are incompatible with facts in evidence, or on facts that are physically impossible."

"Judge, I think that's terribly unfair. That's outrageous," Waples responded.

"I am not directing anything; I am telling them not to speculate," Justice Crane explained.

"You are singling out one argument I made and telling them not to speculate. I think that's grossly unfair," Waples complained.

Justice Crane disagreed. "I think it solves the problem here because it's physically impossible for Mr. Cabey to have been standing and for that bullet to have passed through the jacket in the location it passed through."

"There are too many variables for anyone to say that," Waples argued. "There are an infinite variety of ways this whole thing can be caused."

"We don't know where the gun was and we don't know where Darrell Cabey was," Waples explained. He also remarked, "There are two separate bullet holes in the jacket, Judge. That's sort of QED as far as I'm concerned."

Throughout our deliberations the attorneys and the judge would continue to debate over what could or could not be fairly inferred from the two bullet holes in Darrell Cabey's jacket. Our own discussion about the jacket and the manner in which Cabey was shot, though, was still a few days away.

Chapter 17

Our Deliberations

June 12

Deliberations began on Friday afternoon at 1:20 p.m., after hearing the Justice Crane's two-and-a-half-hour charge: his instructions to us of the legal principles we had to apply to what we judged were the facts of the case. The first thing I remember was a feeling of relief, because now, seven weeks after the trial started and six months to the day since I walked into the courtroom to begin jury service, I was finally free to start discussing the case. After so long a period of imposed silence, talking was a very exciting thought.

We proceeded in a sober and orderly fashion, though, and everyone exercised restraint. No one started making broad statements about the case, for instance, or spouted opinions about Goetz's overall guilt or innocence. I think we were all somewhat humbled by the complexity of the case and of the precepts the judge had given to us to follow. Now that we had our work cut out for us, we knew that there was a heck of a lot to do.

We began, then, by setting the ground rules for the way we would deliberate. James Hurley, our foreman, led this discussion after having met earlier that day with the judge. He explained to us Justice Crane's suggestions for how we should go about our work, and there was in most cases general agreement with few dissenting opinions expressed.

First, there was to be no speaking out of turn. Whenever someone had something to say, the person would have to raise a hand and wait to be recognized by the foreman. There also was to be no talking unless all were present. Discussion was suspended whenever someone had to visit the lavatory or for any other reason had to leave the room. We followed both of these rules carefully throughout.

Smoking and nonsmoking sections of the room were established, rearranging seating positions that had previously revolved around the poker and fan-tan games. Now Hurley sat at the head of the table, at the end of the room farthest from the door. I sat closest to Hurley's left, and to my left, toward the smoking side of the room, were Carolyn Perlmuth, Diana Serpe, D. Wirth Jackson, and James Moseley. On Hurley's right were Cathy Brody, Ralph Schriempf, Erniece Dix, Mike Axelrod, and Frank Figueroa. Across from Hurley, at the opposite end of the table, sat Bob Leach.

We also agreed to deal with the charges against Goetz in numerical order, beginning with count one. Nobody opposed this, although we had some difficulty with it in actual practice because the four separate counts of both attempted murder and assault were in fact so closely tied.

The one issue that did require a some discussion was that of voting openly rather than by secret ballot. Cathy Brody argued that secret ballots should be taken. Citing her experience on a jury in a previous criminal case, she said she was afraid that if a person openly argued one way on an issue, that person might be too embarrassed to change his or her opinion and agree to vote the other way.

The counterargument was that if someone argued one way and then a vote was taken that showed there was a holdout, it would be obvious then who the holdout was; and, when the vote became unanimous, it would be obvious that the person had relented. Also, a person who remained quiet would not be embarrassed but also could not be identified.

The major reason for open votes was to save time by more quickly identifying and confronting the minority opinion and then focusing on the key issues, allowing the minority the chance either to sway the majority or else to be swayed.

Brody soon relented, conceding to the logic of being time efficient. It wasn't that we wanted to rush; we just didn't want to waste time. For the sake of expediency, then, we decided against the luxury of allowing ourselves secret votes.

These issues settled, we began in earnest, discussing count number one, which was possession of a weapon in the third degree. This charge involved the gun Goetz used in the shootings, and it took us only thirty minutes or so to settle on a verdict of guilty, following the procedure we'd established for ourselves.

First James Hurley read us the charge as it was written in the indictment. We then moved directly on to a review of the pertinent evidence because there was little room for disagreement in this case. Even though the gun was never recovered, the evidence was overwhelming that Goetz had possessed a gun on December 22, 1984.

Next we reviewed the legal elements constituting the criminal possession of a weapon in the third degree that the judge had supplied to us in his charge. These simply called for us to decide whether, according to our understanding of the facts, Goetz had "knowingly possessed a loaded firearm in a place outside of his home or place of business." Obviously Goetz had been aware he had the gun; otherwise he wouldn't have thought to use it. Obviously the gun had been loaded because he'd shot four people with it. And obviously the seventh car of a ten-car IRT subway train was neither Goetz's home nor his place of business.

We then took a preliminary vote, and the vote was immediately unanimous, finding Goetz guilty, twelve to nothing. No one had been swayed by Slotnick's argument that Goetz's prior efforts to obtain a license legitimized his carrying an unlicensed weapon. There were no dissenting arguments at all.

James Hurley kept track of our vote on a yellow legal pad rather than marking it on the official verdict sheet. We had also agreed that as part of our procedure we would revote on every charge at our deliberations' end.

We moved on then to counts two and three of the indictment—the criminal possession of a weapon in the fourth degree—concerning the two "Myra" guns.

Because the issues to consider were more complex, this time we took a preliminary vote almost immediately, so that we could identify the points of contention and lines of discussion could be drawn. The vote was approximately eight, guilty; four, not guilty. Mine was one of the guilty votes.

The only elements to the charges at issue were whether Goetz had "knowingly possessed" the firearms: a .38-caliber revolver and a nine-millimeter semiautomatic pistol. Whether the guns were loaded was not an issue; and the place of possession did not have to be outside of the workplace or home. In this case, however, the question of whether Goetz did possess the guns was decidedly less clear than it had been in count one, when "physical possession" (that is, on his person) was undeniable. Here the charges involved "constructive possession," and we discussed the judge's wording of what that entailed at length.

According to Justice Crane, "possession is constructive when the weapon is found not upon the person of the defendant, but instead in a place or thing or person over which he had dominion or control." Justice Crane said the evidence had to establish that Goetz "possessed the weapon to the extent that he had the authority to do with it as he wished, whether to use it, keep it, or otherwise to dispose of it"; and that Goetz's "dominion or control" was such "that it remain[ed] available to him at all times for his use or other disposition in the place where he stored it, secreted it, or concealed it."

Some of those who had voted not guilty argued that Goetz did not have this type of control over the guns once he'd handed them over to Myra Friedman, and that the guns therefore were not within his dominion. Unless Goetz had a key to her apartment, they contended, he had at best only limited access. Also, the judge had said that, according to the law, because the guns were "found in a place to which others besides the defendant have access," that factor "may be considered by you as an indication that he didn't constructively possess [them]." Those supporting a not-guilty vote argued here that not only did Friedman have access, she also used such access to take the guns and hand them over to police.

I argued that this was "splitting hairs": that Goetz was guilty of possessing the guns "on or about December 20" at the time he handed them over to Friedman; and that speculation as to whether Goetz could later have retrieved the guns from her apartment was irrelevant. At this point at least half of the jury agreed with me.

The other major issue we still had to confront, however, was how to define Friedman's role in the possession of the weapons; that is, whether she was an accomplice or not. The reason for this, Justice Crane explained, was because "[o]ur law views with suspicion the testimony of an accomplice in a criminal trial, since by her own testimony she would thereby be a participant in the events charged in the indictment. It is for such reason that the law requires that the testimony of an accomplice must be corroborated by other evidence apart from the accomplice's own testimony. To be sufficient, such evidence standing alone must satisfy the jury that it tends to connect the defendant with the commission of the crime in such a way as may reasonably satisfy you that the accomplice . . . was telling the truth and not lying in order to serve some purpose of her own or to gain some advantage to herself.

"You, the jury, are the sole judges of the sufficiency of such other evidence to satisfy the required tests," Justice Crane continued. "If you find such other evidence insufficient . . . , you must disregard entirely the testimony of the accomplice and strike Myra Friedman's testimony from your minds."

Justice Crane quoted the New York Penal Law definition of "accomplice" as "a witness in a criminal action who, according to evidence adduced in such action, may reasonably be considered to have participated in the offense charged."

"Participation is the key test," Justice Crane told us; and we recalled Friedman's having testified while under cross-examination that she herself had proposed to Goetz her disposing of the guns by throwing them in the river. We eventually decided that even if we chose to believe Friedman's testimony, she had implicated herself as an accomplice to the crime.

Moreover, Bob Leach—one of those who voted not guilty—argued that he didn't believe what Friedman had said. This was the first time we had discussed the credibility of a witness, and we established then a pattern that we followed throughout: if we decided to disbelieve testimony, we needed a plausible motivation for the witness to lie, or a plausible reason why the witness's recall might be wrong.

In Friedman's case, Leach hypothesized that she could have had the guns for an indeterminate length of time prior to December 30, 1984, which was the date she said Goetz brought them to her. For one thing we remembered Goetz saying in his audiotaped statement that he had sold guns to friends at cost; perhaps he had sold Friedman the guns. Her motivation for lying, Leach argued, could have been that she was a writer, and that when she learned that her neighbor was the subway gunman she had concocted her story about the guns with the intent to sell a feature article—which she did, to *New York* magazine for $4,000.

A few hours into this discussion, we sent out our first two notes to the judge. The first requested twelve pens and pads of paper so that we could jot down our own notes during our discussions. These were quickly provided. The second note asked for a rereading of the judge's charge on the law concerning counts two and three. We wanted to hear again the elements constituting constructive possession, and the judge's instructions regarding the testimony of an accomplice to a crime.

We were somewhat confused as to the extent of corroboration needed to validate an accomplice's testimony. Justice Crane reread Section 60.22, subdivision one, of the New York Criminal Procedure Law, which states, "A defendant may not be convicted of any offense upon the testimony of an accomplice unsupported by corroborative evidence *tending to connect* the defendant with the commission of such offense." [Italics mine.] Justice Crane then stated that "[t]he other evidence need not prove that the defendant is guilty of the crime charged. All that the law requires is that the other evidence satisfy you that the defendant was in some manner involved in a criminal transaction and that the accomplice, in involving the defendant, was telling the truth . . ."

Back in the jury room, we discussed whether the other evidence was substantial enough to meet the "tend-to-connect" criteria of the law. What we had were the testimonies of the two men who had originally sold Goetz the guns and the documentation to that effect. We also had the testimony of

Detective Clark that he received a package in the office of Friedman's lawyer, and that the package contained the guns.

In hindsight I believe this other evidence should have been enough to substantiate Friedman's testimony and to have led us to find Goetz guilty on these two counts. George Fletcher, a Columbia law professor who closely followed the case, told me as much after the trial. Fletcher suggested that "tend to connect" was a weaker phrase than we interpreted it to be, and that all the evidence had to do was link Goetz with possession of the guns. When deliberating, though, we believed the evidence had to connect Goetz specifically with having brought the guns to Friedman's apartment "on or about December 30." This, we felt, it did not do.

We therefore searched for further corroboration. I and several others believed we remembered hearing Goetz refer to Friedman and the guns on the audiotapes. Toward the end of the day, at 6:00 p.m., we sent out our next note, requesting a "replaying of the section or sections of the audiotapes relating to Mr. Goetz's description of his delivery of a package to Myra Friedman." We also asked for a rereading of Myra Friedman's testimony "relating to Mr. Goetz's delivery of a package to her apartment at this time."

As it turned out, our memory was faulty. Goetz never did mention Friedman by name, nor did he describe having brought her a package. What he did say—and what was not replayed for us because the judge ruled, despite Waples's urging to the contrary, that it did not pertain to our request—was this: "I'd like to say something. I—I, you know, well, I have—I don't have guns any more. I have other guns . . . But I can't—I'm not willing to tell you about the other guns because it would jeopardize people who I know who are good people and it's not for me, you know—I'm not going to do it."

When we came out the judge informed us that there was nothing on the audiotapes befitting our request. The portion of Friedman's testimony we'd asked for was then reread, and afterward court was adjourned for the day.

June 13

Saturday morning we picked up where we left off, and before we finished with the "Myra" gun counts we made another request, still searching for what Goetz had said in his statements on the subject. This time we asked for a "playing back of any portion or portions of the audio- or videotapes that relate to Myra Friedman" and "that relate to Bernhard Goetz's statements and his actions from when he returned to New York after his visit to Vermont and prior to his trip to New Hampshire."

Out of our presence Justice Crane stated that this was the "same thing as yesterday. They're barking up the wrong tree." He decided to tell us there were "no explicit references" to Myra Friedman on either taped statement. "I think there's something bothering them and if I can tell them that, they'll be able to tell us what they're looking for," Justice Crane said.

Unfortunately, though, it never occurred to us to simply ask to hear Goetz's references to "other guns" he possessed. Because of how we phrased our requests, we never heard the part of his statements we spent half a day searching for; and I'm quite sure that if we had heard it, even though he never mentioned Friedman specifically, it would have made the difference in our final vote.

Ultimately we decided that the other evidence we had apart from Friedman's testimony—the evidence we knew about and could remember, at least—was not substantial enough to tend to connect Goetz with the crime of possessing the guns "on or about December 30," in lieu of our doubts about Myra Friedman's truthfulness, believing she had financial and career motivations for why she might have lied. We settled on a not-guilty verdict on counts two and three shortly before the lunch break Saturday afternoon and moved on then to the attempted murder charges.

The preliminary vote on count four, the attempted murder of Troy Canty in the second degree, was four, not guilty; and eight abstentions. Before the majority of us could make up our minds there was much to consider, much to discuss.

Again we began by reviewing the legal elements that constituted the charge. The definition of second-degree attempted murder actually comes in two parts. The judge had first read the definition of murder in the second degree from New York Penal Law Section 125.25, subdivision one: "A person is guilty of murder in the second degree when with intent to cause the death of another person he causes the death of such person." Then the judge read Section 110.00, the definition of intent: "A person is guilty of an attempt to commit a crime when, with the intent to commit a crime, he engages in conduct which tends to effect the commission of such crime."

Justice Crane told us that in judging Goetz's intent to commit attempted murder, we had to decide that murder was his "conscious aim or objective" when he pulled his gun and shot at the youths. We focused our discussion, then, on what evidence proved or disproved the existence of such intent.

Of course we had Goetz's own statements in both the audio- and videotapes that from the time he saw the smile on Canty's face and the shine in his eyes, his intention was to murder the youths. This seemed fairly conclusive proof of Goetz's intent at first, and I added that any time a person fires a .38-caliber revolver with hollow-point bullets at another person who is less than ten feet away, the intent to murder is clearly there.

We then began discussing the elements of justification, which was by far the most involved part of the judge's charge. Goetz had declared in his statements that he had not feared a robbery, although immediately after the shootings he told Armando Soler, "They tried to rob me and I shot them." If we decided a robbery was not in progress when Goetz fired his weapon, justification relied on Goetz's fear of being beaten, and whether a "reasonable man" in Goetz's position would have also believed that the youths' actions presented an "implied threat of deadly force."

Our discussion of justification was soon halted, though, as well as our discussion of the events surrounding the shootings, because someone pointed out that the judge had instructed us to consider whether justification existed only when we had otherwise agreed that Goetz was guilty of a specific charge. We had not yet settled the issue of whether Goetz was otherwise

guilty of attempted murder, and this was the first thing we had
to resolve.

D. Wirth Jackson, the seventy-four-year-old retired engineer, was the one person who disputed this, saying that he
was not convinced Goetz had intended to murder the youths.
Goetz had no motive to really want the youths dead, Jackson
felt, despite the statements Goetz had made in New Hampshire.

There was then a heated discussion, with me arguing that
the intent was present as I had believed all along. Searching
for a way to convince Jackson, however, I devised an argument
that in fact did the opposite, and I wound up deciding that I
had been wrong.

I concocted an example of a situation in which the intent
to murder is clearly present: a son who tries to kill his father
in order to inherit the family fortune. In such a case if the son
shoots and paralyzes his father, the son's "intent" has not been
satisfied; he needs his father dead in order to satisfy his "conscious aim."

As a result of this example, I switched sides and argued
vehemently that Goetz had not had such a motivation to murder
the youths; what he'd had was a motivation to shoot. The only
scenarios we could come up with where the intent to murder
would have existed were if Goetz may have been out "hunting"
the youths and had not happened upon his situation, or if, as
Waples had suggested, Goetz had been hoping the youths
"would make his day" and give him the pretext for killing
them. Both of these possibilities I had discounted and all the
other jurors had as well. I believed, therefore, that we should
find Goetz innocent of attempted murder, although in the back
of my mind I felt that if we convicted Goetz on count eleven—
the assault in the first degree of Darrell Cabey—I would ask
that we go back and reexamine count seven, the Cabey attempted-murder charge.

My argument convinced all the other abstainers except
Cathy Brody, the English professor who throughout the deliberations proved the hardest to persuade. No one ever voted
guilty on any of the non-gun-possession charges, but many
abstained, and Brody was the staunchest undecided; quite often
she was the last to be swayed.

Brody was also very articulate and often spoke for several of the less vocal members of the jury. Erniece Dix especially often waited for Brody to be convinced before she could make up her own mind; the reservations that Brody would voice were the reservations Dix had felt.

What happened several times, though, was that Brody and the majority would reach an impasse where she would still be unconvinced but would lose the ability to verbalize why. At such times I was usually the person who proved able to flesh out what Brody's reservations were and to help her overcome them. This, of course, was only in the latter stages of a discussion, after I myself had become convinced of Goetz's legal innocence.

In this case, Brody felt that the distinction I'd drawn between the son who would murder his father and Goetz's situation was an unfair test of Goetz's intent. She said that she didn't want to exculpate Goetz on what she considered a technicality, and that she still thought that Goetz might be guilty under the "spirit" of the law.

At about this time we sent out a note requesting People's exhibit one—the scale-model drawing of the subway car—as well as all of the clear plastic overlays that were in evidence on which the eyewitnesses had marked where they and others they had seen had been. We also asked for a rereading of the law concerning the attempted-murder and assault charges, including the elements "regarding all justification tests." The rereading took almost an hour, and we returned to the jury room at 4:46 p.m.

Brody still was not convinced. She was now admitting, after rehearing the law on attempted murder, that Goetz appeared to be technically innocent; but then she said something about feeling that she needed to be right before God as well as according to the law.

Once I heard Brody refer to God in a sincere way, I realized this was an issue that had to be confronted. I suggested to her that she was feeling a moral weight while deliberating on this case, and that she was concerned that someday God was going to judge her on the decisions she made. I told her also that I thought this was an unreasonable and unfair burden to put upon herself. The morality of our decisions must not concern us, I said, arguing that such responsibility was not ours, but that of the creators and overseers of our legal system.

I argued also that the technicalities of the law were decided by wiser individuals than ourselves, and that we had sworn to put aside our personal beliefs and morals and adhere to the law as it was given to us by Justice Crane when we swore our oath as jurors. By forcing that oath upon us, those overseers of our legal system effectively assumed that burden. We were sworn to perform a very specific part of the judicial procedure that we must not presume to act beyond.

This proved enough to satisfy Brody, who finally agreed that it was impossible to prove that Goetz had harbored an intent to commit murder. We unanimously found Goetz not guilty of all four of the attempted charges—counts four through seven of the indictment—and were then were prepared to move ahead to the real core of our deliberations—the assault charges, counts eight through eleven—shortly before the end of Saturday's session.

⚖

Sequestration Notes, June 10-14

Despite some protest by jurors who wanted to continue work, Justice Crane pronounced Sunday a day of rest, citing Section 5 of the New York Judiciary Law, which states that the court can do nothing but take a verdict or discharge a jury on Sunday. Because it was obvious we would be requesting parts of the charge and/or the testimony to be read back, he decided we were better off taking a break.

Whether by luck or by design, the hotel we stayed in Saturday night and all day Sunday was the plushest by far, so our day off was really quite enjoyable. It was the Marriott by LaGuardia Airport, and it had outstanding food and comfortable rooms equipped with pay-TV movie channels. Television, by the way, was supposed to be off limits, except when the court made special provisions for us to watch it—for instance, Thursday night for the basketball game—with an on-duty court officer ready to turn it off should some mention of the case be made. I confess, though, to always being able to figure out how the hotel I was in had managed to disconnect the television and reconnecting it for kicks. The only television I watched during the days of sequestration, however, were the court-approved basketball games and a couple of pay-TV movies, which I knew would be news free.

Away from home, though, I was sleeping badly, suffering through a bout of insomnia that plagued me throughout our deliberations. At night I could not stop thinking about the case and was further bothered by my roommate's snoring the first three nights, Wednesday through Friday.

The hotel on Wednesday had been the worst: a really seedy joint on Tenth Avenue and Fiftieth Street in Manhattan called the Clearview. I heard from someone that several years back the Clearview had been the site of a series of homicides where some guy from New Jersey was chopping prostitutes into pieces. That didn't help my sleeping either.

All the other hotels were located in Queens, near the airports, and except for our two-day stay at the Marriott we were moved to a different hotel each day. We ate dinner in the hotel dining rooms each night, sitting together, while the court officers sat at their own table, close by but separate. When any of us had to go to the bathroom during a meal, a court officer had to provide an escort from the dining room to the lavatory door.

The principal activity after dinner Wednesday night at the Clearview was the continuation of the jury-room card games. Almost everyone piled into my and my roommate's room, and the poker game was played on one bed, the fan-tan game on the other. After the 10:00 p.m. curfew, when everybody was escorted back to their rooms, my roommate turned down his bed to find a pink-and-white woman's nightgown made right into the bed with the sheets, apparently the result of some intense static cling. We had a pretty good laugh over it, and later I got all the jurors to autograph the nightgown and decided to keep it, strange as that might seem.

Thursday night about three-quarters of the jury watched the basketball game in a court officer's room. No news of the Goetz case flashed on the screen. We had a loud, raucous time, with ten or so people in a double-occupancy room lustily cheering for one side or the other. I felt as if I'd been transported back in time to my old college dorm.

Friday night I began to feel sick. The judge's instructions
on the law and the beginning of our deliberations that day had
combined to fatigue me, and then I became queasy during the
ride from the court owing to the motion of the minibus and
problems with the air conditioning that had heat blasting me
in the back while it was ninety-five degrees outside. I also
continued to suffer through my insomnia and my roommate's
snoring. For the third straight night I did not sleep well.

With the day off scheduled for Sunday, Saturday night was
festive and long. At dinner we were told that we had a spending
limit and that we would have to pay the difference if we wanted
to run over it. But since there was very little available that
was under the limit on the Marriott's pricey menu, the Sarge,
Jimmy Lollar, made a phone call on our behalf and the limit
was waived. I had filet mignon and a very good piece of cherry
pie. Those who drank, though, ran up quite a tab since also
on this night the normal two-drink limit was not imposed.

James Moseley, the star drinker of our group, had, like
me, been losing sleep because of his roommate's snoring. So
we decided Saturday to switch roommates and put the snorers
together. Despite the quiet, though, my mind kept racing,
thinking about the case, and I just couldn't seem to turn it off.

I felt myself becoming sicker, my resistance weakening,
and so I was determined to sleep as late as I could. I had little
luck, though. Despite leaving word not to be awakened for
breakfast, I was; and then an incessant metallic clanging from
somebody somewhere making plumbing repairs kept me from
ever falling back asleep.

At about 2:00 p.m. on Sunday I gave up and got dressed.
One of the court officers escorted Ralph Schriempf and myself
downstairs for lunch. I ate a little, but my appetite was bad.

I enjoyed that afternoon's basketball game. I'm a die-hard
Lakers fan, and they beat the Celtics to win the championship
that day. Dan Doelger, my and everyone's favorite court officer
despite his being a loyal Celtics fan, was gracious in defeat.
Another court officer named Cliff, though, ribbed him mercilessly.

That night at dinner I started feeling really sick to my
stomach, but I managed to eat a few bites and keep down my
food. I was not well at this point but I felt committed to not

letting anything stop me from going on with the deliberations. Without me, the jury would be forced to stop and wait until I was able to continue, or to replace me with an alternate and then to start from scratch.

We played poker until 10:00 p.m. but I was unenthusiastic and wound up losing big that night. Once again, I slept badly despite being exhausted. I woke up feeling more tired than when I went to sleep.

⚖

June 15

Now we were getting down to the nitty-gritty, where we were starting to reconstruct the crime in our minds and deciding what had been proven to have happened in the subway car that day. Everything else thus far had been merely preliminaries, warmups for the main event.

Our discussion had actually begun in the final two hours of Saturday's session when, equipped with People's exhibit one and all of the plastic overlays except James Ramseur's, we debated what we knew about where the youths were standing in relation to Goetz. When we resumed our discussion, we immediately requested the subway car chart and the overlays again.

We had been advised to consider each of the charges separately, one by one, but I made a speech early on, spouting a little Eastern philosophy, about how we both had to do this and yet couldn't do this. Although the law viewed each shot Goetz took at the four youths as being a separate crime, I argued that there was also a "through line" that connected all four assault charges. The through line, I said, consisted of Goetz's initial assessment of the danger he faced, the reasonableness of that assessment, and the reasonableness and appropriateness of Goetz's response. Then we would also have to decide whether Goetz ever had the opportunity to reassess his situation and therefore make a second judgment to continue shooting, which we would also have to weigh.

We first discussed what we knew about the initial threat and decided that Canty did approach Goetz, with Barry Allen and/or James Ramseur also closing around him in a semicircle.

In my mind there was always some question about whether
the second youth shot was Allen or Ramseur, and I never
entirely bought Waples's argument that Ramseur was right
beside Cabey, in front of their seat, when Goetz pulled his
gun and opened fire. We knew from the testimony of John
Filangeri that Ramseur was found lying very close to Canty,
and that due to the severity of their injuries, neither of those
two could have moved much once he'd fallen to the floor. This
implied that Ramseur was shot while in front of Goetz, not off
to Goetz's right, meaning that either three youths had been
standing around Goetz before he fired, or that Ramseur's and
Allen's positions were reversed. The majority of credible eyewitness testimony, though, had two youths standing in front of
Goetz.

Next we agreed that most of the eyewitnesses stated they
had also perceived the four youths as a group, adding to the
reasonableness of Goetz's assessment.

We also agreed that the way in which Canty got almost
nose-to-nose with Goetz meant that he had invaded Goetz's
space in a potentially hostile manner. Since in addition to Canty
there was at least a second youth and possibly a third standing
within a few feet of Goetz, and the fourth no more than five
or six feet to Goetz's right, the group represented a danger to
Goetz and the implication of a threat. The big question here,
though, was what was the nature of the threat. Was the threat
one of robbery? Was it one of deadly force?

The laws of justification varied depending on whether
Goetz was faced with a robbery or a beating, and there were
very particular criteria within these laws for what constituted
allowable self-defense. This was why, as Slotnick said, out of
our presence, the laws of justification were "the crux of the
case."

By Monday morning we had already heard the judge's
charge on the justification laws twice. The second time through
he modified his language a bit as the attorneys wrangled for
an advantage. None of us, though, ever noticed the differences,
which had to do with the examples he used from the case to

highlight the issues we had to resolve; he did not alter his description of the law itself.

Justice Crane quoted the New York Penal Law's definition of "deadly physical force" as "physical force which, under the circumstances in which it is used, is readily capable of causing death or other serious physical injury."

"The first question you must consider in deciding whether the defendant was legally justified in using deadly force in defense of his person—that is, in response to the threat of deadly physical force—is whether the defendant reasonably believed that Troy Canty, Barry Allen, James Ramseur, and Darrell Cabey, or any of them, were using or were about to use deadly physical force against him," Justice Crane said. "If the defendant believed that he was being threatened with physical force that did not rise to the level of deadly physical force, then he might have been legally entitled to employ some degree of force to protect himself, but he would not be justified under this provision of law in using deadly physical force."

Justice Crane told us, however, that we could not strictly consider whether we thought Goetz was faced with deadly force; we had to consider first "whether the defendant sincerely and honestly believed in his own mind that he was faced with a deadly threat. If you conclude that the People have failed to prove beyond a reasonable doubt that the defendant lacked this belief, you must then consider whether the defendant's personal belief was reasonable."

In judging Goetz's reasonableness, Justice Crane said we were to consider "the circumstances facing the defendant," including not just the youths' movements, but also "any relevant knowledge the defendant had" about the youths, "the physical attributes of all persons involved, including the defendant," and "any prior experiences he had which could provide a reasonable basis for belief that another person's intentions were to injure him or that the use of deadly force was necessary under the circumstances." Then, given all these facts, we should judge whether "a hypothetical reasonable person who was transported into the subway car on December 22, 1984 and who faced the exact situation which confronted the defendant" would also have held the same beliefs.

"[I]t's not enough that the defendant felt himself that his belief was reasonable," Justice Crane stated. "The question is not just what the defendant believed, but what he had a right to believe." However, Justice Crane also said that Goetz could be mistaken about the threat he perceived and be legally allowed to act against that threat as long as we judged his perception to be reasonable.

The next step in evaluating the reasonableness of Goetz's response, assuming that we judged Goetz's perception of a deadly threat to be reasonable, was to decide whether Goetz "reasonably believed that his use of deadly physical force was necessary to prevent the attack which he reasonably perceived. . . .

"In addition," Justice Crane continued, "such necessary force is limited to whatever is the extent of force he believed to be reasonably necessary. Thus, if the defendant reasonably believed that he could have repelled any threat without firing his gun—for example, by drawing and displaying his weapon—then any use of force beyond that . . . would not be legally justified.

"Moreover, even if the defendant reasonably believed that it was necessary to fire his gun to protect himself, he would be justified only in firing as many shots as he reasonably believed necessary to terminate the threat. . . . If, at some point during the encounter, the defendant continued to use deadly force when he no longer reasonably believed such was necessary to defend himself, you must conclude that he was no longer acting in self-defense."

Once again, if we concluded that Goetz believed his actions were necessary, Justice Crane told us we must also apply "the reasonable man standard that I have described" in judging whether his beliefs were sound. "If you conclude, beyond a reasonable doubt, that any particular shot was an unnecessary or excessive response to whatever threat the defendant perceived, then you must conclude that he was not legally justified in firing that shot."

This is where Justice Crane's language changed between his first reading of this part of the charge and the second reading late Saturday afternoon. In the second reading the judge deleted his example about the possibility of Goetz's drawing and displaying the gun as a less excessive way to repel the threat he faced. Also, in the first reading the judge mentioned the two shots fired at Darrell Cabey, and he told us that we had to "evaluate the question of necessity separately as to each of those two shots." In the second reading, after the defense had accused him of "marshaling the evidence," Justice Crane dropped this reference and added instead, "In assessing [Goetz's] belief and its reasonableness, you may consider the testimony of Dr. Bernard Yudwitz concerning the operation of the autonomic nervous system and its effect on the firing of a weapon in the circumstances you find were facing the defendant. . . . Anger alone, however, no matter how understandable or reasonable, can never justify the use of deadly physical force in self-defense."

The final aspect of the reasonable person standard that we had to consider if we determined that a robbery was not taking place was the "duty to retreat." Even if Goetz reasonably believed that he faced a "deadly peril," and that his use of deadly force was "necessary to repel the threat," he was not legally allowed to shoot if he knew that he could, "with complete safety to himself, . . . withdraw from the encounter" without firing his gun. If a robbery was in progress, Goetz had no such duty to retreat and was legally allowed to stand his ground.

Justice Crane defined "robbery" according to New York Penal Law as "forcible stealing" and said that forcible stealing involves the use or threatened use of physical force "for the purpose of preventing or overcoming resistance to the taking of the property. . . . To constitute robbery," Justice Crane said, "a request or demand for money must be accompanied by both an intent to steal and an implicit or explicit threat of force." He then repeated the Penal Law's definition of "an attempt to commit any crime" as being when a person "engages in conduct which tends to effect the commission of such crime."

In addition, if a person is committing or attempting to commit a robbery and is "aided by another person actually present," the "aider" is then "criminally responsible for the person who is aided in committing the robbery," Justice Crane told us. "This is known as accessorial liability or acting in concert." We were advised to again apply the "reasonable man standard" to determine whether Goetz believed, and had a right to believe, that he was about to be robbed, and also whether Goetz, when he fired the shots in question, reasonably believed that all four of the youths were acting in concert, in order to justify his having shot all four.

Finally, even though in the case of attempted robbery there is no legal duty to retreat, Goetz did have to reasonably believe "that the use of deadly force was necessary to prevent that crime." And, he said, "[t]he legal right to employ deadly physical force" under such circumstances "continues . . . only so long as the defendant reasonably believes that the specific person or persons are still attempting to rob him. . . . [I]f at some point the defendant believed that any robbery attempt had been abandoned or frustrated, then you may consider this factor along with all the other facts in the case in deciding whether he reasonably believed that his resort or continued resort to deadly physical force was necessary."

In all of these justification tests, Justice Crane reiterated to us that "the burden is on the People to establish beyond a reasonable doubt that the defendant was not acting in self-defense." The proof of this had to lie either in Goetz's perception of the threat he faced being unreasonable, or in Goetz's actions to thwart that threat being either unreasonable or excessive. These were the criteria we had to apply to the discernible facts from the evidence in this case.

As I have already said, there was very little argument that Goetz had in fact been presented with a threat. We even generally agreed we could not rule out the possibility that the threat was one of robbery although we never definitively concluded that a robbery was in progress. Most of our discussions involved the way in which Goetz reacted to the threat, with Cathy Brody the most vocal proponent that Goetz should somehow have been able to avoid responding with deadly force.

For one, Brody was reluctant to accept that the threat the youths presented constituted one of deadly force. She argued that the youths did not have weapons (we all agreed that the screwdrivers were intended to be used against video-game machines, not people), and that no overt physical threat had been made. I disagreed with Brody on this issue, and, reminding her that, according to the judge's charge, we were to take the physical attributes of all persons into account, I said I believed that any one of the youths could have beaten Goetz in a fight. As a trained martial artist, I have learned how to assess the threat of multiple opponents; and to be alone against four physically superior men, even without weapons, clearly presented the danger of death.

Brody was not convinced, however, and stated, "I still have trouble with that." We moved on then without fully resolving this issue and discussed whether Goetz had had the option of retreating.

Some jurors argued that even as Goetz first entered the car he should have perceived the potential danger the four youths presented and should not have chosen a seat so near them. Christopher Boucher, remember, testified that when he and Loren Michals boarded the train at Ninety-sixth Street they immediately noticed the youths and "just veered off and went to the front of the car" to avoid them. Other jurors argued against this, though, declaring that Goetz had no obligation to move away or to sit anywhere else than where he felt like sitting, and that were we to deem otherwise we would be making a dangerous implication that a person should be legally compelled to attempt to avoid the chance of confrontation. That would not be a sensible rule.

Once confronted, some thought that Goetz could have just drawn his gun and used it to cover his retreat. Bob Leach, though, made the age-old argument that you don't pull a gun on someone unless you're willing to use it, and others expressed support for its truth. They further contended that the youths were too close for Goetz to draw his gun and wait to see whether Canty would retreat, that if he hadn't started shooting immediately, the gun could have been wrested away and perhaps used against him. When he aimed at Canty, Cabey at least was almost directly behind him, and no matter where the youths were standing, none was more than five feet away.

The situation Goetz had faced the two times he told of on the videotape when he had pulled out his gun and did not choose to fire were different, some argued. In those cases Goetz was on the street, where he had more space between himself and his opponents and decidedly surer footing. Some jurors pointed out that the narrow aisle of a subway car, and especially in a train that is moving, would have been a precarious surface on which to attempt a retreat. Others mentioned the fact that Goetz had tried to flee from his assailants when he was mugged on Canal Street in 1981, and that he had been pursued, over-taken, and subsequently assaulted, which was another substan-tial reason why Goetz would not have felt able to retreat "with complete safety to himself."

We reached a general agreement, therefore—with Brody and a few others remaining uncommitted—that it was not fair to limit Goetz to merely drawing and displaying his weapon. Such an act would have been extremely foolish and dangerous both to himself and the other passengers, had there been a struggle with the youths for the gun. But did Goetz have to shoot all four of the youths? Was this also a necessary and reasonable response?

We did not argue long over the second youth shot once we had agreed on the shooting of Canty. Whether that had been Barry Allen—turning to run or ducking just before Goetz fired—or else James Ramseur—trying to shield himself by raising his arm—the second youth had also moved in front of Goetz, close beside Canty, and there had been little or no pause between the first and second shots. Goetz also could not afford to wait and judge the second youth's reaction because of the other two youths he had to worry about, who were standing behind him and to his right.

The next major issue we discussed, then, was whether Goetz could have stopped after firing the first two shots, when he pivoted and aimed at the second two youths. At this point, some argued, Goetz was no longer surrounded. The first two youths he had shot were down when Goetz turned and faced the other two youths.

Did Goetz have a chance to reassess the danger? Hadn't he by this time terminated the threat? We discussed Goetz's recollections in his taped statements of what the youths were doing when he took aim and fired. The third youth, Goetz said, was "trying to get through the steel wall of the subway car." The fourth, Darrell Cabey, was frozen in fear, standing still in front of his seat, one arm in the air, perhaps holding the strap, "pretending he wasn't with the other guys." Didn't Goetz's statements reflect the comprehension that he no longer needed to fire his gun? Hadn't his actions passed the point of justifiable self-defense?

The pro-Goetz argument relied primarily on Slotnick's oft-repeated phrase, "rapid succession." According to the testimony of virtually every eyewitness, there was no distinguishable gap at least between the first four shots. Whether Christopher Boucher might have been right that there was a pause before the fifth shot was an issue we could ignore for the moment. Boucher himself testified that the shots at first sounded like firecrackers; Armando Soler had said that all the shots were fired in "about a second"; Garth Reid said the duration of the shooting was only "a snap of time." Both Garth Reid and Victor Flores had seen Goetz pivot, but neither had described a discernible pause between the moment Goetz turned and the third and fourth shots.

Also, every eyewitness had been asked to vocalize the speed and rhythm of the shots they'd heard. Overall, the total elapsed time of the shots varied. Some remembered the succession to have been as quick as one-and-a-half seconds, which Joseph Quirk had testified was the fastest speed five shots could be fired from a revolver. Other eyewitnesses spaced the shots so that the total time was approximately three to four seconds. But all of them described hearing the shots in a quick and even rhythm, one after another, indicating to us that Goetz had fired while, arm extended, he rotated rather fluidly, left to right.

At about this time I and a few others began standing up and demonstrating how we thought this all occurred. I tried to show how, even if the shots had taken as much as four seconds, the fact that they were spaced in a steady rhythm did not leave time for Goetz to consider the substantive change in the danger he faced. You can try it yourself. From a sitting position, stand up and take a step to the right. Pull out an imaginary gun, turn around clockwise and point at target number one, then go boom boom boom boom, rotating clockwise and stopping at each target so that the four shots are evenly spaced, taking a total of no more than three to four seconds. It doesn't leave much time to think, does it?

The closer you place the first two targets to one another, the quicker you can hit those, leaving more time to pivot and to then assess targets three and four. But the eyewitnesses did not recall a quick boom boom—pause—boom boom pattern. What they remembered were four or five shots, one after the other, virtually without pause.

In my mind, then, the only time Goetz had to assess whether he would have to shoot four youths or two was in the moments before he pulled his gun. If he had decided then that shooting two would be enough, he would have stopped automatically. He said in his statements, though, that he was aware all four of them were a group, and that when he'd made up his mind to shoot, he had decided to shoot them all.

Of course, I and the others were well aware that this was not all Goetz had said about his decision to shoot the youths. When we had decided Goetz lacked a true motive to commit murder in spite of his professed intention to kill the youths, though, the precedent had been established in our deliberations for how Goetz's words in his taped statements would be weighed. Not that we made any specific rules; everybody decided how much weight to give what when considering any argument. But there was a general consensus that Goetz's recollections were more reliable up until the moment he began shooting than from that moment on, and that more significance should be attached to his statements about actual events than all his hate-filled declarations about what he had been thinking at the time.

James Moseley was one vocal proponent of our being fair to Goetz by considering the circumstances surrounding his statements. He mentioned that Goetz was obviously under stress, that he was exhausted and clearly distraught; that he'd lived with the incident for nine days already, and that for those nine days he had been on the run; and that he had to go through his story three times with police (we had seen in the difference between the audio- and videotapes how much more tired and upset he'd become).

Someone suggested that in Goetz's statements about how he'd wanted to make the youths suffer as much as possible, how he wished he'd put his gun to Cabey's head and fired, and how he'd wanted to gouge Canty's eyes out with his keys, he was expressing the rage he felt for the way in which his encounter with the youths had turned his life upside down and for the emotional turmoil he was suffering as a result. And although Goetz argued fiercely that his actions had been justified, it also seemed possible that these atrocities he accused himself of having thought of or committed had been brought on by a sense of guilt and revulsion for what he had done. They were the statements of a man who felt that his life was ruined, or at least that his life was irrevocably changed; now that the subway gunman had given himself up, everyone would soon know Bernhard Goetz's name.

We had already seen our way past Goetz's pronouncement that his intention was to commit murder; and we had largely agreed that it had not been proved that Goetz did not have a right to shoot at least the first two youths, even though he said that showing the gun would have been enough to thwart their threat. We now discounted his analysis of how Allen, Ramseur, and Cabey were trying to escape as hindsight recollections of what he had seen through what we believed had been an adrenal haze.

Describing on the audiotapes "what it's like to be on the other side of violence," Goetz said "it's like a picture," and that's how we interpreted his recollections about the actions and expressions of the youths. Nine days after the incident, we believed Goetz had stored in his mind four photographs of how the youths looked when he shot them, and since then these snapshots had become motion pictures, his imagination having stretched each moment out. What he was interpreting as "running into the subway car wall," then, might not have been more than a reflexive movement youth number three made when Goetz turned his attention to him and fired.

While still in his seat, Goetz had decided on a plan of action—as he put it, he'd laid down his pattern of fire. We concluded that despite his recollections, it was not reasonable to expect that Goetz could have made a split-second assessment in such a stressful situation that he no longer had to shoot. Under the circumstances, his mind may not necessarily have been on automatic pilot, but certainly his body was working more quickly than his mind.

That afternoon we requested a third reading of the justification laws as they related to first- and second-degree assault. The elements of first-degree assault involve the causing of "serious physical injury" by means of a "deadly weapon," with such serious physical injury being Goetz's "conscious aim or objective." Assault in the second degree (which we had been instructed to consider if we found Goetz not guilty of first-degree assault) does not require proof of such intent to injure, but does require that the causing of the serious injury was the result of a reckless act where the causer "is aware of and consciously disregards a substantial and unjustifiable risk that serious physical injury will result."

In this third time through the justification laws, Justice Crane once again altered his language slightly, although, as I said before, these changes went right over our heads. This time the judge combined his two versions, reinstating his example of Goetz's merely drawing his gun as a lesser form of deterrence than firing it, and also including his example of Dr. Yudwitz's testimony as a possible excuse for why five shots were not excessive. The key here, though, is that the judge was only providing examples of how to apply the law to the issues of the case, and we fully understood that we had to judge the results for ourselves. Neither I nor any of the other jurors, I'm sure, would ever accuse the judge of having marshaled the evidence, although both Waples and Slotnick took exception to his language, and Slotnick directly accused him of such.

After hearing the law read once again, however, Cathy Brody was still undecided about whether Goetz should have used his gun at all, as was Erniece Dix. At this point, though, Brody was having more and more difficulty pinpointing her problem; she just had a strong conviction that the level of violence with which Goetz responded had been unwarranted and inappropriate, and that he had done something terribly wrong.

Quite a few of us, myself included, also did not consider Goetz's actions personally appropriate, but perhaps we had less trouble separating our own convictions about what we would have done in Goetz's position from the justification tests provided by the law. We had to judge Goetz on the law as charged to us, not on any individual moral code. The job before us, then, seemed less to assess the reasonableness of Goetz's actions than to determine whether anything he'd done had been proven to be unreasonable. That's why I believed the case boiled down to the way Goetz shot Cabey, and whether Waples had proved that a separate shot had been fired at a seated target beyond any reasonable doubt.

I had a hunch about what was bothering Brody and speculated that she believed the four youths weren't going to attack or forcibly steal from Goetz, that their tactic was to intimidate him into giving them what they wanted, and that therefore she felt shooting them wasn't appropriate; what was called for was some less violent response. Brody said this was her problem exactly, and she commented that I was the only one who seemed to be able to verbalize her doubts.

I pointed out to her then that legally we did not need to decide whether or not the youths would have resorted to robbery or physical assault. According to the law, the reasonable belief that an implied threat of deadly force was present would be enough to justify Goetz's response.

Still, Brody was not satisfied, saying again that she wasn't convinced the four youths presented the potential threat of death to Goetz in the manner they confronted him and given that they were unarmed.

For the first time the mood in the room became tense, as Brody began to feel more and more isolated and also perhaps that she was being ganged up on. Whenever we sensed these feelings, however, we responded by offering her waves of reassurance—hugs and sundry consoling statements—that we were only trying to persuade her, not to pressure or coerce her in any way. Brody would then insist that she was not feeling put upon, but in truth I think the pressure was there. Everything we were doing at this point was to convince Cathy, all the arguments and demonstrations we made. We were all eager to resolve the situation and needed an idea to break the stalemate.

Brody had requested yet another reading of the law regarding justification, and many of us argued against this, feeling it would be a waste of time. A lot of discussion was going on, though, about what we could do to try to resolve the "deadly force" issue. We seriously considered asking the judge to allow us to revisit the subway car so that we could re-create the shootings. A related suggestion was to request that we be allowed to use the taped outline of the car the defense had made for Joseph Quirk's demonstration that was still on the floor of the well of the courtroom and had been entered into evidence. In order to do this, though, the room would have had to have been cleared, so this also would have been a major hassle. (After the trial I mentioned our idea to Justice Crane, however, and he told me that it would have been allowed.)

I and several others were opposed to both of these schemes, believing that the narrow confines of our deliberation room could serve well enough to illustrate the situation Goetz was in. We could easily stage a re-creation here, I felt, just by pushing the furniture around. We never agreed to do that either, however; several people balked at the suggustion, and we decided we had to be more scientific than that. If it was going to be done at all, everyone wanted to do it right.

I didn't feel, though, that such a re-creation was going to produce any added result. To be honest, I was becoming extremely frustrated that Brody, Erniece Dix, and perhaps also Diana Serpe didn't seem to accept the points I was making; and it looked like we were heading into several more days of what to me would seem pointless arguing.

Small personality conflicts were also beginning to emerge. For instance, I mentioned from my knowledge of martial arts that there are two pressure points at the base of the skull where a person can be killed if hit by a blow, and that this was one way in which Goetz's life was in danger, especially from Darrell Cabey when Goetz stood and faced Canty. I got the definite impression, though, that such talk about what could have happened turned some people off. Mike Axelrod, for one, made it clear that he just didn't want to hear it.

In the nick of time, then, as the tension in the room continued to build and Brody was becoming increasingly defensive and intractable, James Moseley came up with an idea that saved the day. A graphic artist, Moseley drew a small figure on a piece of paper, which he then cut out and showed to us.

"I'd like to introduce you to William Reasonable," Moseley said.

The figure was of a round-headed, bespectacled man with large, droopy eyes, a big nose and sad mouth—a comical character that looked like Ziggy from the cartoons. Moseley then cut out four more figures that he called Unreasonable numbers one, two, three, and four. They were similarly drawn only without the glasses and with angry, threatening expressions on their faces.

Sticking these figures onto a plastic overlay covering the subway chart with small pieces of chewing gum, Moseley then replayed his interpretation of what happened on the train from beginning to end. Done in a deadpan, humorous vein, his presentation really eased our tension and had everybody smiling and laughing again.

Moseley's argument was also extremely persuasive, because for the first time he played out the entire scenario. In all of the eyewitness testimony we had heard, everyone had seen only bits and pieces of what had happened. And, because of all the photographs we'd been shown, there was a tendency to think of the whole confrontation as a series of fragments, like a slide presentation instead of a movie. Instead of, say, Canty is at point A, sitting across from Goetz, then he's at point B, in Goetz's face, Moseley showed us Unreasonable Number One moving across the aisle to approach Bill Reasonable, while Unreasonable Number Two stands and also walks over to him, and Unreasonable numbers three and four stand as well. Unreasonable Number Three then moves into the aisle a bit; the four Unreasonables are slowly closing in.

Bill Reasonable's demeanor also greatly affected us as we watched Moseley manipulate his figures. For the first time as we witnessed this re-creation it was not Bernhard Goetz seated in that car. After having seen and heard four hours of Goetz's taped statements, and after listening to Waples's assessment of Goetz in his opening statement and closing argument, Goetz's personality had been indelibly impressed on us. We had unavoidably become filled with preconceptions after having heard so much emotionally charged rhetoric and witnessing the anger and hatred that on the tapes were almost consuming Goetz.

Now in Goetz's place was this cartoon character who looked like a mild-mannered, average Joe. And as the Unreasonables stood around him it became increasingly clear that anyone could have been frightened in such a position on that train, especially someone who had been mugged before. The compassion we felt for Bill Reasonable, therefore, made it easier to sympathize with Bernhard Goetz, even if we couldn't condone his behavior. We had been told to weigh Goetz's actions against that of a hypothetical reasonable person, and through those instructions, with the help of Bill Reasonable, came our understanding that Goetz had been reasonably afraid.

Brody told Moseley he'd made "a wonderful presentation," and soon after she reluctantly agreed that at least the first three shots at Canty, Allen, and Ramseur had not been proven to be unjustified. We then unanimously voted Goetz not guilty on those three assault charges—counts eight, nine and ten—and focused our discussion exclusively on the one remaining assault charge and the question of how Darrell Cabey was shot.

Our deliberation on count eleven took up about twenty percent of our total time and overlapped with discussions of the other assault counts quite a bit. Even as I argued to acquit Goetz for the assault of Canty, Allen, and Ramseur, then, I felt that the Cabey assault was different and made it clear to everyone where I stood. If Cabey had been shot as part of a single burst of gunfire, I believed Goetz had to be found not guilty given the verified threat he faced. If, however, the evidence proved Goetz had shot Cabey in the way he'd described—after a pause that provided him the opportunity to reflect on and to reassess his situation—I was convinced that Goetz should be found guilty of that crime.

This was the big question of the whole trial. Did Cabey get hit by a bullet that paralyzed him while standing in front of his subway seat, then fall backward into the seat as a second bullet fired at him missed, striking the wall of the conductor's cab? Or was he missed by the first volley and then cold-bloodedly and unjustifiably shot while cowering in his seat?

We began by discussing Christopher Boucher, the only eyewitness whose testimony corroborated Goetz's statements. We discovered that we all had problems with the veracity of parts of his testimony, but if we were to find Waples's reconstruction of the shooting to be credible, then the essential aspects of Boucher's testimony would be true, and its inconsistencies would have to be explained away. Without tangible corroboration, however, we did not find Boucher's testimony terribly convincing. It differed dramatically from that of all the other eyewitnesses, and there were a few glaring inconsistencies within the testimony itself.

The key to the reconstruction was Cabey's jacket, so early Monday afternoon we sent out a note requesting "provision of Darrell Cabey's jacket and the . . . screwdrivers that were found in said jacket for use in the jury room." We also asked for a rereading of any testimony regarding the jacket, which was primarily that of Detective Haase.

Until now whenever we had sent out requests to the judge they were complied with relatively quickly, usually within an hour or so. This time, though, there was a long delay as the attorneys argued with the judge about the instructions he would give us concerning the jacket, which was a carryover of the argument that raged after Waples's summation concerning what the two bullet holes legitimately inferred and what, if anything, could be proved.

Slotnick argued that the judge should tell us "to ignore any argument about two bullets entering into the jacket of Darrell Cabey, as there is no such evidence to that effect in this record and that is impossible under the facts in this case."

Waples repeated his contention that he had made a fair inference based on the evidence, and that if Slotnick "wanted to change the state of the record, he should have done so as part of his case, rather than accusing me of misconduct for making arguments based upon the facts of the record, which is something he is not doing."

The defense team insisted, though, that Waples's demonstration could not be supported by the evidence, and Slotnick cited a previous case in which a conviction was overturned by the New York State Court of Appeals, where "the assistant district attorney, in his summation, improperly indicated to the jury that there was something in evidence that was not." Moreover, Mark Baker added, "the error was exacerbated. The jury requested the very exhibit which was the cause of what was determined to have been unsupportable in the record. That is exactly the case we have here," Baker said. "Absent the jury being told that the district attorney's version was impossible to prove," he stated, "I submit to the Court, most respectfully, if there is a conviction on this count it's absolutely reversible error."

"I think you have to meet this one head on, Judge," Slotnick said.

Justice Crane maintained the same basic position he had held on Friday, that "Mr. Waples has testimony in the record from Detective Haase that licensed him to suggest two separate bullets" because Haase "pinpointed the two holes on the outside [of the jacket] as entrance holes." Justice Crane added, "I can't say, as a matter of law, that the demonstration was fallacious." He did concur with the defense team, however, that, given his understanding of Waples's argument, he didn't believe the second hole through Cabey's jacket could be aligned with "the flat shot against the stainless steel panel" if Cabey was standing at the time. "It seems to me . . . it wasn't possible unless you have a sixth bullet, . . . a separate shot that . . . hit that panel," Justice Crane said, because, he believed, the shot that went through Cabey's jacket would have made "a different kind of impact" on the panel "as far as this record is concerned."

What Justice Crane decided, then—once again, over the objections of both the defense and the prosecution—was to remind us not to speculate about facts not in evidence, particularly about the possibility of there having been a sixth bullet. Slotnick did not think this went far enough.

"I think it's quite clear that what Your Honor is going to allow—and I see it right now—is a misconception and a deception to be sent to the jury," Slotnick said. "There is nothing we can do except to hope their good common sense overcomes that."

After Justice Crane had delivered his instructions to us about the jacket, however, it was Waples who really had a fit.

"You have just heard a read back of all the testimony that existed in the trial about People's exhibit four, Darrell Cabey's jacket," Justice Crane began. "You are asking me to see this jacket in the jury room. As I give it to you, I remind you that during the charge I told you that you must not indulge in speculation or guesswork. I gave you an example but prefaced it with the reminder that you are the sole and exclusive judges of the facts. By referring to this example, I told you that I was in no way dictating to you what the evidence shows or invading your province as the sole and exclusive judges of the facts. I also mentioned that I was neither approving nor disapproving any argument in summation by respective counsel.

"I repeat these remarks as I repeat the example," Justice Crane said, prefacing a discussion of Waples's demonstration. He then told us that, concerning Waples's postulations about the bullet holes and how Darrell Cabey was shot, "[t]here was no testimony, expert or otherwise, to establish these facts, so . . . the demonstration must rest on inferences from the facts in evidence—principally the testimony of Detective Haase.

"Incidentally," Justice Crane added, "in considering inferences I remind you that where two inferences may be reasonably drawn, one consistent with innocence and the other consistent with guilt, the defendant is entitled to the inference of innocence."

Justice Crane then reminded us that Haase's testimony asserted the bullet that dented the stainless steel panel "impacted more or less flatly" and said, "[Y]ou are not to speculate . . . that, for example, there was yet another unaccounted-for bullet. Neither are you to speculate on matters not in evidence, nor reasonably inferrable from facts in evidence; and . . . you must not rely on inferences that are incompatible with other facts you have . . . unless you are honestly able to reconcile them. Finally, you must not draw inferences that are physically impossible. Thus, any suggestions conveyed to your minds of things not in evidence or reasonably inferrable therefrom should be resolutely removed from any consideration by you."

He excused us then, sending the jacket with us, and we interpreted his instructions to be a stern reminder of our duty

to maintain a presumption of innocence if more than one
scenario for the jacket's having two bullet holes could be fairly
inferred. None of us presumed that his words were guiding us
toward an interpretation of the evidence. Neither Waples nor
Slotnick, though, was satisfied with what Justice Crane had
said.

"Your Honor should have told the jury to ignore the
statement in summation," Slotnick repeated after we'd left.

"I don't see how Mr. Slotnick can protest that charge,
because that amounts to the direction to the jury to disregard
that portion of my summation," Waples countered angrily. "I
think what I just heard was the most one-sided and most
unwarranted instruction that I have ever heard given to a jury.
It's completely unfair. I made a perfectly proper argument
based on the evidence again repeated here, and I just cannot
fathom how Your Honor can give that instruction to this jury."

"Same way I couldn't fathom how Mr. Waples could have
given his statement to the jury in summation," Slotnick said,
gloating perhaps.

Listening to the rereading of Haase's testimony, I realized
it did not clearly support or refute Waples's reconstruction of
the way in which Cabey was shot. I found it to be extremely
ambiguous and ultimately inconclusive. Often when a witness
was demonstrating something, the judge would ask the examining attorney to "make a record" by describing what was
being demonstrated so that it would be recorded on the trial
transcript. When Haase testified about the bullet holes, however, he did not specify the direction in which the bullets
passed through the jacket, whether it had been outside in or
inside out. I felt that the record had to clearly state that the
bullet Waples said missed Cabey and then hit the panel entered
through the inside part of Cabey's jacket and exited the outside.
But what Haase had said when pointing out the bullet holes
was their respective locations on the left side of the jacket and
in each case that the bullet had entered "here" and exited
"here." We could only surmise, since the bullet that struck
Cabey had to have passed from the outside in, that he had
indicated the second bullet had passed in that direction as well

or else he would have more clearly distinguished between the two.

I was the first to try on the jacket when it arrived in the jury room. Inserting the screwdrivers and zipping the pockets, the weighted flap of the jacket did hang loose from my body when I leaned far enough forward; and when I lifted my arm as if holding a subway strap and standing facing the "Cabey" seat, the location of the bullet hole under the armpit was fractions of an inch forward of my chest. James Moseley then tried on the jacket to see what he could see.

For me, though, the possibility of finding Goetz guilty on the Cabey shooting had been dealt a serious blow. I decided I could not support a conviction based on Waples's reconstruction, owing mostly to the inconclusiveness of Haase's testimony. Of course, we were not aware of the defense's theory that one bullet made both bullet holes. But I came up with another theory that I soon considered more probable than the one that coincided with Waples's hypothesis, given that Haase seemed to have indicated two bullets had passed from the outside in: Cabey could have been standing in front of his seat, facing the aisle, and been hit by the fourth shot that Goetz fired. That shot could have been the one that paralyzed him and, as he was falling backward into the seat, Goetz's gun, following his fall, could have fired again. The fifth bullet could have just missed hitting Cabey's body, passed through the left side of his jacket, forward of his chest, and then struck the panel "more or less flatly," leaving the dent on the conductor's cab wall.

Sequestration Notes, June 15

During the day I was feeling worse and worse. Despite the air conditioning that kept the jury room quite cool, I was sweating and feeling feverish. I had no appetite at all for lunch.

On the bus ride to our hotel that evening, I really had to struggle not to vomit and succeeded in making it all the way to my room before I started throwing up what little there was in my stomach. I lay on my bed then and tried to relax.

The court officers on duty that night, showing concern for my condition, wanted to bring me to a doctor. I refused, however, not wanting anything to hold up our deliberations. To me this was like the big game, and if I was going to be taken out it would have to be on a stretcher. And anyway I was feeling pretty sure that tomorrow was going to be the last day.

In bed, then, I sweated out the fever for a couple of hours and from time to time wondered how the Michael Spinks-Gerry Cooney fight was going. I was hoping Spinks would win.

About the same time that Cooney hit the canvas and stayed down for the count of ten, I felt my fever break. Moseley and I played crazy eights for a while, and then I slept decently for the first time in a week.

I wasn't feeling like Superman when I woke the next morning, but I did manage to eat some breakfast, and after that my condition noticeably improved. Then I had a sandwich at lunchtime, and forgot all about how lousy I'd been feeling in the excitement of that afternoon.

June 16

Our discussion of Christopher Boucher's testimony was focused on its many inconsistencies and the impossibility of some of what he claimed. The most glaring error was his recollection of what Cabey was doing when he saw Goetz fire the final shot. Boucher said Cabey was sitting and gripping the front edge of the seat with "a frightened look on his face," his hands just outside of his knees. He placed Goetz perpendicular to Cabey, two or three feet directly in front of him, with his right arm extended and crooked at the elbow, the gun held slightly above the waist. When Goetz pulled the trigger, Boucher said Cabey "just tightened"; he did not see Cabey jerk his arm, twist, or flinch in any way. But it was obvious to us that unless Cabey did twist to the right, he could not have been hit at the angle of the bullet that entered his body.

Even granting room for error in Boucher's depth perception as he looked at the scene from the south end of the car, and therefore placing Goetz a few feet south of Cabey's seat instead of perpendicular to Cabey, that still would not make it possible for the shot Boucher saw to coincide with Cabey's wound. Cabey would have to have moved, and Goetz himself said that he fired reflexively when Cabey jerked his arm. Boucher didn't see that, perhaps because, as Waples had emphasized, Boucher's attention was riveted on the gun.

For Boucher's account to be correct, there also would have been an audible separation between the fourth and fifth shots, and that separation had not been noticed by *any* of the eight other eyewitnesses who had testified before us. We considered this to be highly improbable, given the circumstances and the loudness of the shots. Armando Soler had heard the shots clearly from where he was standing, at the south end of the car in front of the one in which the shots were fired. Mary Gant, the eyewitness seated nearest to Goetz, said that the shots were the loudest noise she ever heard. Gant also had been knocked to the floor while most of the other eyewitnesses were scrambling to escape. One would certainly think that in such a situation, when people are fearful and hoping that the shooting will stop, they all should have heard, after a pause, that fifth and final shot.

Tuesday morning we requested a rereading of both Boucher's and Loren Michals's testimonies, and we also asked to review the police report of Boucher's statement that was made on the day of the shootings.

There were many minor discrepancies between their two accounts of what happened, and the one major one: Michals did not see nor remember hearing the final shot that Boucher swore he saw.

Michals was sitting to Boucher's right, and to Michals's right was Andrea Reid. When the shots were fired, Michals said his view was blocked by Reid, who was "holding her baby and starting to get up, so I didn't have a clear view instantly." At the same time, Michals said, "Christopher and I were starting to get up and move towards the door."

Once Andrea Reid had moved past him, Michals said he could then see down the center of the car. He saw one youth "slumping to the floor in a kind of fetal position near the bench that was across from me," and another youth "slumping in a seat." From their descriptions Michals would appear to have seen Barry Allen and Darrell Cabey, and at this moment Cabey had already been shot. Goetz, he said, was "pretty much just standing still" near the center of the aisle, making "a motion like he was perhaps putting something in his pocket. I only looked at him really for a couple of seconds," Michals added, "then turned to try to get out of the car."

Michals also testified that he had been approximately forty feet from Goetz when he looked back and saw him, that "there quickly had been a number of shots" although the precise number had "faded with time," and that his friend Christopher "really seemed shaken up" after the incident, "so we went . . . to a bar and had a quick drink."

Comparing this with Boucher's version, I had more faith in the accuracy of Michals's account. Both at first had not recognized that the noises they were hearing were gunshots. Michals said he was "half-dozing" and thought the sounds were coming "from outside the car." Boucher said that he "heard popping" and thought "the kids at the other end of the train were shooting off firecrackers."

The next thing Boucher noticed was that Andrea Reid, with her baby, "jumped up and had fallen over Loren." Michals then "was assisting her up," and at this time, Boucher said, his view was still blocked. Once Michals and the woman had moved out of the way, Boucher, still seated, saw Goetz standing before Cabey and "in just a matter of seconds" Goetz then fired.

Discrepancy number one, then, was the issue of Andrea Reid's "falling over" Loren Michals. Michals did recall this happening and Andrea Reid insisted it did not. Next, Michals said he and Boucher together stood up to exit the car. According to Boucher, he remained seated until after Michals and Reid had moved away. Also, when Waples asked him how many shots he had heard altogether, Boucher said he was "positive" that there had been "three."

Under cross-examination Boucher denied that the shots had occurred in rapid succession, saying he had heard definite pauses between the shots. He admitted to having been "shocked" and "shaking" on the subway platform but said he had not been overly traumatized by what he had seen.

Slotnick also asked Boucher if he had discussed his testimony with Michals. Boucher said that they had not gone over it in detail but admitted they had "discussed little bits." Minutes later Slotnick asked Boucher how far he had been from where Goetz was standing. Without hesitation, Boucher responded with the precise answer Michals had given to this question: "About forty feet."

Recalling Boucher's testimony back in the jury room, I did not remember Boucher admitting he had ever discussed his testimony with Michals and believed that very quick, assertive answer to be a clear indication that he had. In hindsight I can see that Boucher was not lying, but that is how I interpreted this detail at the time.

According to the police report that was written on the day of the shootings, Boucher told the officer who wrote the report that two youths were in the small seat when Goetz shot at Cabey. When testifying, Boucher denied having made that statement, but in weighing the credibility of Boucher's testimony, we also took that discrepancy into account.

Overall we agreed that there was a great deal of reasonable doubt as to the veracity of Boucher's testimony. No one really felt that Boucher was lying, but we believed he could have been mistaken about what he thought he had seen.

I thought Boucher's greatest weakness as a completely credible witness was that he often acted too sure of himself compared, for example, with Loren Michals. For instance, where Michals claimed to have heard "three or four" or even five shots, he excused his uncertainty by simply saying that time had made his memory suspect. And, after all, this was two and a half years after the fact. Boucher, however, said he was certain three shots had been fired. Such statements made one wonder what other details Boucher was recalling inaccurately that he said he was certain about.

Despite the lack of tangible physical evidence and our doubts about Boucher's testimony, there remained Goetz's own description of how he shot Cabey. Even without substantial corroborating evidence, we still had to explain away the tapes.

By this time, we had already generally agreed to disregard Goetz's inflammatory remarks. When Goetz made these statements (for example, "For a period of time, I was a cold-blooded murderer"; "I wanted to kill those guys; I wanted to maim those guys; I wanted to make them suffer in every way I could"; and "If I had more bullets, I would have shot 'em all again and again"), were these the comments of a man with a score to settle, a man who held the entire city of New York in contempt, and a man who had decided to take the law into his own hands and deliver his own brutal brand of justice? Or were these the words of a frightened, confused, bitter man who was just coming to terms with the fact that, as a result of what he'd done, his life had been irrevocably changed; and the manifestations of internal turmoil, guilt, self-deprecation, self-directed rage? On the one hand, there really was no way for us to know for certain. And on the other hand it really did not matter, because although it might have made a difference concerning intent, we primarily had to judge Goetz on his actions; not on his words but on his deeds.

In some cases, though, we did find Goetz's statements unintentionally exculpatory. For instance, when Goetz said on the audiotapes about shooting Cabey, "If I was a little more under self-control—I was so out of control—I would have put the barrel against . . . his forehead and fired," Goetz's admission that he was out of control made it seem more likely his recollections could be wrong.

"I don't believe in all this insanity stuff, because you know what you're doing," Goetz said at another point. "But if you can accept this: I was out of control . . . [M]aybe you should always be in control, but if you, if you put people in a situation where they're threatened with mayhem, several times, and then if . . . a person . . . turns into a vicious animal, I mean . . . what do you expect, you know?"

In fact, on the audiotapes Goetz admitted to quite a bit of uncertainty and disorientation about what had happened once he started while firing his gun. He said, for one, that he "hardly heard the gun firing." And when Detective Domian asked him, "Did you just shoot each one of these people just once?," Goetz responded, "Well, you see, that's why I—that's— that's one of the things that puzzles me." Later he added, "[T]hat's what must have happened. That's what did happen. . . . Because that's the way to do it. It's—It's the only—It's the only logical way."

Goetz also complained about news reports in which the police had said he'd fired four shots when he was certain he'd actually fired five. It seemed very possible to us, however, that Goetz realized he'd fired five shots sometime after he'd fled the subway, when he had an opportunity to check his gun and see that all five bullets were gone. Then, in explaining to himself what had happened, he might have fabricated something he had not done.

Could it, however, be merely a coincidence that the erroneous scenario Goetz composed was the same one remembered by an eyewitness? As Waples said in his closing argument, could Boucher and Goetz both have had "the exact same terrible dream?" Several jurors argued this just didn't seem possible, pointing out also how frighteningly accurate Goetz's recollection was concerning so many other details of the events on that train. How could we know that so much of what he said was correct and yet choose to disbelieve such a significant event as the shooting of a seated person?

Once again, our ultimate decision rested on the concept of reasonable doubt. Cathy Brody was the final convert, as she had been throughout; but she acquiesced because we agreed we just couldn't be certain of what had happened. Maybe Goetz did shoot at Cabey when he was seated. I still think it is possible that that in fact is what occurred. But neither Goetz's own incriminating statements, the corroborative testimony of Christopher Boucher, nor the two bullet holes in Cabey's jacket was enough to *convince* me that it had happened. And all the other jurors, ultimately, were unconvinced as well.

We made one very bad—in fact, inexcusable—mistake, however, as we searched for a reason to justify how Goetz and Boucher had come up with the same fabrication, if a fabrication was what it was. Despite all of the judge's admonitions against speculating on facts not in evidence, we surmised that perhaps, since we knew from the tapes that Goetz had been reading and listening to news reports about the shootings, Goetz might have learned of Boucher's version and concocted his story as a result. I have since learned that Boucher's version was not reported until he testified before the grand jury; so not only were we wrong to speculate, but we drew a conclusion that was absolutely false.

After all of this discussion, we still had to have one final round of discussion to convince Cathy Brody that Goetz faced the threat of deadly force. She was holding out on acquitting Goetz of the assault of Cabey on this issue because Cabey was the last youth shot.

We more or less repeated all our previous arguments; and I contended that at the moment when Goetz started firing it was from Cabey that he had the most to fear. I reiterated that when Goetz pulled his gun and turned to face Troy Canty, Cabey had the opportunity to grab Goetz from behind. All Cabey had to do was to have reacted quickly enough, and I argued that the fact that this hadn't happened did not eliminate it as a danger and something that Goetz could have reasonably feared. I urged Brody to accept the threat that the youths represented as one that could have resulted in Goetz's death.

Finally, Brody reluctantly agreed that there was too much reasonable doubt to support a conviction either on the basis of how Goetz shot Darrell Cabey or because of a nagging belief that the shooting of four unarmed youths on a subway train is not a reasonable act, and that somehow Goetz must have overstepped that which the law allows.

We did not need a very long time to reach agreement on the two remaining charges. First, though, we did have the law reread to us concerning counts one and twelve—the criminal possession of a weapon in the third and second degrees, respectively—both involving the gun that Goetz used in the subway.

Hearing the legal elements that constituted count one again, no one quarreled with our prior guilty verdict. The distinguishment in the law between counts one and twelve, though, involved the "intent to use the [gun] unlawfully." In order to find Goetz guilty of the criminal possession of a weapon in the second degree, we would have had to agree that the unlawful use of the gun against another person was Goetz's "conscious aim or objective."

We had rejected, however, the prosecution's suggestion that Goetz had been hoping for trouble on the subway that day, and we had agreed, by virtue of our not-guilty verdicts on all the assault charges, that Goetz's use of his gun had not been proven to have been illegal. We also believed, therefore, that there was no substantial proof of any unlawful intent. The only thing that had been proven was Goetz's illegal possession of the gun.

Similarly, with count thirteen, reckless endangerment in the first degree, which was limited to the lives of the train-car passengers other than the four youths Goetz shot, we had already decided that Goetz's actions had not been proven to to have been unjustified; therefore they could not be judged to have been entirely "reckless" or committed with a conscious disregard of "substantial and unjustifiable risk." As with the four assault counts, we considered second-degree reckless endangerment as well, the difference being that in the first-degree charge, the reckless acts also had to "evinc[e] a depraved indifference to human life."

With no dissenting argument, then, we voted not guilty on these last two counts.

Afterword

Goetz Is Sentenced

By the end of our deliberations, several members of the jury nicknamed me Barry, Jr., for having argued Goetz's case as well as Slotnick. The truth is that I can be very vocal and I think I also can be quite persuasive. Mike Axelrod called me "the mouth that roared."

I sincerely believe that if the evidence had borne out Waples's case, I would have been able to convince the others to reach a verdict of guilty on one or more of the assault counts. The jurors could have just as easily been calling me Greg, Jr., in my opinion.

To you who have read this book and believe in Goetz's guilt on the assault and attempted murder charges, I suggest that the fault in failing to convict him lies not with the jury nor the judge nor the prosecutor, but with a deficiency in the justification laws. The law, I think, is not specific enough about the alternatives Goetz should have been required to seek before being allowed to fire his gun as a legitimate act of self-defense.

According to the law, as explained by Justice Crane, once the implied threat of deadly force is present a person can shoot to defend himself if he cannot retreat "with complete safety to himself." When a person is confronted by two or more persons within the close confines of a moving subway car, a strong argument can always be made that the person's safety is not ensured. I believe that a truly reasonable person with a proper respect for the sanctity of human life should do more than Goetz did to try to avoid shooting preemptively. Nothing more, however, is required by the law.

As Slotnick said throughout the case, Bernhard Goetz did what the law allows. I agree with that statement, and I think that the law is flawed.

In the days immediately following the verdict, I and many of my fellow jurors discussed the case with the press. We spoke of the lack of divisiveness on the jury, explaining that we had simply been meticulous, and that was why we'd deliberated so long. The verdict was reached "without shouting, without screaming, without rancor," Mike Axelrod said on "Nightline" Tuesday night. "There were no teams," Diana Serpe said to a *New York Newsday* reporter, and, she pointed out, there also "were no holdouts, only people who were indecisive."

We described Goetz's condition when the audio- and videotapes were made to explain why we'd chosen not to believe him. "The man was near hysteria," Brody told the *Daily News.* And the *New York Post* quoted Mike Axelrod as saying Goetz was "a broken man" who seemed on the verge of a nervous breakdown as he relived a nightmare again and again.

Concerning what Goetz had done, we explained that the evidence showed he had been trapped, and that we certainly didn't feel he'd gone out hunting. But Axelrod for one called him "a pathetic man," and James Moseley's somewhat cryptic comment to the *New York Post* may have actually explained our decision about Goetz best: "A reasonable man put in that position may not be a reasonable man."

The key distinction that should be understood is that we were not asked to judge Goetz as an individual. I think it was clear to most of us that Goetz was not a typical or model citizen and that he was deeply emotionally disturbed. We had been asked whether a reasonable person in Goetz's place would have feared what Goetz had feared, and whether Bernhard Goetz therefore had the legal right to react in the way he had.

Of course there was a good deal of praise for Slotnick. We had, after all, acquitted his client on twelve of thirteen charges, and we had largely adopted his argument that stress caused Goetz to make all those statements on the tapes. I called Slotnick "a hell of a lawyer," and I really do think he did an outstanding job. Whether or not you agree with some of the tactics he employed, he was relentless in the defense of his client, conceding nothing and fighting for every edge.

On the other hand there were some harsh words for Waples. Many jurors had commented during deliberations that they had thought Waples's summation unreasonable when he suggested that Goetz had been looking for an opportunity to "take a lifetime of revenge out on [the youths]." I suppose he had to suggest this to us in order to support count twelve of the indictment, possession of a weapon in the second degree. But such an inference was really insupportable, and I think Waples would have been better off conceding that point. If Goetz had really been an emotional powderkeg waiting to detonate ever since his mugging incident, how had he managed to carry a gun every day for over three years before having used it? In New York that constitutes a pretty long fuse.

Many of us were also irked by the way Waples depicted the youths in summation, saying that they were merely being "rambunctious" and that their actions amounted to "life's petty annoyances" that a reasonable person would have simply ignored. We believed Goetz had faced a serious threat that was not one the prosecutor should have passed off so lightly, and we found his suggestion extremely inappropriate that Goetz should "pack his bags" and leave New York. For us, it was the kind of comment that reinforced the image of the uncaring municipal justice system that Goetz had complained about in the tapes.

Mine was one of the critical voices that disparaged Waples's summation after the trial. I hope this book makes it clear, however, how fine a job Waples did overall. He impressed me as a man of tremendous integrity who believes in his soul that Goetz was guilty, and that alone leads me to suspect that Waples might be right. I harbored an image of Waples throughout the trial as an incorruptible shining white knight, and indeed I think it's fair to say that he pursued justice for Darrell Cabey as if he were on a holy quest. I believe he was in a no-win situation, though, lacking the tangible physical evidence needed to corroborate Goetz's statements, or at least a few more eyewitnesses who had seen or heard a separate fifth shot.

I also believe that because of the thirteen-count indictment Waples was forced to spread himself too thin. He began his

summation by practically conceding that Goetz may have been
justified in shooting Canty and Allen and perhaps even James
Ramseur. I think that if from the beginning he had conceded
that Canty was up to no good, and that Canty was abetted by
Allen and Ramseur, Waples could have avoided being saddled
with Canty's protracted and unhelpful testimony and the non-
testimony of Ramseur and focused attention on the argument
that the shooting of Cabey was unjustifiable. His case might
have seemed more convincing then. Of course, without the
testimonies of Canty and Ramseur before the second grand
jury there might not have been an indictment against Goetz.
So Waples, as I said, had no way to win.

Justice Crane, I thought, was the essence of fairness, and
he resolutely withstood any temptation to manipulate the trial
for political gain. In the short speech he made discharging us
from jury service I first learned of Justice Crane's political
leanings, as he caught us up on current events. "The jury is
no longer constrained to avoid reading the newspapers," he
said, then added, "By the way, during the lengthy period I
have been reading the newspapers. There's been a convention
in Venice. The President successfully avoided any definitive
pacts or treaties in that encounter. We have had—Perhaps you
were unaware of a tragic episode in the Persian Gulf. I know
you are aware of the sports."

After the trial, Justice Crane lost a bid for the Democratic
nomination for a New York State Supreme Court seat, reportedly because the Democratic delegates who voted on the matter
thought he had been too soft on Goetz. That personally dis-
heartens me. I feel that court is being deprived a great judge.

After we were discharged there was an open-court conversation between Justice Crane and the lawyers to schedule
a date for Goetz's sentencing. Waples requested that it be in
the third week of July because he planned to be away for the
month of August.

"When are you coming back?" Justice Crane asked.

"Well, I'm not sure," Waples replied. "I don't quite know
where I'm going."

"Hopefully I'm going to heed Mr. Waples's advice and
leave New York for a while too," Slotnick said. "May we have
the first week in September, Judge?"

Waples went to Alaska in August, backpacking in the Brooks Range, north of the Arctic Circle. Slotnick did not get away, however, and had his wrist broken when assaulted that summer outside his office building by two men on a motorcycle. In the skirmish he also lost his $15,000 watch.

After several reschedulings, Goetz was sentenced on Monday, October 19, 1987, which was also Black Monday, the day of the 508-point stock market plunge. Three members of the jury-in-chief—Cathy Brody, Frank Figueroa and Ralph Schriempf—and one alternate—Augie Ayala—attended. Brody wrote me over the summer telling me that if I wanted to write a letter to Justice Crane concerning Goetz's sentence, doing so was considered appropriate. I declined, however. I would liked to have attended the sentencing, but I couldn't get away from work that day.

At the sentencing, both Waples and Slotnick made preliminary speeches. Waples pressed for Goetz to serve a jail term, citing that Goetz was a flagrant offender who by his own admission had been illegally carrying a gun on a regular basis since 1981. Moreover, he said, Goetz had shown no remorse for the crime. "He knew he was breaking the law," Waples said, "he just didn't care." He called Goetz "unworthy" and "unsuitable" for probation because of his "blatant defiance" of the law. And he claimed that because of Goetz's "strong opinions and high intelligence," the only sentence that would affect him was "one with the jail door swinging shut."

Waples said he hoped the sentence would "disarm [Goetz] forever" and argued that Justice Crane did not have "unbridled discretion" to avoid giving Goetz the mandatory one-year jail term that the law dictates for this crime. Even for a first offender, Waples said, the only loophole in the law was if the judge felt that, given the circumstances, a jail sentence would be "unduly harsh."

Slotnick then cited the probation department report on Goetz that had recommended Goetz not serve a jail term and asked the judge to "believe our pain." Goetz, he argued, had "suffered greatly" since the incident, losing his anonymity, the viability of his electronics calibrations business, and "two and

a half to three years of peaceful existence." He argued that
for Goetz "the real sentence began December 22, 1984" because of the intense publicity of the case. The first three weeks
after the verdict the "entire press corps camped outside his
door," Slotnick said, and he called that "a horrible way to
live."

Concerning the issue of whether a jail sentence for Goetz
would have a deterrent effect on the public at large from
carrying illegal handguns, Slotnick quoted a news report that
declared, "Bernhard Goetz is not contagious" and he quoted
Mayor Koch as having said there was "no greater deterrent
than what happened to Goetz." He argued that "individual
defendants should not be punished because [of] high publicity"
and asked Justice Crane to treat Goetz "as anyone else." Then,
however, he pleaded with the judge to not "break the heart
of the people of the city of New York" and to "understand
the feeling of the people out there" who did not want Goetz
to go to jail.

Slotnick recommended for Goetz a conditional discharge but
said to Justice Crane that if Goetz must receive some kind of
sentence, it should be in the form of community service. Goetz's
"intention is to leave this city," but, Slotnick said, "I'd like
him to stay. I think he's an asset to this city." Goetz, he said,
is "a talented man."

The sentence Justice Crane settled on, I thought, was quite
harsh. He gave him a split sentence that included both a six-
month jail term and five years' probation, plus 280 hours of
community service, a $5,000 fine or another year in jail, and
an order to seek psychiatric help. Justice Crane explained that
if he gave Goetz a "definite" one-year sentence, after sixty
days Goetz could be freed on a conditional release. But, he
said, there was no precedent for such commutations with split
sentences, and that he expected Goetz would have to serve
the full six months.

Justice Crane said that one of the considerations on which
he based his sentence was the concept of "general deterrence"
and the "presumed effect of the sentence on others. . . . To
this Court, a nonjail sentence would invite others to violate
the gun laws who, misguided or not, feel the need to arm
themselves without first securing a license," Justice Crane said.

Concerning the one-year mandatory sentence called for by law for the illegal possession of a weapon in the third degree, Justice Crane said, "Whether one agrees with this statute or not, that was the law [in 1984] and it remains the law today."

Other considerations, according to Justice Crane, were Goetz's statements on the tapes that he had sold other guns to his friends and that he had twice drawn his gun in other incidents. He also cited Goetz's use of a quick-draw holster and hollow-point ammunition as well as the reports of two court-appointed psychologists who had examined Goetz. The final straw, though, if I know Justice Crane, was the fact that in Florida in 1985—some months after the shootings—Goetz "made preliminary efforts to obtain another gun."

The sentence was appealed and arguments were heard on May 20, 1988 before the New York State Appellate Division, First Department, of New York County. Goetz's attorneys contended that Justice Crane's sentence was "illegal" and "improper" and, surprisingly, Waples concurred. He asked that Goetz receive at least the mandatory one-year sentence, even though this might mean a shorter jail term for Goetz. The appeals court's decision may be handed down at any time. Goetz may have hurt his chances to win his appeal, though, when he told a reporter from The Associated Press over the telephone on the day he was sentenced that he would defend himself "completely" if threatened again.

There was a certain amount of outrage voiced by those who found the sentence too lenient. Those people obviously felt that Goetz was guilty of far worse crimes than the one charge on which he was convicted. Was he? Did Goetz shoot a helpless Darrell Cabey while Cabey cowered in his subway seat? Or was that the fantasied reconstruction of a disturbed man who was piecing together the fragments of his memory? Perhaps neither Bernhard Goetz nor Darrell Cabey knows for sure.

Meanwhile the end of the criminal proceedings against Goetz will not mark the conclusion of his troubles. There remain the civil cases by the youths whom he shot which, although set back perhaps by the result of the criminal trial, are definitely going forward. In February 1988 a Bronx judge ruled not to reconsider her earlier decisions that the civil suits be consolidated into one case and that Goetz must stand trial in the Bronx because it would be too big a hardship for Darrell Cabey to commute into Manhattan. Cabey is suing Goetz for $50 million; Canty and Ramseur for over $5 million each.

In March 1988 Goetz's civil attorney, Joseph Keltner, filed with the court to be allowed to withdraw from the case. Keltner claimed he wanted to quit because Goetz was being uncooperative; my sources said, however, that Goetz in effect had fired him. The problem is that an attorney cannot simply exit a case once it's in its pretrial stages. If Keltner is granted leave, Goetz will then be given "a reasonable period of time, one or two months" to find new representation, according to Ronald Kuby, one of Darrell Cabey's lawyers. At any rate, Kuby said, the civil trial against Goetz most likely will begin toward the end of 1988.

About two months after the sentencing, in December 1987, the jury held a reunion at a pricey East Side restaurant, which was actually a mistake because the cost ($35 a head) may have been the reason why a few people didn't attend. Those who came enjoyed it, though. It was nice to see each other again.

We all shared in a unique experience, one that we will remember always, and I'd like to think I made a few friends. Justice Crane came to the restaurant, by the way, as did Robert Hamkalo. Justice Crane had insisted on being invited, and I had an interesting discussion with him. He called Goetz "a very sick man."